ENDLESS HOPE OR HOPELESS END

The Bible and the End of Human History

James Rochford

Visit xenos.org for bulk orders and author access

Cover design by Ian Adams

International Standard Book Number

New Paradigm Publishing

Contents

Preface

Modern cinema can't help from speculating about the end of the world—though with little agreement on *how* the world will end. Will flesh-eating zombies tear humanity to pieces? Will an extraterrestrial race invade the Earth? Will we die from communicable disease? Dystopian government? Sentient machines? Nuclear war?

Can Will Smith really save us from all of these horrors? (A brief look at his acting career will show you that he has...)

But what about the real world?

Humanity only recently crawled out from under the debris of two world wars, and we wonder if we can really survive a third. Threats bombard us on all sides: disease, terrorism, nuclear war, poverty, racism, genocide—the list could go on. As we look at our *past* and our *present*, we can't help ourselves from peering anxiously into our *future*. Where is the world headed? How will it all end?

The Bible gives us a unique vision of the future—a picture that is not only true, but also desirable. It not only conforms to reality, but it offers us hope. Scripture tells us what the future holds, but more importantly, it introduces us to the One who holds the future: Jesus Christ.

Jesus will return to Earth, and he's bringing Heaven with him. With such an inspiring message, we owe it to ourselves to study, reflect, contemplate, meditate, pray, and dwell on the Bible's vision of the future. Yet most Christians remain surprisingly ignorant on this topic. If you talk to ten different Christians about biblical prophecy, you're likely to hear eleven different opinions!

That's why I wrote this book. I wanted to write a concise book that would clearly communicate this complex subject for the average reader. I left the more complicated material in the footnotes, so more advanced readers could go deeper, without burdening newer students of Scripture.

You might not agree with every conclusion that I've reached here, but I trust that you will "examine everything carefully" for yourself, and "hold fast to that which is good" (1 Thess. 5:21).

I'm thankful for Eric Chabot, Gaelan Shively, Stephanie Wise, Maggie Van Keuls, Drew Sweet, Ross Meeker, Curt Meeker, Roscoe Robinson, Dennis McCallum, and all of the students from my Leadership Training Class for their help in reading, reviewing, and editing this book. I'm also thankful to my wife for her patience, encouragement, love, and support.

Finally, I'd like to dedicate this book to my son, Jack. In the past two years, you have brought more joy and happiness to your mother and me than you'll ever know. I look forward to the day that we can read this book together.

I love you,

Dad.

Introduction

"Heaven and earth will pass away, but My words will not pass away"—*Jesus Christ*[1]

"I think the odds are no better than fifty-fifty that our present civilisation on Earth will survive to the end of the present century."—*Martin Rees, Cambridge Agnostic cosmologist and physicist*[2]

"Another book on the end times? *Uggh!*"—*said every person ever*

Many people view end times prophecy like a late night infomercial: Both might provoke interest and fascination, but we can't help thinking that someone is just trying to get our credit card information. Even the words "end times" conjure up images of fanatical street preachers, hurling fear and panic to passersby. You know the type: wide-eyed bearded gurus wearing signs that say **THE END IS NIGH!** They appear in their natural habitat of populated urban centers, waving illustrated pamphlets in one hand and King James Bibles in the other, screaming like they're scalping football tickets.

Yet street preachers aren't the only ones to predict the end of the world; people have been doing it for millennia. An ancient Assyrian clay tablet dating to 2800 BC warns, "Our Earth is degenerate in these later days; there are signs that the world is speedily coming to an end."[3]

Pope Innocent III (AD 1284) predicted the end of the world during the fifth crusade on Jerusalem, depicting the prophet Muhammad as the Antichrist. He wrote, "A son of perdition has arisen, the false prophet Muhammad... The end of this beast is approaching, whose number, according to the Revelation of Saint John, will end in 666 years, of which already nearly 600 have passed."[4]

In 1844, the Baptist preacher William Miller predicted Jesus' return. He famously wrote, "I believe the time can be known by all who desire to understand and to be ready for His coming. And I am fully convinced that

---

[1] Matthew 24:35.
[2] Martin J.Rees, "Our Final Hour: A Scientist's Warning: How Terror, Error, and Environmental Disaster Threaten Humankind's Future" in *This Century on Earth and Beyond*. (New York: Basic, 2003) 8.
[3] Mark Strauss, "Ten Notable Apocalypses That (Obviously) Didn't Happen." *Smithsonian Magazine*. October 12, 2012. http://www.smithsonianmag.com/history/ten-notable-apocalypses-that-obviously-didnt-happen-9126331/?no-ist
[4] Mark Strauss, "Ten Notable Apocalypses."

sometime between March 21, 1843 and March 21, 1844... Christ will come."[5] Followers of Miller left their jobs to attend church meetings, anxiously expecting Jesus to descend from heaven. But after no one appeared on the clouds of heaven in 1844, Miller's infamous prediction became known as the "Great Disappointment."

The Watchtower Society (the Jehovah's Witnesses central organization) has made a multitude of false predictions about the return of Christ:[6]

> 1877: "THE END OF THIS WORLD... is nearer than most men suppose."

> July 15, 1894: "We see no reason for changing the figures—nor could we change them if we would. They are, we believe, God's dates not ours. But bear in mind that the end of 1914 is not the date for the beginning, but for the end of the time of trouble."

> 1904: "The stress of the great time of trouble will be on us soon, somewhere between 1910 and 1912 culminating with the end of the 'times of the Gentiles,' October 1914."

> May 1, 1914: "There is absolutely no ground for Bible students to question that the consummation of their gospel age is now even at the door... The great crises... that will consume the ecclesiastical heavens and the social earth, is very near."

> 1933: "The incontrovertible proof that the time of deliverance is at hand."

> 1939: "The battle of the great day of God Almighty is very near."

These recurring false predictions couldn't convince followers forever. Ankerberg and Weldon write, "Thousands of Jehovah's Witnesses have left the Watchtower after having lived through the high expectations and heartbreaking disappointments of these false prophecies."[7]

In recent years, prophecy crusaders have only risen in fervor. Christian teacher Edgar Whisenant wrote his infamous pamphlet *88 Reasons Why the Rapture is in 1988*, selling 4.5 million copies worldwide (Not surprisingly, Whisenant's sales dropped dramatically in 1989!).

In 2011, the late Christian radio broadcaster Harold Camping made multiple predictions of Christ's return. Camping's organization paid for billboards, commercials, and thousands of pamphlets to publicize the return of Christ

---

[5] William Miller, *Signs of the Times,* (January 25, 1843).
[6] These are all documented in John Ankerberg and John Weldon, *The Facts on Jehovah's Witnesses* (Eugene, OR: Harvest House, 1998), 57-59.
[7] John Ankerberg and John Weldon, *Cult Watch* (Eugene, OR: Harvest House, 1991), 84.

with the statement: **"JUDGMENT DAY: MAY 21, 2011—THE BIBLE GUARANTEES IT!"** In the process, Camping's ministry accumulated millions of dollars from Christian supporters. Yet May 21, 2011 came and went. But Jesus never *came* to Earth, and no believers *went* to heaven. It served as the final failed prediction of Camping's ministry before he died in 2013.

Prophecy fanatics seem to be fulfilling Aesop's fable of the boy who cried wolf, rather than biblical prophecy. Every few years we hear of a new doomsday prediction, but nothing ever happens. Rather than feeling a sense of *divine awe* in regards to biblical prophecy, it feels more like *déjà vu*. Doesn't this discredit the entire project of biblical prophecy? Shouldn't we just give it up?

Is cynicism the answer?

While it's easy to be cynical about biblical prophecy, the Bible predicts such cynicism. Roughly two thousand years ago, Peter wrote, "In the last days scoffers will come... They will say, '*What happened to the promise that Jesus is coming again?* From before the times of our ancestors, everything has remained the same since the world was first created'" (2 Pet. 3:3-4 NLT).

Sound familiar?

Like a pile of dung attracts flies, Jesus knew that religious fanatics would flock to his teaching about the end of human history, misleading many in the process. He warned, "See to it that no one misleads you. For many will come in My name... and will mislead many (Mt. 24:4-5; cf. 24:24; 2 Thess. 2:3). False predictions about the return of Christ have so inundated us that when history really does come to an end, we might not treat the Bible's warnings seriously. The 19th century philosopher Søren Kierkegaard once wrote,

> A fire broke out backstage in a theatre. The clown came out to warn the public; they thought it was a joke and applauded. He repeated it; the acclaim was even greater. I think that's just how the world will come to an end: to general applause from wits who believe it's a joke.[8]

As we study this subject, we might feel uncomfortable because it's associated with such sensationalism and mania. Yet what's the alternative? Yes, prophecy profiteers have tried to exploit the Bible's teaching on the

---

[8] Søren Kierkegaard, *Either/or: A Fragment of Life* (London: Penguin, 1992), 49.

future, *but they have also tried to distort every other teaching in the Bible!* Think about it: which biblical teaching have false teachers *not* tried to distort?

The only way to combat prophecy fanatics is to actually understand the subject better than they do. By retreating from the discussion, we leave ourselves vulnerable to those who would hijack the subject for their own purposes. In the end, if we ignore biblical prophecy, the false teachers will have accomplished their mission: *keeping us from God's truth.*

"I like the Bible, but I don't like prophecy..."

Theologians refer to the study of the end of human history with the term *eschatology*. This comes from the Greek term *eschaton* which means "last." So eschatology is the study of the "last things."

The Bible contains history and theology, but also a considerable portion of its teaching is prophecy. Old Testament (hereafter OT) Scholar Walter Kaiser writes, "So important is prediction to the very nature of the Bible that it is estimated that it involves approximately 27 percent of the Bible."[9] God predicted the first destruction of the world, during Noah's time (Gen. 6:13); he predicted that the Jews would be enslaved for 400 hundred years under Pharaoh—centuries beforehand (Gen. 15:13); and Jesus even predicted his own death and resurrection on a number of occasions (Mt. 16:21; Mk. 8:31; Lk. 9:22; Jn. 2:18-22). Should any believer in the Bible ignore the reality of these predictions? Surely not, considering that prophecy fills the pages of Scripture from one end to the other.

According to scholar Robert Saucy, the New Testament (hereafter NT) authors refer to Jesus' return roughly 300 times—or one out of every twenty-five verses. He writes, "Beginning in the Gospels with Christ's own prediction, it is included in all but four books (Galatians, Philemon, 2 and 3 John)."[10] Likewise, theologian Mark Hitchcock notes, "For every time the Bible mentions the First Coming, the Second Coming is mentioned *eight times.*"[11] If we purge the return of Christ from our Bibles, it would be like reading a novel without the final chapter. How does the story end? If God lays such emphasis on this subject, we owe it to ourselves to understand it.

---

[9] Walter C. Kaiser, *The Messiah in the OT* (Grand Rapids, MI: Zondervan Pub., 1995), 235.
[10] Robert Saucy, "The Eschatology of the Bible." In F. E. Gaebelein (Ed.), *The Expositor's Bible Commentary, Volume 1: Introductory Articles* (Grand Rapids, MI: Zondervan Publishing House, 1979), 110.
[11] Emphasis mine. Mark Hitchcock, *The End: A Complete Overview of Bible Prophecy and the End of Days* (Carol Stream, IL: Tyndale House, 2012), 4.

Many Christians study the Bible for its teaching on God, forgiveness, and eternal life—and rightly so—but many remain ignorant of its teaching on eschatology. Frequently, Christians claim, "We won't know how the prophecies about the Second Coming are fulfilled until they actually happen so there's no use wasting time trying to figure out what they're saying." But Jesus expected the people of his day to be ready for his First Coming by reading predictive prophecy (Lk. 19:44). If we're not supposed to understand prophecy before it occurs, why include it in the first place?

It's ironic (and sad) that many Christians have never studied (or even read) the book of Revelation. Why not? If the book of Revelation is simply an encoded enigma that cannot be understood, then why would God offer a special "blessing" for those who read it (Rev. 1:3)? Moreover, if the book is completely mysterious, then why call it a "revelation" at all? Hitchcock observes, "The word revelation (*apokalupsis*) means 'to unveil, reveal, or remove the cover from something.' This implies that prophetic truth can be substantially understood. The Lord has given prophecy, not to confuse us or hide the truth, but to help us understand it and be transformed by it."[12]

Eschatology doesn't exist for some sort of "spiritual elite" in the Christian community; everyone can study this topic. Paul taught eschatology to the Thessalonians, even though he had visited them for only a short time. In his first letter to them, he wrote, "About times and dates we do not need to write to you, for *you know very well* that the day of the Lord will come like a thief in the night" (1 Thess. 5:1-2 NIV; cf. 2 Thess. 2:5). Paul thought that all believers should take the time to study eschatology—even those who have only known Christ for a short time.

The full details of eschatology might take years to grasp, but don't let that discourage you: the main message is clear enough. In one of his lectures, NT professor Stanley Toussaint tells about teaching his graduate students the complexities of the book of Revelation all semester. As he was leaving his classroom late one night, he walked past the janitor reading the book of Revelation in his Bible. Out of curiosity, Toussaint asked him, "Do you understand what you're reading in there?"

The man's face lit up. "Oh, of course..." he said casually. "We're gonna win!"[13]

Some aspects of eschatology may confuse us, but the Bible couldn't be any clearer on the main message: Christ is coming back! History rushes toward an endless hope—not a hopeless end.

---

[12] Mark Hitchcock, *The End*, 51.
[13] Hitchcock writes about this story as well. Mark Hitchcock, *The End*, 42.

Part One: Why Believe in Prophecy?

The Bible gives many prophecies about the end of human history, but why should we trust these predictions? Do we accept their reliability on blind faith or wishful thinking?

Not at all. God used his ability to know the future as a means of demonstrating his unique existence. Scripture claims that God alone knows the future, and the ancient Jews discerned the authenticity of their prophets based on their ability to accurately predict forthcoming events (Deut. 18:22). In the book of Isaiah, we read:

> Present the case for your idols... let them tell us what the future holds, so we can know what's going to happen. 23 Yes, tell us what will occur in the days ahead... But no! You are less than nothing and can do nothing at all... Who told you from the beginning that this would happen? Who predicted this, making you admit that he was right? No one said a word! 27 I was the first to tell Zion... See, they are all foolish, worthless things. All your idols are as empty as the wind. (Isa. 41:21-29 NLT)

> I am the Lord; that is my name! I will not give my glory to anyone else, nor share my praise with carved idols. 9 Everything I prophesied has come true, and now I will prophesy again. I will tell you the future before it happens. (Isa. 42:8-9 NLT)

> I expose the false prophets as liars and make fools of fortune-tellers. I cause the wise to give bad advice, thus proving them to be fools. (Isa. 44:25 NLT)

Here we see that God claims to know the future, and separates himself from false gods on this basis. Undeniably, not all of the predictions in the Bible have come to fruition, but some have, giving us confidence in the unfulfilled future predictions. One of the best reasons for trusting the Bible's predictions about the *future* is to look at its track record in the *past*.

Consider the science fiction film *Knowing* (2009) in which an elementary school unearths a 50 year time capsule only to discover a paper with a series of encoded numbers. The main character, an MIT astrophysics professor, decodes the numbers, discovering that the document accurately predicted the time, location, and number of fatalities in a string of disasters over the last fifty years. The document predicts three more fatalities—all of which occur in the immediate future.

I don't want to ruin the end of the film, but consider this situation for a moment. If the time capsule really did predict hundreds of events in sequential order, wouldn't this boost your confidence in the three remaining predictions? Seeing the track record of the fulfilled predictions, wouldn't this cause you to take the unfulfilled predictions seriously?

This same situation confronts us in the case of biblical prophecy. Before we consider what the Bible predicts about the future (i.e. unfulfilled prophecy), we should first reflect on what it has accurately predicted in the past (i.e. fulfilled prophecy). In this first section then, we will consider a number of remarkable biblical predictions that have already been fulfilled: (1) details about Jesus of Nazareth, (2) the regathering of Israel, (3) the destruction of cities and nations, and (4) the proper succession of the great world empires.

Chapter 1. Fulfilled Predictions of Jesus of Nazareth

Jesus Christ's mission to Earth wasn't God's last ditch effort to rescue humanity. Instead, God prepared his plan "before the foundation of the world" (Eph. 1:4; cf. Rom. 1:2-3). As we read through our Bibles, we discover many predictions anticipating the career of Jesus of Nazareth.

The Messiah would destroy the work of the Serpent (Gen. 3:15)

> I [God] will cause hostility between you and the woman, and between your offspring and her offspring. He will strike your head, and you will strike his heel. (Gen. 3:15 NLT)

Who is this mysterious person whom God himself predicted immediately after the moral fall of humanity?[1] The oldest Jewish commentaries of Genesis 3:15 understood this prophecy to refer to the destruction of Satan by the Messiah—a Reigning Ruler who would bring peace and justice to the Earth.[2] While the Serpent would harm this man ("You will strike his *heel*"), this messianic figure would ultimately defeat the Serpent ("He will strike your *head*"). Oddly enough, Genesis 3:15 predicts that this mysterious person would come from the line of a woman—not a man ("*her* offspring"). Theologian Arnold Fruchtenbaum writes,

> There are many genealogies in Scripture... virtually all of them are lists of men's names. Legal descent, national and tribal identity, were always taken from the father, never from the mother (the sole exception to this is found in Ezra 2:61 and Nehemiah 7:63). It is very rare that a woman's name would be included at all unless she figured very prominently in Jewish history, and even then she would warrant only a passing reference.[3]

---

[1] It is certainly a singular person, because the Hebrew uses the masculine singular. Walter C. Kaiser, *The Messiah in the OT* (Grand Rapids, MI: Zondervan Pub., 1995), 39.
[2] Wenham writes, "The oldest Jewish interpretation found in the third century BC Septuagint, the Palestinian targums (*Ps.-J., Neof., Frg.*), and possibly the Onqelos targum takes the serpent as symbolic of Satan and look for a victory over him in the days of King Messiah." Gordon Wenham, *Genesis 1—15* (Dallas: Word, Incorporated, 1998), 80.
[3] Arnold G. Fruchtenbaum, *Messianic Christology*. 14.

The Jewish people were a patriarchal society—not matriarchal—so it's odd that this prediction would exclude Adam's descendants, but include Eve's; unless, of course, this messianic figure would be born without the help of a human father. This prophecy comes into focus when we remember that Jesus had no human father—only a human mother (Mt. 1:18, 23; Gal. 4:4). Scholar Duane Lindsey notes, "It is significant that there is no mention of Messiah's human father in the Old Testament."[4]

The Messiah would be God's Son (Ps. 2; 2 Sam. 7:14)

Psalm 2 describes a future Conquering King, whom the Jewish people called the Messiah. This psalm mentions God's "anointed" (Hebrew *masiah*) who would rescue Israel from the cruelty of the Gentile nations (Ps. 2:2), which is why Jewish rabbis universally held it to be a messianic psalm until the 11th century AD.[5] But who is "the Son" mentioned in verse 12?

> Do homage to the Son, that He not become angry, and you perish in the way, for His wrath may soon be kindled. How blessed are all who take refuge in Him! (Ps. 2:12)

Surely this person is the Son of God—the future Messiah. Earlier in the text, God installed his king (v.6) and his son (v.7); at the end of the psalm, we see that we are to serve the Lord (v.11) and kiss the Son (v.12). The two titles are synonymous with one another. As you might expect, it shouldn't surprise us to understand the Messiah as the Son of God, because 2 Samuel 7:14 predicts an eternal ruler who would be the Son of God ("I will be a father to him and he will be a son to me").

The KJV and NIV render "homage" as kiss. To "kiss" a king meant to give him respect or honor (1 Kings 19:18; Hos. 13:2; 1 Sam. 10:1). The point is this: When the Son comes to Earth, pay him his due respect.[6]

---

[4] F. Duane Lindsey, "The Commission of the Servant in Isaiah 49:1-13." *Bibliotheca Sacra* (April-June, 1982), 132.

[5] The renowned Jewish rabbi Rashi interpreted it to be fulfilled by King David in the eleventh century AD. George A. Gunn "Psalm 2 and the Reign of the Messiah." *Bibliotheca Sacra* (October-December, 2012), 428.

[6] Some critical scholars argue that Psalm 2:12 shouldn't be translated as "son" (Aramaic *bar*), but instead, it should be translated as the Hebrew word *bor* meaning "purity." However, Abraham Ibn Ezra understood this to mean "son," Proverbs 31:2 translates *bar* as son, and the psalm begins and ends with the son. See Michael L. Brown, *Answering Jewish Objections to Jesus: Messianic Prophecy Objections*. Volume Three (Grand Rapids, MI: Baker, 2003), 113.

The Messiah would be God incarnate (Ps. 45:7; Isa. 9:6; Mic. 5:2)

The term "incarnation" comes from the prefix "in" meaning "inside," and the Latin root *carne* which means "meat" or "flesh." To incarnate, therefore, means "to enter flesh," just as the term *reincarnate* means to "reenter flesh." Theologians refer to Jesus' birth as the incarnation, where the eternal God entered into space and time—flesh and blood. While many people believe that the concept of the incarnation is a NT invention, we find various predictions of this event throughout the OT.

The Psalmist addresses the human king—the future Messiah—in Psalm 45:1. He writes, "Your throne, O *God*, is forever and ever" (v.6) and "Therefore God, Your God, has anointed You" (v.7). Naturally, we must ask an important question: how can a human king be called "God"? That is, of course, unless this human king was also divine. Hebrew scholar Michael Brown tells the following anecdote regarding Psalm 45:

> When I first started studying Hebrew in college, I asked my professor, a very friendly Israeli rabbi, to translate for me the words *kis'aka 'elohim 'olam wa'ed*. He replied immediately, 'Your throne, O God, is forever and ever,' explaining, 'These are praises to the Almighty.' I then asked him to read the rest of the psalm, clearly addressed to the king, and his face dropped. How could this earthly king be called *'elohim*? To repeat: This is the most natural and obvious meaning of the Hebrew, and no one would have questioned such a rendering had the entire psalm been addressed to God.[7]

Isaiah predicted the incarnation when he wrote, "A child will be born to us, a son will be given to us; and the government will rest on His shoulders; and His name will be called Wonderful Counselor, Mighty God, Eternal Father, Prince of Peace" (Isa. 9:6). But how could a little baby be called "Mighty God"? Some critics argue that the title "Mighty God" is hyperbolic for a powerful human leader. Yet Isaiah uses each and every one of these titles to refer to Yahweh—not a human being—including Wonderful

---

[7] Michael L. Brown, *Answering Jewish Objections to Jesus: Theological Objections*. Volume Two (Grand Rapids, MI: Baker, 2003), 43.

Counselor (Isa. 25:1; 28:29),[8] Mighty God (Isa. 10:21), Eternal Father (Isa. 63:16b),[9] and Prince of Peace (Isa. 26:3, 12).

Zechariah predicted, "They will look on Me whom they have pierced; and they will mourn for Him, as one mourns for an only son, and they will weep bitterly over Him like the bitter weeping over a firstborn" (Zech. 12:10). Notice what the text says: "They will look on *Me* whom they have pierced." Up until this point, Yahweh has been speaking in the first person (Zech. 12:1-9). How could people pierce God? In light of the incarnation, this prediction comes into focus at the Cross of Christ (Jn. 19:37; Rev. 1:7). Interestingly, some Jewish interpreters held Zechariah 12:10 to be about the future Messiah.[10]

Many Jewish theologians struggled with the thought that God could be pierced by human beings. As a result, some Jewish copyists changed the pronoun from "me" to "him" ("They will look on *him* whom they have pierced").[11] However, the most reliable texts of Zechariah 12:10 state that the people pierced Yahweh himself.

Micah foresaw that the Messiah would be an eternally ancient being: "One will go forth for Me to be ruler in Israel. His goings forth are from *long ago*, from the *days of eternity* [Hebrew *'olam*]" (Mic. 5:2). It is true that *'olam* can be

---

[8] The OT uses the Hebrew word "wonderful" (*pālā'*) 80 times, and "the vast majority… refer to the Lord, himself and his works. It is the nearest word Hebrew has to the idea of 'supernatural.'" Alec Motyer, *Isaiah: an introduction and commentary*. Vol. 20. (Downers Grove, IL: InterVarsity Press, 1999), 101-102.

[9] Critics argue that this passage calls Jesus the "Father," which doesn't seem to fit with a Trinitarian understanding of him as the "Son." However, this title means that he brought eternal life to others. Fruchtenbaum writes, "The Son who is to be born will be the Father of Eternity, meaning that He is the source of eternal life. Clearly this is to be no mere man." Arnold G. Fruchtenbaum, *Messianic Christology*, 40. In the same way, Jabal was called the "father of those who dwell in tents," and Jubal was the "father of all those who play the lyre and pipe" (Gen. 4:20-21; c.f. 1 Pet. 3:6; Jn. 8:44 for similar usages).

[10] In the *Talmud*, *Succah* 52a, we read, "Why is this mourning in Messianic times? …One opinion is that they mourn for Messiah Ben Joseph who is killed, and another explanation is that they mourn for the slaying of the evil inclination. It is well according to him who explains that the cause is the slaying of the Messiah since that well agrees with this verse. If it refers to the slaying of the evil inclination, it must be asked, is this an occasion for mourning? Is it not rather an occasion for rejoicing? Why then should they weep?" Rashi—the great Jewish exegete—seems to agree with this interpretation, citing this early tradition. http://www.chabad.org/library/bible_cdo/aid/16216#showrashi=true&v=10

[11] Baldwin writes, "The early translators evidently found this verse an embarrassment, for their versions show marked variations on the Hebrew… Evidently some early copyist(s) felt that the prophet could not have intended to put into the mouth of the Lord the apparent contradiction that he had been put to death, and therefore changed the pronoun." J. G. Baldwin, *Haggai, Zechariah and Malachi: An Introduction and Commentary*. Vol. 28 (Downers Grove, IL: InterVarsity Press, 1972), 205.

rendered in a temporal—not eternal—way (see Micah 7:14). However, this term is also applied to God's eternal nature (Ps. 90:2; 25:6), and Micah uses it for eternity as well (Mic. 2:9; 4:5, 7). Moreover, the great Jewish theologian Rashi interpreted '*olam* in Micah 5:2 as eternal.[12] Fruchtenbaum writes, "The Hebrew words for 'from long ago, from the days of eternity' are the strongest Hebrew words ever used for eternity past... What is true of God the Father is also said to be true of this One who is to be born in Bethlehem."[13]

The Messiah would be born in Bethlehem (Mic. 5:2)

Micah predicted that the Messiah would come from the little city of Bethlehem. Jewish rabbis viewed Micah 5:2 as a messianic prediction,[14] as did the NT authors (Mt. 2:6; Jn. 7:42), because the Messiah would be the son of David who had also been born in Bethlehem (1 Sam. 17:12).

The Messiah would die by Crucifixion (Ps. 22:16)

David described the gruesome act of crucifixion for a future Righteous Sufferer: "A band of evildoers has encompassed me; *they pierced my hands and my feet*" (Ps. 22:16). The Jews didn't crucify their criminals; they stoned them.[15] Moreover, crucifixion wasn't even known to the Jewish people at this point in history, and it wasn't popularized until the Roman Empire put it into practice centuries later. In fact, the first recorded act of crucifixion

---

[12] Rashi cites Psalm 72:17 as a cross reference for understanding "his origin is from of old." http://www.chabad.org/library/bible_cdo/aid/16191#showrashi=true

[13] Arnold G. Fruchtenbaum, *Messianic Christology*, 64.

[14] Carson and Beale write, "The Targum of the Minor Prophets very explicitly takes this text as messianic: 'And you, O Bethlehem Ephrathah, you who were too small to be numbered among the thousands of the house of Judah, from you shall come forth before me the anointed One, to exercise dominion over Israel, he whose name was mentioned from of old, from ancient times.' ...Other post-Christian rabbinic literature recognized that the Messiah was to be born in Bethlehem (e.g., Tg. Ps.-J. Gen. 35:21), so there is no reason to reject the claim of the Gospels that this information was recognized already in the first century." G. K. Beale & D.A. Carson, *Commentary on the NT Use of the OT* (Grand Rapids, MI; Nottingham, UK: Baker Academic; Apollos, 2007), 6.

[15] Lockyer writes, "The Jews executed their criminals by stoning. Crucifixion was a Roman and a Grecian custom, but the Grecian and Roman empires were not in existence in David's time. Yet here is a prophecy written 1,000 years before Christ was born by a man who had never seen or heard of such a method of capital punishment as crucifixion." Herbert Lockyer, *All the Messianic Prophecies of the Bible* (Grand Rapids: Zondervan Pub. House, 1973), 150.

was in 519 BC by Darius of Persia—five hundred years after David wrote this.[16] Thus, David pictured a form of death, which hadn't even been invented yet.

The Messiah would die in AD 33 (Dan. 9:24-26)

The prophet Daniel predicted that the Messiah would die in AD 33 before the destruction of the second Temple.[17]

> Seventy weeks have been decreed for your people and your holy city, to finish the transgression, to make an end of sin, to make atonement for iniquity, to bring in everlasting righteousness, to seal up vision and prophecy and to anoint the most holy place. [25] So you are to know and discern that from the issuing of a decree to restore and rebuild Jerusalem until Messiah the Prince there will be seven weeks and sixty-two weeks; it will be built again, with plaza and moat, even in times of distress. [26] Then after the sixty-two weeks the Messiah will be cut off and have nothing, and the people of the prince who is to come will destroy the city and the sanctuary. (Dan. 9:24-26a)

DANIEL 9:24-27 TIMELINE

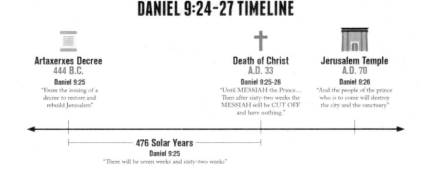

Daniel's reference to a "decree" occurred in Nehemiah 2, when King

---

[16] Hoffmeier writes, "Herodotus, the fifth-century Greek historian, describes a case in which Darius the Great (522-486 BC) crucified 3,000 Babylonians." James Karl Hoffmeier, *The Archaeology of the Bible* (Oxford: Lion, 2008), 158.

[17] For a longer treatment of this prophecy, see my earlier work: James Rochford, *Evidence Unseen: Exposing the Myth of Blind Faith* (Columbus, OH: New Paradigm Publishing, 2013), Chapter 7.

Artaxerxes allowed the Jews to rebuild their city ("from the issuing of a decree"). This was in the spring of 444 BC. The years Daniel predicted ("seven weeks and sixty-two weeks") add up to 483 years (69 x 7 = 483). Of course, we must remember that the Jewish people didn't use our modern calendar system. They used a *360 day calendar year* and a 30 day month—not a *365 day calendar year* (Num. 20:29; Gen. 7:11; 8:3-4; Rev. 11:2; 13:5; 12:6; 11:3). When we adjust the calendar accordingly, we find that Daniel predicted 476 years on the solar calendar, bringing the prediction to AD 33—the preferred date for Jesus' death.

The prophet Haggai predicted that the glory of the second Temple would be greater than the first (Hag. 2:8-9). Obviously, Solomon's Temple contained much more *physical* beauty than the second Temple of Jesus' day. The only reason we can believe that the second Temple had more "glory" than the first is due to the fact that God himself would fill the second Temple, as he did the first Temple (2 Chron. 7:1-4). Scholar Michael Brown notes, "The expression 'fill with glory' always refers to the divine manifestation in the Bible."[18] Malachi wrote that the Lord would "suddenly come to His temple" before it was destroyed (Mal. 3:1), and Jerusalem would become a "heap of ruins" after this occurred (Mic. 3:12).

If Jesus didn't fulfill this prophecy, then who did? No other messianic candidate came into the second Temple before its destruction in AD 70.

The Messiah as the Servant of God (Isa. 42, 49, 50, 53)

Isaiah explains a future Servant in four chapters of his book. His descriptions of the Servant offer a stark similarity with Jesus of Nazareth. Isaiah states that the Servant will:

-be loved by God and endowed with God's Spirit (Isa. 42:1).

-have a global influence (Isa. 42:1, 4; 49:1; 52:15).

-be gentle and quiet (Isa. 42:2-3).

-represent the nation of Israel (Isa. 49:3), but be separate from it (Isa. 49:6)

-appear to fail in his mission, but actually succeed (Isa. 49:4; 53:1).

---

[18] Michael L. Brown, *Answering Jewish Objections to Jesus: Messianic Prophecy Objections*. Volume Three (Grand Rapids, MI: Baker, 2003), 146.

-be God's salvation (Isa. 49:6).[19]

-help the weary (Isa. 50:5).

-be innocent in God's eyes (Isa. 50:7-9; 53:9).

-be exalted like a King (Isa. 52:13; cf. 6:1).

-not look like a King (Isa. 53:2).

-be beaten beyond recognition (Isa. 50:6; 52:14; 53:5).

-not defend himself from false accusations (Isa. 53:7).

-be killed (Isa. 53:8).

-be buried in a rich man's tomb (Isa. 53:9).

-be a sin offering for the people (Isa. 53:10-11).

-come back to life (Isa. 53:10).

Critics argue that the Servant cannot refer to Jesus, because Isaiah identified the Servant with the nation of Israel (Isa. 41:8; 42:19; 43:10).[20] However, this interpretation is more of a recent view—not an ancient one. In fact, it wasn't held for 1,000 years after the time of Jesus.[21] The nation of Israel is clearly distinct from the Servant after Isaiah 49:6. Here we read, "It is too small a thing that You should be *My Servant* to raise up the *tribes of Jacob* and to restore the *preserved ones of Israel…*" (Is. 49:6). Later in Isaiah 53:6, we read, "All of *us* [the people] like sheep have gone astray, each of *us* has turned to his own way; but the LORD has caused the iniquity of *us all* to fall on *Him* [the Servant]." And in Isaiah 53:8, we read, "But *he* [the Servant] was struck down for the rebellion of *my people* [the nation of Israel]"

---

[19] The Hebrew states that the Servant doesn't just *bring* salvation, but rather, he himself *is* the salvation. J. A. Motyer, *The Prophecy of Isaiah: An Introduction & Commentary* (Downers Grove, IL: InterVarsity Press, 1996), Isaiah 49:6.

[20] See David Klinghoffer, *Why the Jews Rejected Jesus: the Turning Point in Western History* (New York: Doubleday, 2005), 165. Samuel Levine. *You Take Jesus, I'll Take God: How to Refute Christian Missionaries* (Los Angeles, Ca.: Hamoroh, 1980), 25. Tovia Singer. *Outreach Judaism: Study Guide to the "Let's Get Biblical!" Tape Series, Live!* (Monsey, NY: Outreach Judaism, 1998), 27. Asher Norman, *Twenty-six Reasons Why Jews Don't Believe in Jesus* (Los Angeles, CA: Black White & Read, 2007), 229-239.

[21] Brown writes, "For almost one thousand years after the birth of [Jesus], not one rabbi, not one Talmudic teacher, not one Jewish sage, left us an interpretation showing that Isaiah 53 should be interpreted with reference to the nation of Israel." Michael L. Brown, *Answering Jewish Objections to Jesus: Messianic Prophecy Objections*. Volume Three. (Grand Rapids, MI: Baker, 2003), 41.

(NIV).[22] Thus later in his book, Isaiah makes it clear that the Servant is distinct from Israel—being a singular person.

The Messiah's message would spread globally (Isa. 49:6)

Jesus claimed that his message of love and forgiveness would reach the entire globe (Mt. 24:14). Just imagine if you were standing there when Jesus said this. Days later, soldiers butchered him like an animal on a Roman Cross, and his movement seemed defeated. However, over the last two millennia, Jesus' message of love and forgiveness has reached billions of people.

Isaiah likewise predicted that the Messiah's message would be global in scope. Regarding the Suffering Servant, he wrote, "It is too small a thing that you should be My Servant to raise up the… preserved ones of Israel; *I will also make You a light of the nations so that My salvation may reach to the end of the earth*'" (Isa. 49:6; c.f. 61:1-3; Gen. 49:10). He also wrote that "the coastlands will wait expectantly for His law [or teaching]" (Isa. 42:4). In his massive book *World Christian Trends*, David Barrett writes,

> In 1900 over 80% of all Christians were White. Most were from Europe and North America. Today that percentage has fallen to 45%. The demographic center of Christianity is now found in Latin America, Africa, and Asia. Over the next 25 years the White portion of global Christianity is expected to continue to decline dramatically… The country with the fastest Christian expansion ever is China, now at 10,000 new converts every day… From only 3 million in 1500 A.D., evangelicals have grown to 648 million worldwide, 54% being Non-Whites.[23]

Robert Newman writes,

> [Jesus of Nazareth] is also the only person claiming to be the Jewish Messiah who has founded a world religion among Gentiles.

---

[22] Arguing for the national interpretation of Isaiah 53, critics claim that this entire passage is from the perspective of the Pagan kings in Isaiah 52:15. Therefore, from this view, Isaiah 53 is about the Pagan nations gasping at the suffering of Israel ("Kings will shut their mouths on account of Him [Israel]"). However, Isaiah 53:8 stands in contrast to this view, because Isaiah refers to the participants as "my people." Isaiah also uses the covenant name for God (YHWH) in 53:6, which would be highly odd for a Pagan king to us. In addition, all of the arguments against Israel being the Servant also apply.

[23] David Barrett (et al.), *World Christian Trends, AD 30-AD 2200: Interpreting the Annual Christian Megacensus* (Pasadena, CA: William Carey Library, 2001), 3.

This accomplishment would have been very difficult to stage. Furthermore, the prophecy envisions quite an unusual event. Here is a figure who is to be a light to Gentiles, but is abhorred by the nation Israel. Who would ever have expected that the Jewish Messiah would be generally rejected by Jews but widely accepted by Gentiles?[24]

Ask yourself: *What person in human history has caused more non-Jewish people to come to faith in the God of Israel?* Isn't it odd that so many Christians come from a non-Jewish background, yet believe in the God of the Jewish people? Through his death, Jesus Christ brought more Gentiles to faith in the God of the Bible than any other person in human history.

Roughly seven billion people fill the Earth today. According to the United States Center for World Mission (USCWM), the message of Christ has reached roughly four billion of these people (4.06), and the number rises daily.[25] With the rise of mission services and globalization, we can expect these remaining groups will hear about Christ in the near future.

Were these "predictions" made after the time of Christ?

Many marvel at biblical prophecy until skepticism sets in. Some wonder if these "prophecies" were actually written after the fact. However, even skeptics of the Bible freely admit that the OT existed long before the time of Christ. Translators created the Septuagint (a Greek translation of the OT) sometime between 250 and 132 BC.[26] Moreover, the Dead Sea Scrolls contain a citation of every OT book (except Esther), and they also date from before the time of Christ.[27] For these reasons, even skeptic Jim Lippard admits, "Prophetic statements do not post-date the events being predicted. In the case of the OT prophecies… we have documents (e.g., the

---

[24] Robert C. Newman "Chapter 13: Fulfilled Prophecy as Miracle." Douglas Geivett and Gary Habermas, *In Defense of Miracles: A Comprehensive Case for God's Action in History* (Downers Grove, IL: InterVarsity, 1997), 223.

[25] The Joshua Project is a ministry of the United States Center for World Missions. Joshua Project "Great Commission Statistics." http://www.joshuaproject.net/great-commission-statistics.php.

[26] Harris notes that the 250 BC date is inferred from tradition—a translation done under Ptolemy Philadelphus. The 132 BC date comes from the prologue of Ecclesiasticus in the apocrypha, which refers to the OT being dressed in Greek. R. Laird Harris, *Inspiration and Canonicity of the Scriptures* (Greenville, SC, 1995), 76.

[27] Walter C. Kaiser, *The OT Documents: Are They Reliable & Relevant?* (Downers Grove, IL: InterVarsity, 2001), 45.

Dead Sea Scrolls) which do predate the time at which the historical Jesus is believed to have lived."[28]

Additionally, the Jewish people fretted over their transmission of the Bible. They believed that they were copying the very words of God. Rabbi Ishmael told his son, "Be careful, because your work is the work of heaven; should you omit [even] one letter, the whole world would be destroyed."[29] With statements like these, we might consider it an understatement to say that the Jewish people copied the Bible with meticulous care! In fact, their scribes followed a number of failsafe procedures to ensure accuracy, and if these were not followed, the scribes would have the faulty manuscripts "condemned to be buried in the ground or burned; or... banished to the schools, to be used as reading books."[30] When we consider the book of Isaiah, for example, we discover that the book was copied and recopied over the course of a millennium with "only three words exhibiting a different spelling... [in] a book that runs about one hundred pages and sixty-six chapters in our English text."[31]

Did Jesus or the disciples self-fulfill these prophecies?

Other skeptical thinkers ask themselves: "How do we know that these are true supernatural predictions? What if Jesus intentionally self-fulfilled these predictions to start a new religion?" This is a worthy question to consider.

Yet, it wouldn't have been in Jesus' interest to self-fulfill these predictions. This might sound like the overstatement of the century, but think about it: why would Jesus desire to be tortured and crucified? Josephus referred to crucifixion as "the most wretched of deaths."[32] Even our modern word *excruciate* draws its roots from the original Latin, which means "out of the Cross." Instead of trying to self-fulfill the prophecies about being a crucifixion victim, why didn't Jesus try to fulfill those about being a conquering king?

In addition, Jesus' closest disciples were imprisoned, tortured, and killed for their faith. They were enemies of the government (the Roman Empire) and

---

[28] Jim Lippard "The Fabulous Prophecies of the Messiah" (1993) *http://www.infidels.org/library/modern/jim_lippard/fabulous-prophecies.html.*
[29] B. *Sota*, 20a.
[30] Frederic Kenyon, *Our Bible and the Ancient Manuscripts* (New York: Eyre and Spottiswoode. 1897), 34.
[31] Walter C. Kaiser, *The OT Documents: Are They Reliable & Relevant?* 45-46.
[32] Josephus, *Jewish War*. 7.203.

the religious establishment (rabbinic Judaism). And remember, all of Jesus' closest disciples were Jewish. By lying, they would have believed that Yahweh would judge them for being false teachers (Dan. 12:2; Deut. 18:15-22).

The notion that the disciples were nefariously trying to ignite a false religion isn't even held by most critical scholars today. Even the notorious NT critic Bart Ehrman writes, "It is *undisputable* that some of the followers of Jesus came to think that he had been raised from the dead,"[33] and atheistic scholar Gerd Ludemann states, "It may be taken as *historically certain* that Peter and the disciples had experiences after Jesus' death in which Jesus appeared to them as the risen Christ."[34] In fact, after compiling a bibliography of 3,400 historical scholars on the subject, Gary Habermas authoritatively writes, "It seems clear that the disciples were utterly persuaded that the risen Jesus had appeared to them. The data are strong enough that *this is granted by virtually all critical scholars.*"[35]

Conclusion

The Bible offers a number of fulfilled prophecies about Jesus of Nazareth, making multiple predictions about his life, death, and resurrection:

---

[33] Emphasis mine. Bart Ehrman, *Did Jesus Exist?* (New York: Harper One, 2014), 183-184.
[34] Emphasis mine. Of course, Ludemann chalks this up to a hallucination or vision. Gerd Ludemann and Alf Ozen, *What Really Happened to Jesus: a Historical Approach to the Resurrection* (Louisville, KY: Westminster John Knox, 1995), 80.
[35] Emphasis mine. Gary Habermas, *Experiences of the Risen Jesus: The Foundational Historical Issue in the Early Proclamation of the Resurrection* Originally published in *Dialog: A Journal of Theology*, Vol. 45; No. 3 (Fall, 2006), pp. 288-297; published by Blackwell Publishing, UK.

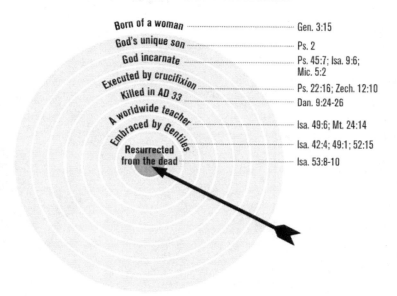

PROPHECIES ABOUT THE MESSIAH

Born of a woman	Gen. 3:15
God's unique son	Ps. 2
God incarnate	Ps. 45:7; Isa. 9:6; Mic. 5:2
Executed by crucifixion	Ps. 22:16; Zech. 12:10
Killed in AD 33	Dan. 9:24-26
A worldwide teacher	
Embraced by Gentiles	Isa. 49:6; Mt. 24:14
Resurrected from the dead	Isa. 42:4; 49:1; 52:15
	Isa. 53:8-10

If the predictions of the First Coming of Jesus were fulfilled with such accuracy, then we should anticipate the prophecies about his Second Coming to be fulfilled as well.

Discussion questions

1. Not all prophecies offer the same amount of evidential weight in apologetics. Which prophecies do you feel are the strongest for demonstrating the truth of Christ? Why or why not?

2. If all you had was a Bible and a pen and paper, would you be able to explain the prophecy of Daniel 9:24-27? As an exercise together, pair up into groups and try to explain the prophecy.

3. How would you respond to the claim that Jesus or the disciples self-fulfilled these prophecies? Which key arguments would you offer?

Chapter 2. Fulfilled Foreshadowing of Jesus

Good writers fill their books or movies with foreshadowing—little hints that point toward the future. These aren't *predictions* per se; instead, they are more like *clues* that allow the reader or viewer to wonder about where the plot is headed. Consider just a few examples **(WARNING: Spoiler alert!)**:

> *The Empire Strikes Back* (1980): After Luke Skywalker fights an image of Darth Vader in the cave on Dagobah, Yoda says: "Much anger in him… Like his father." Later, we discover that Vader is Luke's dad.

> *Back to the Future: Part Two* (1989): Biff sits in a hot tub watching *A Fist Full of Dollars*, where Clint Eastwood tricks men into shooting him in the chest with a metal plate. Marty McFly uses this exact trick in the third film.

> *The Shawshank Redemption* (1994): The evil warden shows Andy a Bible, and he says, "Salvation lies within." Later, Andy uses the Bible to hide a small chisel and pick to find "salvation" from the prison.

> *Fight Club* (1999): After beating himself up in his boss' office, Edward Norton's character says, "For some reason… I thought of my first fight… With Tyler." Later, we discover that he *is* Tyler Durden, beating himself up the entire time.

> *The Dark Knight* (2008): When Harvey Dent and Bruce Wayne sit at dinner together, Dent says, "You either die a hero, or live long enough to see yourself become the villain." At the end of the film, Bruce Wayne (Batman) watches Dent die before he can be revealed as the villain Two-Face.

Why do good writers place foreshadowing in their books or films? It gives the audience "Aha!" moments, when they view the work a second or third time. In the same way, the Bible contains extensive foreshadowing of Jesus. That is, while the Bible includes *predictions* about Jesus, it also has *pictures* of him—subtle hints that prefigure his person and work.

Abraham and Isaac foreshadowed the Cross of Christ (Gen. 22)

God promised that Abraham would bless the world through his many descendants (Gen. 12:1-3). However, when God finally gave Abraham a son named Isaac, he told this old man to travel three days to the land of Moriah and sacrifice Isaac on an altar (Gen. 22:2-4). Of course, before Abraham could sacrifice Isaac on a makeshift altar on Mount Moriah, God stopped him.

Yet what a strange story! We could imagine Jewish readers asking themselves: "What was *that* all about?" Why would God command Abraham to sacrifice his only son, especially when he forbids human sacrifices as horribly immoral (Lev. 18:21; 20:2-5; Deut. 12:31; Ezek. 16:20-21; 20:31; Jer. 7:31)? But after we read about the Cross of Christ, we discover that this entire event foreshadowed Jesus' work on our behalf.

> -Genesis 22:2 is the first use of the word "love" in the Bible, and it is given in the context of a father loving his son. Likewise, the first use of the word "love" in the gospel of John is in John 3:16.

> -Abraham had only one son, whom he loved, and he was asked to sacrifice him to God (Gen. 22:2). Likewise, God has only one son, whom he loves, and he sacrificed him for humanity (Jn. 3:16).

> -When Abraham passed this test, the angel of the Lord said, "I know that you fear God, since you have not withheld your son, your only son, from Me" (Gen. 22:12). Likewise, 1 John 3:16 states that we know God loves us by looking to the Cross ("We know love by this, that He laid down His life for us").

> -Isaac carried the lumber for his sacrifice up the mountain (Gen. 22:6), and Jesus carried his Cross to Golgotha (Jn. 19:17).

> -Isaac willingly lay down as the sacrifice (Gen. 22:9). At this point, he had grown stronger than his elderly father—but he *willingly chose* to lay down his life. Likewise, Jesus said, "I lay down My life so that I may take it again. [18] No one has taken it away from Me, but I lay it down on My own initiative. I have authority to lay it down, and I have authority to take it up again" (Jn. 10:17-18).

> -Abraham spent three days grieving the death of his son, believing that he was as good as dead as they travelled to Mount Moriah (Gen. 22:4). Jesus was literally as good as dead for three days, but God raised him from the dead (Mt. 12:40; cf. Heb. 11:19).

These are certainly some interesting *parallels*, but are they *prophecies?* Yes! Later in history, we discover that this divine drama took place *in the very spot where Solomon built the Jewish Temple*—on Mount Moriah (2 Chron. 3:1). That's not a coincidence. Historically, Jesus was crucified just to the north of this mountain. Kidner notes that Moriah "is the vicinity of Calvary."[1] Thus the veiled summary statement in Genesis 22:14 really makes sense when we consider the geographic location: "On the mountain of the Lord it will be provided." On Mount Moriah, where Abraham *almost* sacrificed his son, God *really* sacrificed his Son for human sin.

While Abraham believed that God would provide a lamb for the burnt offering (Gen. 22:8), God provided a ram instead (Gen. 22:13). God didn't provide this lamb for the sacrifice until Jesus came as "the Lamb of God who takes away the sin of the world" (Jn. 1:29).

Traditional Jewish prayer circles would frequently read the story of Abraham's sacrifice of Isaac.[2] We might imagine them asking themselves, "Why would God ask Abraham to kill his son? *That's unthinkable!*" However, after the Cross, we can see that God did the "unthinkable" for each of us.

The Passover foreshadowed Jesus (Ex. 12)

When the Jews were about to escape slavery in Egypt, God commanded them to celebrate the festival of the Passover. In this feast, they would sacrifice an innocent lamb, smearing the blood over their doorpost. When God came to judge the people of Egypt, he would "pass over" the houses where he saw the blood. In other words, if he already saw blood on a house, he would see that a death had already taken place. Those beneath the blood of the innocent animal—the lamb—would be spared from judgment. This event foreshadowed the work of Christ in several ways.

> -Exodus records, "[The Passover] is to be the first month of the year to you" (Ex. 12:2). Similarly, the work of Jesus gives believers a new beginning (2 Cor. 5:17).

> -God chose a "lamb" which was offensive to the Egyptians (Gen. 46:34), because it was a furry animal. Likewise, Jesus was thought to be a "stumbling block" to the people in his time (1 Pet. 2:8; 1 Cor. 1:23).

---

[1] Derek Kidner, *Genesis: An Introduction and Commentary*. Vol. 1. (Downers Grove, IL: InterVarsity Press. 1967), 154.
[2] Brown writes, "[This account was] referred to daily in the traditional Jewish prayer service." Michael L. Brown, *Answering Jewish Objections to Jesus: Messianic Prophecy Objections*. Volume Three, 4.

-God told the people that the "lamb shall be an *unblemished* male" (Ex. 12:5). In the same way, Jesus was a *perfect* substitute (2 Cor. 5:21; Jn. 1:29).

-God commanded, "They shall take some of the blood and put it on the two doorposts" (Ex. 12:7). The blood represented the life of the animal (Lev. 17:11; Heb. 9:22). Here, the blood needed to be shed and also applied for each individual household (v.8). Similarly, while Jesus' blood was shed for all people (1 Jn. 2:2), we each individually need to apply his work to our own lives (Jn. 1:12).

-God said that the lamb should be "roasted with fire" (Ex. 12:9), which was symbolic of judgment. Similarly, Jesus paid for our sins so that he could pay for God's judgment that we deserved (Heb. 12:29).

-When God saw the blood, he would "pass over you, and no plague will befall you to destroy you when I strike the land of Egypt" (Ex. 12:13). Jesus' blood keeps us from coming under the judgment of God (1 Pet. 1:18-20).

-When they ate the Passover, they were not allowed to "break a bone of [the lamb]" (Ex. 12:46; Num. 9:12). None of Jesus' bones were broken on the Cross (Jn. 19:32-36; Ps. 34:20).

For centuries, and still today, the Jewish people have celebrated the Passover. Gallons upon gallons of blood were shed, but what does it all mean?

As we flash forward to the life of Christ, we ask ourselves, "What was the last meal Jesus took before he took up the Cross?" You guessed it: *The Passover* (Lk. 22:13-20). Here we discover Jesus interpreting the Passover to be symbolic of himself. As Jesus took the Passover meal, he said, "Do this in remembrance of *Me*" (Lk. 22:19). He held up the wine and said, "This is my blood shed for you." Then, instead of abstaining from drinking the blood, Jesus encouraged his disciples to drink the "blood" (i.e. the wine), which symbolizes our need for partaking of his spiritual life.

The Tabernacle (Ex. 26)

Ancient people believed they could meet with the divine in specific places called *temples*. The supernatural and the natural intersected in temples—like a nexus between worlds—a crossroads. Virtually all ancient people believed that you couldn't just stumble into the presence of the divine. Instead, you had to meet your deity in a temple of some kind. Comparative religion scholar Mircea Eliade writes,

> The dividing structure between sacred and profane space… also serves the purpose of preserving profane man from the danger to which he would expose himself by entering it without due care. The sacred is always dangerous to anyone who comes into contact with it unprepared, without having gone through the 'gestures of approach' that every religious act demands.[3]

The ancient Jews held to a similar concept, but their Temple was different. It was portable. It followed them. Or rather, they followed *it*.

Before the Jewish people built their massive Temple under King Solomon, God had them build a simple tabernacle. Instead of a massive and immovable Temple, God wanted a portable tent—a mobile home—that the people could carry with them wherever they went. Even the Hebrew term for the Tabernacle (*miškān*) is a derivation of "the word 'to dwell' (*šākan*) and is the place where God dwells among his people."[4] Since God is omnipresent (Ps. 139:7-10; 1 Kings 8:27), it's odd to think of him uniquely dwelling in a portable tent, but it's only symbolic of his presence. He wanted a picture that would point to how people can relate to him.

We discover the fulfillment of the Tabernacle in the person of Jesus. When Christ came, God revealed that the Tabernacle—this moveable tent—foreshadowed the incarnation. At the incarnation, Jesus "became flesh, and *dwelt* among us" (Jn. 1:14). Regarding this passage, scholar D.A. Carson comments, "More literally translated, the Greek verb *skenoo* means that the Word pitched his tabernacle, or lived in his tent, amongst us."[5] Just as God *dwelt* in the portable tent with his people in the OT, God *dwelt* in a human body in the person of Christ.

The Jewish people believed that they could only come to God through the Temple. Thus when Jesus claimed that he *was* the Temple, he was claiming that people could only come into God's presence *through Him*. Indeed, Jesus said, "Destroy this temple, and in three days I will raise it up" (Jn. 2:19). John explains, "[Jesus] was speaking of the temple of His body" (Jn. 2:21).

---

[3] Mircea Eliade, *Patterns in Comparative Religion* (Cleveland, OH: The World Publishing Co, 1958), 370.
[4] Walter Kaiser, *Exodus*. In F. E. Gaebelein (Ed.), *The Expositor's Bible Commentary, Volume 2: Genesis, Exodus, Leviticus, Numbers* (Grand Rapids, MI: Zondervan Publishing House, 1990), 453.
[5] D.A. Carson, *The Gospel According to John* (Grand Rapids, MI: Inter-Varsity Press, 1991), 127.

Jesus wasn't merely claiming that we could come to God through his body, but through the death and resurrection of his body. Quite a claim indeed!

Within the Tabernacle, we find a number of articles of worship that also point forward to Christ's work.

The Priests (Ex. 28:29-38)

At the very center of the Tabernacle there was a place called "The Holy of Holies." This was where God dwelt uniquely. Only one man—the high priest—could enter the Holy of Holies, and only once a year on Yom Kippur ("The Day of Atonement"). When he entered the Holy of Holies, the high priest would "carry the names of the sons of Israel in the breastpiece of judgment over his heart" (Ex. 28:29), and he would "bear the guilt involved in the sacred gifts the Israelites consecrate... they will be acceptable to the Lord" (Ex. 28:38 NIV).

This, too, prefigured what Jesus would do for us, as our high priest and mediator (1 Tim. 2:5). Jesus interceded for us permanently, as the ultimate high priest (Heb. 7:23-28; 9:11-15). He represents us to God so completely that he even records our names in the book of life in heaven (Rev. 21:27). Because Jesus was the perfect high priest (Ex. 30:18-21), we can now have bold access to God through his intercessory work (Heb. 4:16).

The Ark of the Covenant (Ex. 25:10-22)

Maybe you've seen the movie *Indiana Jones: Raiders of the Lost Ark* (If you haven't, you should close this book right now, and watch it, because you apparently haven't lived life yet!). This fictional movie follows Indiana Jones in a battle with the Nazi regime over the Lost Ark of the Jewish people. While the story is obviously fictional, it was based on the OT concept of the Ark of the Covenant.

The Ark was a golden box inside the Holy of Holies. Inside, the people placed a number of specific items: (1) a jar of manna, (2) Aaron's rod, and (3) the Law. Why were each of these placed in the Ark?

The jar of manna stood for God's provision for the people (Ex. 16:32-34; Deut. 8:3), which the people rejected (Num. 21:4-9); Aaron's rod stood for God's leadership (Num. 16), which the people rejected (Num. 17:10); and the Law stood for God's moral direction (Deut. 10:5), which the people rejected (Ex. 32). Thus the Ark of the Covenant was a box of evidence that convicted the people of their sin. They rejected God's *provision*, *leadership*, and *moral direction*. What was God supposed to do with these people who had rejected him, and why collect this legal evidence against them in the Ark?

The Cherubim and Mercy Seat (Ex. 25:20-22)

Cherubim (angels) looked down from the top of the Ark into this box of legal evidence (Ex. 25:20-22). This, no doubt, symbolized the angelic order looking down at humanity from heaven. According to the Bible, an innumerable race of angels exists (Rev. 5:11), who can witness events on Earth (1 Pet. 1:12). Knowing the just nature of God, these angels must have wondered what God would do to the sinful people of Earth. How would he solve the problem of their rebellion?

Bloody forgiveness (Lev. 17:10-11)

Ancient people could see that an animal needed its blood to live. Therefore, God used blood as a symbol for life: "The life of the flesh is in the blood and I have given it to you on the altar to make atonement for your souls; for it is the blood by reason of the life that makes atonement" (Lev. 17:11). Once a year, the high priest was to pour the blood of the innocent substitute onto the atonement cover. In Leviticus we read, "[The high priest] shall take some of the blood of the bull and sprinkle it with his finger on the mercy seat …Then he shall slaughter the goat of the sin offering which is for the people, and bring its blood inside the veil and do with its blood as he did with the blood of the bull, and sprinkle it on the mercy seat" (Lev. 16:14-15). The priest was to do this "because of the impurities of the sons of Israel and because of their transgressions" (v.16).

What a graphic picture of sin and forgiveness! In order to have forgiveness for their sins, the people saw that an innocent and perfect animal needed to die as their substitute. When Jesus died on the Cross, he fulfilled these symbols. John the Baptist called him "the Lamb of God who takes away the sin of the world" (Jn. 1:29). He was the perfect substitute that could pay for our sins in a unique way. Thus it shouldn't surprise us that after Jesus died on the Cross, the veil to the Temple was torn in two (Mt. 27:51)—visibly demonstrating that Christ had fulfilled the ceremonial symbols found there.

Conclusion

In the movie *The Usual Suspects* (1995), Verbal Kint (played by Kevin Spacey) tells the story of the events surrounding the infamous villain Keyser Söze. After the movie ends, the audience discovers that Verbal Kint *is*

Keyser Söze—hiding in plain sight. We find many hints throughout the film:

> -In the opening of the film, the villain Keyser Söze stands over Keaton (Gabriel Byrne) with a gold watch, lighter, and a pack of cigarettes. At the end of the film, Agent Kujan's officer issues Verbal Kint "one watch gold, one gold cigarette lighter, and one pack of cigarettes."

> -Verbal Kint tells Agent Kujan that Keyser Söze was "Turkish." The translation of "Söze" in Turkish is "to speak too much." When Keaton asks Kint how he received his nickname ("Verbal"), he tells him, "People say I talk too much."

> -Verbal Kint tells Agent Kujan, "A man can convince anyone he's somebody else, but never himself." As a result, Kint spends the entire film convincing Kujan that he isn't Keyser Söze.

> -Verbal Kint tells Agent Kujan that the greatest trick the Devil ever pulled was to convince the world that he didn't exist. Then he says, "And like that... *poof!* He's gone." By the end of the film, Verbal had successfully convinced Kujan that Keyser Söze was a myth, and Kujan lets him go, disappearing forever.

After watching the movie on a second or third viewing, these hints and many others come alive to the careful viewer. The identity of the main character had been staring us in the face the entire time, but it isn't until the end that we see how all of the pieces fit together. Similarly, after seeing the work of Christ on the Cross, we realize that Jesus was hiding in plain sight throughout the stories and symbols of the OT Scriptures.

Discussion questions

1. What is the difference between prediction and foreshadowing? In what ways are predictions better? In what ways are pictures (or foreshadowing) better?

2. Explain the significance of the Ark of the Covenant. Offer three ways that it foreshadows Jesus.

3. Abraham and Isaac have many similarities with God and Jesus: How do we know that we're not reading into the text to find these similarities? What textual clues reveal that God meant to foreshadow the work of Christ?

4. Why do you think God might have waited to explain the work of Christ? Why did God sometimes work through foreshadowing, rather than being more explicit? Why all of the subtlety?

5. Some people say that studying evidence for Jesus like this isn't important. We should just have faith. How do you think this material helps to bolster your faith?

Chapter 3. Fulfilled Predictions of Israel's Regathering

The Bible predicts the regathering of the nation of Israel at the end of human history. For years, this seemed to be an absurd prediction. No other nation had ever been globally dispersed, and then regathered in such a way. Yet in 1948, after the horrors of the Holocaust, the Jewish people regained their land exactly as the Bible had predicted for millennia.

Just to put this in perspective, this would be akin to the government giving back the United States to the surviving Native American population. Actually, this would be far *more* likely—given the fact that Native Americans were not globally dispersed and have only been oppressed for a couple of *centuries*, rather than a couple of *millennia*. The Bible, however, predicted Israel's national regathering numerous times—thousands of years before it occurred.

The Regathering in Isaiah

> Then it will happen on that day that the Lord will again recover *the second time* with His hand the remnant of His people, who will remain, from Assyria, Egypt, Pathros, Cush, Elam, Shinar, Hamath, and *from the islands of the sea.* [12] And He will lift up a standard for the nations, and will assemble the banished ones of Israel, and will gather the dispersed of Judah *from the four corners of the earth.* (Isa. 11:11-12)

Isaiah states that the Jewish people will be regathered "a *second* time." Some interpreters argue that the first gathering refers to the Exodus from Egypt (citing verse 16), and the second gathering refers to the return from the Babylonian Exile.[1]

However, this "second" gathering cannot refer to the return from Babylon in the sixth century BC. First of all, Isaiah promised that a "remnant" will be regathered a second time. Yet the Exodus from Egypt was not a *remnant*, rather God gathered *all* of his people in the Exodus. Moreover, the context of Isaiah 11 reveals that this event will occur toward the end of human history, when Christ returns to judge and rule the Earth (vv.5-10). As scholar Alec Motyer accurately notes, Isaiah typically uses the expression "in

---

[1] Anthony A. Hoekema, *The Bible and the Future* (Grand Rapids, MI: Eerdmans, 1979), 206.

that day" to refer to the end of history.[2] Since Isaiah wrote this before the
Exile in the eighth century BC, the return from the Babylonian and Assyrian
exile was the *first* regathering—not the *second* (cf. Isa. 10:20-27; 44:26-45:8).

Isaiah 11 also states that this event will be a *global* regathering ("from the
islands of the sea... from the four corners of the earth"), rather than a *local*
regathering like that from the Babylonian Exile. Isaiah 11 doesn't fit with
the Babylonian Exile in 538 BC which "was only from Babylon and not
from these other lands."[3] The first regathering under Ezra and Nehemiah
only contained about 50,000 Jewish exiles from only a few surrounding
nations.[4] Even John Goldingay (who interprets the second regathering to
refer to the Babylonian Exile) frankly admits, "There has not been one
particular moment when all the people of Israel have been brought back to
Palestine from the four corners of the world, as is evidenced by the fact that
most of the Jewish people do not live there."[5]

While even today this prophecy has not been completely fulfilled, we've
seen this prediction coming to fruition:

---

[2] J. A. Motyer, *The Prophecy of Isaiah*, Isaiah 11:10-11.
[3] John N. Oswalt, *Isaiah: The New Application Commentary* (Grand Rapids, MI: Zondervan, 2003), 189.
[4] Eugenie Johnston writes, "About 50 thousand Jews from Babylon returned immediately under Zerubbabel (Neh. 7:6-7, 66-67). Nearly a century later, Nehemiah led another group from Shushan in Persia (Neh. 1:1; 2:1-11). No other places are mentioned from which Jews returned. Among the names of Jews who returned, we find a number of Babylonian and Persian names, indicating that the Jews had lived in these areas, but no evidence of return from other regions." Robert C. Newman, *The Evidence of Prophecy: Fulfilled Prediction as a Testimony to the Truth of Christianity* (Hatfield, PA: Interdisciplinary Biblical Research Institute, 1988), 90.
[5] John Goldingay, *Isaiah* (Peabody, MA: Hendrickson, 2001), 86. To avoid the prediction, critical scholars hold that the nations besides Egypt and Assyria are scribal additions. See Joseph Blenkinsopp. *Isaiah 1-39: A New Translation with Introduction and Commentary* (New York: Doubleday, 2000), 267-268.

Population of Modern-day Israel		
Nation	**Jewish Population (1948)**	**Jewish Population (Today)**
Egypt	66,000 Jews.	A few hundred.
Assyria & Babylon **(modern day Iraq)**	150,000 Jews	Fewer than 10!
Hamath **(modern day Syria)**	15,000 Jews.	Fewer than 100.
Elam **(modern day Persia, then Iran)**	95,000 Jews.	20,000 to 25,000.[6]

The Regathering in Jeremiah

> Days are coming… when the city will be rebuilt for the LORD *from the Tower of Hananel to the Corner Gate.* [39] The measuring line will go out farther straight ahead *to the hill Gareb*; then it will turn to *Goah.* [40] And the whole valley of the dead bodies and of the ashes, and all the fields *as far as the brook Kidron, to the corner of the Horse Gate toward the east*, shall be holy to the LORD; *it will not be plucked up or overthrown anymore forever.* (Jer. 31:38-40)

This cannot refer to the regathering in the sixth century BC, because Jeremiah predicts that the Jews will never be dispersed again after this time ("it will not be plucked up or overthrown anymore *forever*"). Surely this cannot refer to the regathering after the Babylonian Exile, because the people lost the land after this point.

Jeremiah even describes the borders of the real estate God promised to Israel. Scholar John Walvoord comments, "Jerusalem will be built in a certain area which had formerly never been used for building purposes. It is

---

[6] These figures all come from the website, www.jewishvirtuallibrary.org/jsource/anti-semitism/

remarkable that this precise area has been built into a portion of the modern city of Jerusalem in fulfillment of this prophecy."[7]

Some interpreters argue that the nation of Israel has been replaced by believers in Christ (a subject we will thoroughly address in later chapters). However in context, we read that God would no sooner revoke his promise to national Israel than he would eliminate the sun, moon, and stars (Jer. 31:35-36).

The Regathering in Ezekiel

In Ezekiel 37, God gives the prophet Ezekiel a vision of bones that gain flesh and come to life. In verse 11, he interprets the meaning of the vision:

> These bones are the whole house of Israel… [12] I will bring you *into the land of Israel*… [14] I will put My Spirit within you and you will come to life, and *I will place you on your own land*. Then you will know that I, the LORD, have spoken and done it… [21] Behold, I will take the sons of Israel *from among the nations where they have gone*, and *I will gather them from every side and bring them into their own land* [22] and I will make them one nation *in the land*… [25] They will live *on the land* that I gave to Jacob My servant, in which your fathers lived; and they will live on it, they, and their sons and their sons' sons, forever; and *David My servant will be their prince forever*. (Ezek. 37:11-12, 14, 21-22, 25)

God gives the bones joints, then flesh, and then covers them with skin. Then finally, God breathes into them, giving them life (cf. Gen. 2:7). Dwight Pentecost suggests that this passage implies a process, rather than an overnight event.[8] Similarly, the modern regathering of Israel has been a slow process—not an overnight event. Modern Israel is largely secular, but since the Hebrew prophets anticipated a spiritual awakening of Israel at the end of human history, we should expect this to occur as well (Zech. 12:2-13:1). David Garland writes, "Just as these events in the vision are miraculous, so will be Israel's restoration."[9]

Ezekiel's prediction cannot refer to the regathering after the Babylonian Exile in the sixth century BC, because he mentions that the Messiah would be there ("David My servant will be their prince *forever*…" v. 25).

---

[7] John F. Walvoord, *Israel in Prophecy* (Grand Rapids: Zondervan Pub. House, 1978), 68.

[8] J. Dwight Pentecost, *Things to Come: a Study in Biblical Eschatology* (Grand Rapids, MI: Academie, 1964), 345.

[9] David E. Garland (et al.), *Jeremiah-Ezekiel* (Grand Rapids, MI: Zondervan, 2010), 849.

The Regathering in Hosea

> You shall stay with me for many days. You shall not play the harlot, nor shall you have a man; so I will also be toward you. ⁴ For the sons of Israel will remain for many days without king or prince, without sacrifice or sacred pillar and without ephod or household idols. ⁵ Afterward the sons of Israel will return and seek the Lord their God and David their king; and they will come trembling to the Lord and to His goodness in the last days. (Hos. 3:3-5)

God commanded Hosea to marry Gomer—a prostitute. He has several kids with her, but she leaves him to sleep with other men (2:2-7). In chapter 3, God commands Hosea to renew his relationship with Gomer. This becomes a dramatic picture of God's dealings with Israel. God married Israel, Israel left him for idols, and yet God still remained faithful. In chapter 3, Hosea makes a remarkable prediction about Israel: "The sons of Israel will remain for many days (1) without king or prince, (2) without sacrifice or sacred pillar and (3) without ephod or household idols" (Hos. 3:4).

> (1) **"Without king or prince…"** The people will cease to have a political ruler for this gap of time.

> (2) **"Without sacrifice or sacred pillar…"** The people will be without true religious practice during this gap of time.

> (3) **"Without ephod or household idols…"** The people will be without idolatry for this gap of time (c.f. 2 Kings 23; Ezra 2:63).

Hosea remarkably predicts that the Jewish people would retain their ethnic identity even though they lacked leadership, a temple, or even false religious practices. Thousands of years after this prediction, we observe that the Jewish people have retained their identity—even without these essentials. Hosea then predicts, "Afterward the sons of Israel will return and seek the LORD their God [spiritual restoration] and David their king [political restoration]; and they will come trembling to the LORD and to His goodness in the last days" (Hos. 3:5).[10]

The Regathering in Zechariah

> I will whistle for them to gather them together, for I have redeemed them; and they will be as numerous as they were before. [9] When I scatter them among the peoples, they will remember Me in far countries, and they with their children will live and come back. [10] I will bring them back from the land of Egypt and gather them from Assyria; and I will bring them into the land of Gilead and Lebanon until no room can be found for them. (Zech. 10:8-10; cf. Zech. 14:10)

This prediction cannot refer to the Babylonian Exile, because this book post-dates the exilic period, dating anywhere between 520 and 480 BC. Critics date it even later.[11] Also, Zechariah mentions the "far countries"— not merely Egypt and Assyria (c.f. Zech. 12:6). Furthermore, at the end of history, Zechariah pictures Jerusalem being in the hands of the Jewish people once again (Zech. 12 and 14).

The Regathering in Jesus' teaching

> They [the Jewish people] will fall by the edge of the sword, and will be led captive into all the nations; and Jerusalem will be trampled under foot by the Gentiles UNTIL *the times of the Gentiles are fulfilled.* (Lk. 21:24)

As a Jewish rabbi, Jesus followed what the Hebrew Scriptures had always taught, believing that the nation of Israel would see a regathering at the end of human history. The operative word here is "until…" The Romans destroyed Jerusalem and the Temple in AD 70. However, while the Jews were going to be *temporarily* removed from the land, they would *ultimately* receive the land.

---

[10] Critics claim that Hosea's primary ministry was only to the North (Ephraim), rather than the south (Judah). Ephraim, however, amalgamated with the southern kingdom; therefore, it appears that Hosea had the entire nation in mind. If he only had this northern kingdom in mind (Ephraim), then some have argued that the Samaritans could also be a fulfillment of this passage, because they have similar hallmarks in their history, as well. See Robert C. Newman, *The Evidence of Prophecy: Fulfilled Prediction as a Testimony to the Truth of Christianity* (Hatfield, PA: Interdisciplinary Biblical Research Institute, 1988), Chapter Seven.
[11] Gleason Archer, *A Survey of Old Testament Introduction* (Chicago: Moody, 1974), 433.

What if the regathering of Israel is just a self-fulfilled prophecy?

Skeptics claim that the Jewish people merely self-fulfilled the prophecies about their regathering as a nation. Atheist Douglas Krueger writes, "Does it take divine inspiration to state that at some unspecified point in the future people will come together and found a state? It is not clear that this is so much a prophecy as an expression of hope."[12] But consider three serious counterarguments to this view:

First, the regathering of Israel was largely a secular movement—not a religious one. Religious zealotry can explain fervent and unrelenting motivation. But it doesn't explain the regathering of Israel, because Israel was (and is) largely a secular state—not a religious one. According to a recent study, half of Israel is "non-religious" or "anti-religious." In fact, only 12% identify themselves as religious and 5% as orthodox.[13]

Second, the regathering of Israel faced inconceivable opposition. Josephus estimated that the Romans killed 1.1 million Jews in AD 70.[14] Later in AD 135 Emperor Hadrian "destroyed 985 towns, slaughtered a further 580,000 Jews, expelled the remainder from Jerusalem, [and] prohibited circumcision and Sabbath observance."[15] In the fourth century AD, Emperor Constantine made it illegal to convert to Judaism. Later in the Polish Legislation of 1562, the Jewish people "were to dress differently from Christians; they were prohibited from owning Christian serfs or domestics and from holding public office."[16] In 1648, Russian Cossacks tortured and killed Jews who refused to convert to the Orthodox faith. The Jewish people were "were flayed alive, split asunder, clubbed to death, roasted on coals, or scalded with boiling water. Even infants at the breast were not spared... Scrolls of the Law were taken out of the synagogues by the Cossacks who danced on them while drinking whiskey. After this Jews were laid upon them and butchered without mercy."[17] Pope Pius VI (1775-1799)

---

[12] Douglas E. Krueger, *What Is Atheism?: A Short Introduction* (Amherst, NY: Prometheus, 1998), 100.

[13] Shlomit Levy (et al.), "A Portrait of Israeli Jewry: Beliefs, Observances, and Values Among Israeli Jews 2000." Conducted by *The Guttman Center of the Israel Democracy Institute* for *The AVI CHAI Foundation*, 2002.

[14] Josephus, *The Wars of the Jews*, 6.9.3.

[15] Barry E. Horner, *Future Israel: Why Christian Anti-Judaism Must Be Challenged* (Nashville, TN: B&H Academic Publishing, 2007), 17.

[16] Barry E. Horner, *Future Israel*, 27.

[17] P. E. Grosser and E. G. Halperin, *The Causes and Effects of Anti-Semitism* (New York: Philosophical Library, 1978), 181. Cited in Barry E. Horner, *Future Israel*, 28.

issued his *Edict to the Jews* that commended forced baptism and even abduction of Jewish babies from their parents.

Sadly, many so-called Christians carried out much of this persecution and anti-Semitism. Yet religious people weren't the only ones to persecute the Jews. Voltaire spoke of the Jews as "our masters and our enemies, whom we at once detest."[18] He wrote, "We find in [the Jews] only an ignorant and barbarous people, who have long united the most sordid avarice with the most detestable superstition and the most invincible hatred for every people by whom they are tolerated and enriched. Still, we ought not to burn them."[19] Samuel Kellogg writes,

> Nearly every influence which might obliterate a people has come upon the Jews over the centuries, as upon no other nation in history, and yet they still survive today… The Nazi holocaust wiped out about six million Jews according to the best estimates, about two-thirds the Jewish population of Europe at that time.[20]

If the Jewish people self-fulfilled this prophecy, they did so under the worst possible conditions. Other dispersed people (facing much less opposition) have tried to reclaim their land, but this isn't as easy as skeptics cavalierly claim. If it's so easy to globally regather a nation, then why haven't other people been able to do so?

Consider for a moment the difficulty of keeping a national or cultural identity without a king or prince to govern the nation (Hos. 3:4). Ezekiel predicted that the kingly line would be suspended until the Messiah came. He states, "Remove the turban and take off the crown… this also will be no more until he comes whose right it is" (Ezek. 21:25-27). There has been no king in David's line since this time (587 BC). Even without a centralized national or cultural identity, the Jewish people reclaimed their land almost two millennia after they were banished from it.

Third, the regathering of Israel was fulfilled by non-believing nations. The Roman government usually didn't scatter conquered nations; they dominated them, letting them stay in their land.[21] Moreover, until the United Nations voted

---

[18] Voltaire, *Dictionnaire Philosophique*. "Abraham."

[19] Voltaire, *Dictionnaire Philosophique*. "Jews."

[20] Robert C. Newman, *The Evidence of Prophecy: Fulfilled Prediction as a Testimony to the Truth of Christianity* (Hatfield, PA: Interdisciplinary Biblical Research Institute, 1988), 55, 62.

[21] Samuel Kellogg writes, "Generally they [the Romans] allowed these nations to remain in their own land if they would submit to Rome." Robert C. Newman, *The Evidence of Prophecy: Fulfilled Prediction as a Testimony to the Truth of Christianity* (Hatfield, PA: Interdisciplinary Biblical Research Institute, 1988), 58.

for Israel's sovereignty, the Jewish people could not buy or import weapons. In actual fact, Great Britain set up a naval blockade on Israel, confiscating guns that Jewish settlers smuggled in. Were these nations trying to fulfill biblical prophecy, too? This places us in the very awkward position of believing that atheistic governments (like the USSR) were trying to fulfill biblical prophecy![22]

Conclusion

Remarkably, the Bible repeatedly predicted the restoration of Israel toward the end of human history—not just in *one* passage but in *dozens*. In the last century, we have seen this remarkable prediction come to fruition. This, of course, bolsters our confidence that the rest of the predictions in Scripture will likewise be fulfilled.

Discussion questions

1. When Israel was regathered in 1948, some theologians believed that this was a sign that history was about to come to an end. Based on these prophecies above, do you think that conclusion is warranted?

2. Some skeptics point out that not *all* Jewish people live in Israel today, as the Bible predicts. Thus these are false predictions. How would you respond to this argument?

3. With the Palestinian-Israeli conflict raging, some wonder if God is authorizing violence in favor of Israel. Do you think these biblical predictions warrant such violence?

---

[22] Incidentally, this is why conspiracy theorists believe that the Holocaust was a hoax, falsely believing that the Jews deluded the world to regain their land. It might go without saying, but such claims are not only racist, but are bizarre and do not accord with the evidence in any conceivable way.

Chapter 4. Fulfilled Predictions of the Destruction of Cities and Nations

The Bible doesn't restrict its predictions to the life of Jesus or the nation of Israel. In fact, the Hebrew prophets made a number of accurate prophecies about the unique demise of many ancient cities, nations, and empires. As Isaiah wrote, "Everything I prophesied has come true, and now I will prophesy again. I will tell you the future before it happens" (Isa. 42:9 NLT).

Throwing Tyre into the Mediterranean Sea

The city of Tyre was an affluent seaport in the ancient world. The Greek historian Herodotus claimed that the city had existed for 2,300 years before he visited it,[1] and the prophet Isaiah concurred that it had existed "from antiquity" (Isa. 23:7). The historian Strabo claimed that Tyre was "the largest and oldest city of the Phoenicians."[2] The Tell al-Amarna correspondence tells us that Tyre was an "important, fortified city."[3] Yet despite the fact that "Tyre was at the height of its commercial prosperity in the seventh century BC,"[4] Ezekiel predicted its unique and specific destruction (Ezek. 26:3-14).

Many nations would destroy Tyre. Ezekiel wrote, "I will bring up *many nations* against you... She will become spoil for the *nations*" (Ezek. 26:3, 5).

These nations would make Tyre a bare rock. Ezekiel predicted, "They will destroy the walls of Tyre and break down her towers; and I will scrape her debris from her and make her a bare rock" (Ezek. 26:4).

These nations would throw Tyre into the sea. Ezekiel wrote, "She will be a place for the spreading of nets *in the midst of the sea*... They will make a spoil of your riches and a prey of your merchandise, break down your walls and destroy your pleasant houses, and *throw your stones and your timbers and your debris into the water*" (Ezek. 26:5, 12).

---

[1] Herodotus, *Histories*, II, 44.
[2] Strabo, *Geography*, 16.2.22.
[3] Trudy Ring (et al.), *International Dictionary of Historic Places: Middle East and Africa, Volume 4* (Fitzroy Dearborn Publishers: Chicago, IL, 1996), 711.
[4] Trudy Ring (et al.), *International Dictionary of Historic Places: Middle East and Africa, Volume 4* (Fitzroy Dearborn Publishers: Chicago, IL, 1996), 711.

When did Ezekiel predict this?

Most scholars—whether critics or Christians—date Ezekiel's prediction to 587 BC. Robert Manweiler writes, "Ezekiel is probably the most carefully dated of all OT books... we here note that the majority of biblical scholars, *even of those who reject the inspiration and unity of the Bible*, believe most of the book was written in the sixth century BC by the prophet Ezekiel."[5] Even the arch-skeptic Richard Carrier assumes a sixth century date for this prophecy.[6] Thus the date of this prophecy is fairly fixed—even by critics.[7]

Was it fulfilled?

The Babylonian King Nebuchadnezzar attacked Old Tyre as Ezekiel predicted (Ezek. 26:7-11).[8] Josephus records that his siege lasted for thirteen years, but he was unsuccessful in looting the city (585-573 B.C.).[9] He eventually broke through Old Tyre's defenses, but the people retreated to New Tyre (or "Insular Tyre"), which was an island about a half mile from the coast. The new island city was impenetrable. Historian Lewis Cummings comments, "From the dawn of time... the city, impregnable behind its high walls, and located upon a rocky island two miles in circuit and half a mile offshore, had successfully repelled all attempts at invasion."[10]

---

[5] Emphasis mine. Robert C. Newman, *The Evidence of Prophecy: Fulfilled Prediction as a Testimony to the Truth of Christianity* (Hatfield, PA: Interdisciplinary Biblical Research Institute, 1988), 21. OT scholar Gleason Archer confirms this dating. After commenting on the biblical criticism of C.C. Torrey regarding a late dating of Ezekiel, he writes, "Few scholars, however, have followed him in this skepticism, and in more recent years the cumulative data of Palestinian archaeology... point to a complete cessation of Israelite occupation in Palestine during the greater part of the sixth century." Gleason Archer, *A Survey of Old Testament Introduction: Third Edition*, (Chicago: Moody Press. 1994), 412.

[6] Richard Carrier, *Sense and Goodness Without God: A Defense of Metaphysical Naturalism* (Bloomington, IN: Authorhouse, 2005), 249.

[7] After commenting on the biblical criticism of C.C. Torrey regarding a late dating of Ezekiel, Gleason Archer writes, "Few scholars, however, have followed him in this skepticism, and in more recent years the cumulative data of Palestinian archaeology... point to a complete cessation of Israelite occupation in Palestine during the greater part of the sixth century." Gleason Archer, *A Survey of Old Testament Introduction: Third Edition*, 412.

[8] According to the 2010 World Book Encyclopedia, "In 573 B.C., the Babylonians crushed a Tyrian revolt after laying siege to the city for 13 years. Badly weakened, Tyre fell to the Persians in 538 B.C." *The World Book Encyclopedia*. Vol. 19 (Chicago, IL: World Book, 2010), 541-542.

[9] Josephus, *Against Apion*, 1:21.

[10] Lewis Vance Cummings, *Alexander the Great* (New York: Grove, 1968), 175.

Naturally, skeptical readers see nothing supernatural about this portion of Ezekiel's prophecy, because it was fulfilled only a few years after it was written. However, the truly remarkable element comes *two hundred years* later, when Alexander the Great came through and conquered New Tyre (332 B.C.).

THE SIEGE OF TYRE

November 333–August 332 B.C.

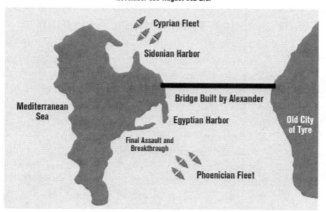

Historians tell us that Alexander the Great didn't want to continue conquering onto Egypt without first securing Tyre behind him. Historian Philip Freeman writes, "If he left Tyre unconquered, it would continue to serve as a base for the Persian navy and, even worse, as a glaring emblem of his failure."[11] Since New Tyre was a half mile from the coast, he ordered his men (and neighboring nations) to build a causeway to the city, which was 200 feet in width (thus fulfilling verse 12 regarding the "many nations" involved).[12] Freeman writes, "Alexander was present every day, conferring with the engineers, encouraging his men, and carrying stone after stone into the sea himself."[13] To build the causeway, Alexander had his men tear down

---

[11] Philip Freeman, *Alexander the Great* (New York: Simon & Schuster, 2011), 133.
[12] Cummings writes, "Diodorus claims to know that is was two hundred feet wide when it was finished." Lewis Vance Cummings, *Alexander the Great* (New York: Grove, 1968), 176.
[13] Philip Freeman, *Alexander the Great* (New York: Simon & Schuster, 2011), 131.

the buildings of Tyre, thereby fulfilling Ezekiel's prediction that they would throw the "stones and timbers and even [their] dust into the sea" (v.12; c.f. Zech. 9:3-4; Isa. 23:2-3, 8, 18).[14]

Today you can still see Alexander's causeway from the air, just under the surface of the Mediterranean. Surely, the pagan Alexander had no motive in fulfilling biblical prophecy, but his conquest of Tyre precisely fulfilled what Ezekiel had predicted centuries before him.

Didn't Ezekiel predict that Nebuchadnezzar would loot the city, rather than Alexander?

Ezekiel predicted that Nebuchadnezzar would attack the city of Tyre: "I will bring upon Tyre from the north Nebuchadnezzar king of Babylon, king of kings, with horses, chariots, cavalry and a great army" (Ezek. 26:7). Skeptic Richard Carrier argues that the third person plural ("they") in verse 12 does not refer to later conquerors (like Alexander); it refers to the "chariots" (v.10) and "horses" (v.11) of Babylon.[15] In other words, Ezekiel never predicted Alexander—only Nebuchadnezzar.

However, Ezekiel very clearly predicted that Nebuchadnezzar would *not* plunder the city: "Nebuchadnezzar king of Babylon made his army labor hard against Tyre… *But he and his army had no wages from Tyre* for the labor that he had performed against it" (Ezek. 29:18). Carrier claims that here Ezekiel had to "retract his prediction" in this verse because it failed.[16] But why does Carrier assume this? If this was really the case, why wouldn't Ezekiel simply edit chapter 26 to fit with what happened? It was his book after all! Moreover, even in chapter 26, Ezekiel very clearly predicted that "*many* nations" would take Tyre (Ezek. 26:3, 5), not just Nebuchadnezzar. Ezekiel's mention of "they" in verse 12 does not refer to the chariots and horses. Instead, it serves as a chiasm with the "many nations" in verses 3-5.

Hasn't Tyre been rebuilt?

Other critics of this prophecy argue that modern Tyre has been rebuilt— despite Ezekiel's prediction that "[Tyre] will be built no more" (v.14). However, since Old Tyre was destroyed and thrown into the sea (as Ezekiel

---

[14] Historian Philip Freeman writes, "The siege of Tyre began with the demolition of older parts of the town on the mainland for construction materials for a causeway to the island." Philip Freeman, *Alexander the Great*, 131.

[15] Richard Carrier, *Sense and Goodness Without God*, 249.

[16] Richard Carrier, *Sense and Goodness Without God*, 249-250.

predicted), the old city has never been rebuilt. Ezekiel had predicted that the "great waters [will] cover you" (Ezekiel 26:19), and he writes, "I will make you dwell *in the lower parts of the earth*, like the ancient waste places, with *those who go down to the pit*, so that you will not be inhabited" (Ezek. 26:20).

Based on this passage, the city of Tyre refers to the inhabitants and materials of the city—not the real estate. No one has pulled the stones and bricks from under the silt; these still rest at the bottom of the Mediterranean Sea. Indeed, an ancient traveler named Benjamin of Tudela commented that he could see the old city buried beneath the shallow sea in AD 1169.[17]

While the current dwellers of Tyre live on the same real estate as Old Tyre, they really have little to do with the ancient city other than being in the same location. Robert Newman adds, "Remembering that Ezekiel spoke against a Tyre that was a world-trade center and naval empire, the fact that the site now has museums and resorts in addition to its fishing village hardly constitutes regaining her former title 'Queen of the Seas.'"[18]

The decline of Egypt (Isa. 19; Ezek. 30)

The Egyptian civilization dominated the ancient world. Many ancient people were hoping to gain Egypt as a military ally (Ezek. 17:15-17; 2 Kings 17:4-7). Thus it's odd that the Hebrew prophets would predict Egypt's political demise. Yet the Hebrew prophets predicted exactly this.

Civil war. Egypt reigned with a unified and centralized government for millennia. Yet in the eighth century BC, Isaiah predicted, "I will incite Egyptians against Egyptians; and they will each fight against his brother and each against his neighbor, city against city and kingdom against kingdom" (Isa. 19:2).

Spoiled canals in the Nile River. Isaiah predicted that the plant life around the Nile would become putrid and withered (Isa. 19:6-7; Ezek. 30:12). Barfield writes, "Today, most canals remain covered—clogged with sand and debris from centuries of neglect."[19]

Spoiled trade and exports. While ancient people considered Egyptian linens a costly treasure (1 Kings 10:28; Ezek. 27:7), Isaiah predicted, "The

---

[17] Benjamin of Tudela, AD 1165. Cited in Wallace Bruce Fleming, *The History of Tyre* (New York: Columbia University Press, 1915), 101.

[18] Robert Newman, "Public Theology and Prophecy Data: Factual Evidence that Counts for the Biblical Worldview." *JETS* 46/1 (March 2003), 96.

[19] Kenny Barfield, *The Prophet Motive: Examining the Reliability of the Biblical Prophets* (Nashville, TN: Gospel Advocate, 1995), 37.

manufacturers of linen made from combed flax and the weavers of white cloth will be utterly dejected" (Isa. 19:9).

Breach of Thebes. Ezekiel predicted multiple "judgments on Thebes" (Ezek. 30:14). The Persian king Cambyses defeated the city in 525 BC—at the height of their prosperity. Ezekiel did not predict that Thebes would be annihilated—just "breached" (v.16).

Destruction of Memphis. Unlike the *breach* of Thebes, Jeremiah predicted the *annihilation* of Memphis. He wrote, "Memphis will become a desolation; it will even be burned down and bereft of inhabitants" (Jer. 46:19). While Memphis was much larger than Thebes, it was completely annihilated. Barfield writes, "Memphis' end came swiftly and silently. Modern scholarship still cannot answer when the city disappeared or why. So complete was the obliteration that even the site of ancient Memphis became a matter of dispute."[20]

Loss of a monarchy. The ancient world recognized Egypt for her centralized government around a single pharaoh, but even though this was the norm, Ezekiel predicted, "There will no longer be a prince in the land of Egypt" (Ezek. 30:13). Egypt has lost the strength of a centralized pharaoh since this time. While Farouk was called a king in Egypt, he was not himself Egyptian; he was of Albanian, French, and Turkish descent.[21] Barfield writes, "With Farouk's overthrow in the 1950s, Egypt's leaders spurned royalty. Nasser found the title offensive, as did Sadat and Mubarik."[22] Egypt abolished the monarchy in 1953.

Decline of Egypt as a world power. Ezekiel predicted, "It will be the *lowest of the kingdoms*, and it will never again lift itself up above the nations. And I will make them so small that they will not rule over the nations" (Ezek. 29:15; 30:4, 6). After the Assyrian Esarhaddon conquered Egypt in 670 BC, several nations conquered Egypt—one after another (e.g. Nebuchadnezzar, Cambyses, Alexander the Great, the Ptolemies, the Turks, and Napoleon). While other ancient peoples have not survived today, Ezekiel predicted that the Egyptian people—much like the Jewish people—would continue as "a *lowly* kingdom" (Ezek. 29:14). Of course, the nation of Egypt still exists today—even as a shadow of the great civilization that it once was.

---

[20] Kenny Barfield, *The Prophet Motive*, 47.
[21] Arthur Goldschmidt, *Biographical Dictionary of Modern Egypt* (Boulder, CO: Lynne Rienner Publishers, 2000), 191.
[22] Kenny Barfield, *The Prophet Motive*, 49-50.

The permanent destruction of Babylon (Isa. 13:19-20; Jer. 51:24-26)

In its day, Babylon dominated the ancient world. The ancient historian Herodotus stated that the walls of Babylon were fourteen miles long, 300 feet tall, and 75 feet thick.[23] More than 50 temples filled the inside of the city. Builders constructed the central 280 foot tall ziggurat with seventeen metric tons of gold.[24] Yet despite all of its decadence and security, the Hebrew prophets foretold Babylon's permanent annihilation and demise.

Many northern nations would conquer Babylon. Jeremiah predicted, "I am going to arouse and bring up against Babylon a horde of great nations from the land of the north, and they will draw up their battle lines against her" (Jer. 50:9). King Cyrus of the Media-Persian Empire ("from the land of the *north*") conquered Babylon in 539 BC.

Babylon will be permanently abandoned. Isaiah predicted, "It will never be inhabited or lived in from generation to generation" (Isa. 13:20). Jeremiah predicted, "You will be desolate *forever*" (Jer. 51:26). When he predicted this, the Hanging Gardens of Babylon were one of the Seven Wonders of the World, and the city itself was an extravagant monument to human achievement. Today, however, an Iraqi tour guide web site notes, "Babylon lies completely in ruins. A large and splendidly carved stone lion is all that remains of its former glories."[25] Indeed, the Hanging Gardens of Babylon are the only ancient wonder whose location is unknown.

Stones will not be plundered from the city. Jeremiah predicted, "They will not take from you even a stone for a corner nor a stone for foundations" (Jer. 51:26). Newman writes, "Interestingly, as Jeremiah predicted, natives who work the site for building materials only take bricks; they burn the stones they find for lime."[26]

People will not take their animals there to graze. Isaiah predicted, "No Arab will pitch his tent there, no shepherd will rest his flocks there" (Isa. 13:20 NIV).

---

[23] Herodotus, *Histories*, 1, 178.
[24] Herodotus records that they used 800 talents, which translates to 16.8 metric tons. Herodotus, *Histories*, 1, 178.
[25] http://middleeastarab.com/iq/cities-iraq-babylon.html.
[26] Robert Newman, "Public Theology and Prophecy Data: Factual Evidence that Counts for the Biblical Worldview." *JETS* 46/1 (March 2003), 94.

Again Newman writes, "Even today, Arabs are afraid to live at the site of Babylon, and its soil is too poor to provide grass for grazing."[27]

Annihilation of Philistia

Gaza would be burned and abandoned. Amos predicted, "I will send fire upon the wall of Gaza and it will consume her citadels" (Amos 1:7). Alexander the Great fulfilled this prophecy in the fourth century BC. Most of the cities surrendered to Alexander, but not Gaza, which fought tenaciously. After being wounded twice in the battle with Gaza, Alexander's fury resulted in the capture and burning of the city, fulfilling Zephaniah's statement that "Gaza will be abandoned" (Zeph. 2:4; cf. Jer. 47:5).

Ashkelon would be abandoned. The Hebrew prophets foresaw that Ashkelon would be "a desolation" (Zeph. 2:4), "ruined" (Jer. 47:5), and "not inhabited" (Zech. 9:5). Barfield writes, "After the Babylonian period, Ashkelon disappeared from historical records. She reappeared in the Hellenistic period and endured a violent and bloody history for 1,500 years."[28]

Ekron would be abandoned. Zephaniah predicted, "Ekron will be uprooted" (Zeph. 2:4). This was surely a play on words, because "the city's name means 'firm-rooted.'"[29] Likewise, Amos predicted, "I will even unleash My power upon Ekron, and the remnant of the Philistines will perish" (Amos 1:8). Barfield writes, "Babylon's military pushed the Philistines from Ekron at the end of the seventh century. Her citizens faced deportation. Those few who managed to escape mixed with other people in the region. Ekron disappeared, along with her Philistine inhabitants."[30]

Destruction of Jerusalem (Dan. 9:26; cf. Lk. 21:20-24)

Daniel predicted the destruction of Jerusalem and the Jewish Temple. He wrote, "The people of the prince who is to come will destroy the city and the sanctuary" (Dan. 9:26). Certainly, it's odd for a Jewish author to predict the destruction of his nation's own capitol and religious temple. And yet, Daniel predicted this centuries in advance. The Roman armies viciously

---

[27] Robert C. Newman "Fulfilled Prophecy as Miracle." Douglas Geivett and Gary Habermas, *In Defense of Miracles: a Comprehensive Case for God's Action in History* (Downers Grove, IL: InterVarsity, 1997), 220.

[28] Kenny Barfield, *The Prophet Motive*, 79.

[29] Kenny Barfield, *The Prophet Motive*, 80.

[30] Kenny Barfield, *The Prophet Motive*, 80.

destroyed the city of Jerusalem, fulfilling these predictions in AD 70. Since even critical scholars date Daniel to 164 BC, Daniel's prediction occurred at least a full two centuries before its fulfillment.

Conclusion

What can we say about this survey of biblical prophecies? Is this good evidence that a transcendent God knows and communicates the future to us through the pages of Scripture? Atheist Douglas Krueger offers several criteria for what would constitute a valid supernatural prediction. He writes, "Some criteria are needed in order to distinguish cases of lucky guesses from those of true prophecy. Let us define a genuine prophecy as one that satisfies the following five criteria."[31]

CRITERION #1: The prophecy must be clear, and it must contain sufficient detail to make its fulfillment by a wide variety of possible events unlikely.

Unlike prophecies from non-biblical sources,[32] you can see for yourself that the Bible offers clear and understandable predictions of the future.

CRITERION #2: The event that can fulfill the prophecy must be unusual or unique.

The Bible predicts unique details about the demise of specific cities and civilizations. For instance, in the case of the destruction of Tyre, it predicted that "many nations" (Ezek. 26:3, 5) would throw Tyre into the Mediterranean Sea (Ezek. 26:5, 12). Likewise, while it predicts the *permanent* demise of many nations (e.g. Moab, Philistia, Babylon, etc.), it only predicts the *temporary crippling* of nations like Egypt (Ezek. 29:10-14). While Ezekiel predicted that Egypt would be "the lowest of the nations" (Ezek. 29:14-15), he predicted that it would still be a nation in the future (cf. Dan. 11:42; Mic. 7:12; Zech. 14:18; Isa. 11:11; 19:22-25). When was the last time you met a Moabite? What about a Philistine? Bumped into any Babylonians recently? Of course not. These civilizations have disappeared from the face of the Earth, but Egypt still remains—just as the Bible predicted.

---

[31] Douglas E. Krueger, *What Is Atheism?: A Short Introduction* (Amherst, NY: Prometheus, 1998), 96-98.
[32] See my earlier work for a survey of so-called predictive prophecy from other non-biblical sources. James Rochford, *Evidence Unseen*, 111-128.

CRITERION #3: The prophecy must be known to have been made before the event that is supposed to be its fulfillment.

The Hebrew prophets made their predictions centuries (or in some cases millennia) before their fulfillments.

CRITERION #4: The event foretold must not be of the sort that could be the result of an educated guess.

While we might feel uncomfortable giving exact probabilities to these predictions above, we can intuitively see that these predictions are surely not "educated guesses." How could they have guessed on these specific global events?

CRITERION #5: The event that fulfills the prophecy cannot be staged, or the relevant circumstances manipulated, by those aware of the prophecy in such a way as to intentionally cause the prophecy to be fulfilled.

Most of these prophecies could not be self-fulfilled. It would be incredibly odd to think that a bloodthirsty pagan king like Alexander the Great would have any interest in fulfilling biblical prophecy. Furthermore, some of these predictions even inflicted judgment on Israel herself, predicting the destruction of Jerusalem and the Temple (Dan. 9:26). Surely the people of Jerusalem did not incite the Jewish War in order to fulfill biblical prophecy! Such a thought borders on insanity.

Thus if we follow Douglas Krueger's criteria, we would need to regard these passages as cases of "genuine prophecy."

Discussion questions

1. Some of these predictions are more remarkable than others. Which do you find to be the most persuasive? Why or why not? Do you find these predictions more or less persuasive than those covered in earlier chapters?

2. Skeptics argue that given enough time *every* city will be destroyed. After all, empires crumble all the time. Therefore, these prophecies aren't that spectacular. How would you respond?

3. Do you think you could present this material to a friend if you only had ten minutes to do so? How would you make a quick and convincing case if you only had your Bible and maybe a pen and paper?

Chapter 5. Fulfilled Predictions of World Empires

Imagine if you could predict the next five hundred years of world history. Would it be a blessing or a curse? Would you want to know what would happen, or would you be content with blissful ignorance?

The Hebrew prophet Daniel didn't have a choice.

In the sixth century BC, the Babylonian Empire invaded Israel, capturing Daniel and his three friends. Nebuchadnezzar—the king of Babylon—deported these young men to be brainwashed viceroys, leading Israel for him as an occupied state. But instead of brainwashing Daniel, Nebuchadnezzar ended up coming to him for help. After having a terrifying dream of a giant statue, Nebuchadnezzar asked Daniel to interpret his nightmare. Daniel claimed that the king's dream predicted the future—a remarkable forecast of the next several centuries of global politics. This young Jewish prophet told the king, "Let the name of God be blessed forever and ever, for wisdom and power belong to Him. It is He who changes the times and the epochs; He removes kings and establishes kings; He gives wisdom to wise men and knowledge to men of understanding" (Dan. 2:20-21).

Three Successive Visions (Dan. 2, 7, 8)

Daniel told the king that God "has made known to King Nebuchadnezzar what will take place *in the latter days*" and "what would take place *in the future*" (Dan. 2:28-29). Clearly, Daniel believed that the king's dream predicted the future. OT scholar Stephen Miller concurs, "Virtually all scholars agree that the different parts of the statue represent empires or kingdoms."[1]

In addition to Nebuchadnezzar's dream, Daniel saw visions of these world empires. Miller notes, "Virtually everyone agrees that the vision of chapter 7 parallels the dream image of chapter 2 and that both passages should be interpreted in the same manner."[2] This much, at least, isn't debated by interpreters. The three visions in Daniel 2, 7, and 8 hang together in a unit.

---

[1] Stephen R. Miller, *Daniel*. New American Commentary. Vol. 18. (Nashville, TN: Broadman, 1994), 92-93.

[2] Stephen R. Miller, *Daniel*. New American Commentary. Vol. 18. (Nashville, TN: Broadman, 1994), 218.

In his dream, Nebuchadnezzar saw a statue with a head of gold, chest and arms of silver, belly and thighs of bronze, legs of iron, and feet of iron mixed with clay (Dan. 2:31-33). Finally, a stone collided with the feet of the statue, crushing it (Dan. 2:34-35). In chapters seven and eight, Daniel himself sees visions of various animals and beasts. Instead of leaving us to speculate about the meaning of these visions, Daniel explains them, predicting the succession of world empires with clarity.

DANIEL 2 PROPHECY

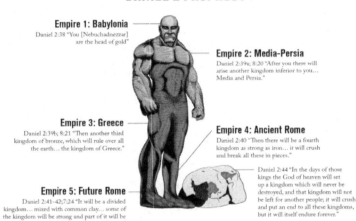

Empire 1: Babylonia
Daniel 2:38 "You [Nebuchadnezzar] are the head of gold"

Empire 2: Media-Persia
Daniel 2:39a; 8:20 "After you there will arise another kingdom inferior to you... Media and Persia."

Empire 3: Greece
Daniel 2:39b; 8:21 "Then another third kingdom of bronze, which will rule over all the earth... the kingdom of Greece."

Empire 4: Ancient Rome
Daniel 2:40 "Then there will be a fourth kingdom as strong as iron... it will crush and break all these in pieces."

Daniel 2:44 "In the days of those kings the God of heaven will set up a kingdom which will never be destroyed, and that kingdom will not be left for another people; it will crush and put an end to all these kingdoms, but it will itself endure forever."

Empire 5: Future Rome
Daniel 2:41-42; 7:24 "It will be a divided kingdom... mixed with common clay... some of the kingdom will be strong and part of it will be brittle... out of this kingdom ten kings will arise."

EMPIRE #1. BABYLONIA: Head of Gold, Winged Lion (Dan. 2:38; 7:4)

> You [Nebuchadnezzar] are the head of gold. (Dan. 2:38)

> The first was like a *lion* and had the *wings of an eagle*. I kept looking until its wings were plucked, and it was lifted up from the ground and made to stand on two feet like a man; *a human mind also was given to it*. (Dan. 7:4)

Daniel makes no mention of Babylonia in chapter 8, because it was already deposed as an empire at that point (Dan. 8:1). However, in 2:38, Daniel clearly equates the head of gold with Babylon ("You [Nebuchadnezzar] are the head of gold").

Just as Daniel saw a vision of a "lion" with the "wings of an eagle," Jeremiah symbolized Nebuchadnezzar as a "lion" (Jer. 4:7; 49:19, 22; 50:17, 44) and various prophets characterized him as an "eagle" (Jer. 49:22; Lam. 4:19; Ezek. 17:3; Hab. 1:8). Archer writes, "The lion symbol was characteristic of Babylon, especially in Nebuchadnezzar's time, when the Ishtar Gate entrance was adorned on either side with a long procession of yellow lions on blue-glazed brick."[3] Moreover, the expression "a human mind was given to it" refers to Nebuchadnezzar getting his sanity back after God took it from him (Dan. 4:28-37) for seven years (Dan. 4:16).

Nebuchadnezzar's reign ended in 562 BC—a number of decades after Daniel made this prediction. Several kings reigned after him, but the Persians ultimately defeated Babylonia in 539 BC.

EMPIRE #2. MEDIA-PERSIA: Breast and Arms of Silver, Bear, Ram (Dan. 2:39a; 7:5; 8:3, 20)

> After you there will arise another kingdom inferior to you. (Dan. 2:39a)

> Behold, another beast, a second one, resembling a bear. And it was raised up on one side, and three ribs were in its mouth between its teeth; and thus they said to it, 'Arise, devour much meat!' (Dan. 7:5)

> Then I lifted my eyes and looked, and behold, a ram which had two horns was standing in front of the canal. Now the two horns were long, but one was longer than the other, with the longer one coming up last... The ram which you saw with the two horns represents the kings of Media and Persia. (Dan. 8:3, 20)

Daniel doesn't explicitly name this kingdom in chapter 2. However in his second and third vision, he identifies it as Media-Persia (Dan. 8:20).

Historically, Media-Persia ruled from 539 to 331 BC. Daniel describes this second kingdom as "inferior" to Babylon (Dan. 2:39a), which probably refers to its moral quality. When he records the bear being "raised up on one side" (Dan. 7:5), this refers to the Persians being greater than the Medes, absorbing them into their great empire. The "three ribs... in its mouth" (Dan. 7:5) describe how the Media-Persians subdued the three empires of Babylonia (539 B.C.), Lydia (546 B.C.), and Egypt (525 B.C.).

---

[3] Gleason Archer, *Daniel*. In F. E. Gaebelein (Ed.), *The Expositor's Bible Commentary, Volume 7: Daniel and the Minor Prophets* (Grand Rapids, MI: Zondervan Publishing House, 1986), 85-86.

Finally, by describing Media-Persia as a ram (Dan. 8:5), Miller comments that this "was a fitting symbol of the empire... the Persian ruler carried the gold head of a ram when he marched before his army."[4] Just as modern day football teams have animals as their mascots, the Persians used a golden ram to symbolize the strength of their great army.

EMPIRE #3. GREECE: Belly and Thighs of Bronze, Four-Winged Leopard, Shaggy Goat (Dan. 2:39b; 7:6; 8:21-22)

> Then another third kingdom of bronze, which will *rule over all the earth*. (Dan. 2:39b)

> Behold, another one, *like a leopard*, which had on its back four wings of a bird; the beast also had *four heads*, and dominion was given to it. (Dan. 7:6)

> The shaggy goat *represents the kingdom of Greece* 22 The *four horns* that replaced the one that was broken off represent *four kingdoms* that will emerge from his nation but will not have the same power. (Dan. 8:21-22)

Daniel sees Greece as a leopard: an animal known for its *speed*, rather than its *strength*. Alexander conquered the known world at an alarming rate—within 10 to 15 years. The Grecian Empire held its reign from 333 to 63 BC.

Daniel mentions that there were "four horns that replaced the one that was broken off," and he states that these "represent four kingdoms that will emerge from his nation but will not have the same power" (Dan. 8:22 NIV). Since Alexander didn't have a living heir to inherit his empire,[5] four of his generals tried to usurp power after his premature death (Dan. 8:8). His generals were (1) Antipater in Macedon-Greece, (2) Lysimachus in Thrace-Asia Minor, (3) Seleucus in Asia, and (4) Ptolemy in Egypt, Cyrenaica, and Palestine, which split the Greek Empire into four factions—just as Daniel predicted.[6]

---

[4] Stephen R. Miller, *Daniel*. New American Commentary. Vol. 18. (Nashville, TN: Broadman, 1994), 222.
[5] Alexander had two sons (Alexander IV and Herakles), but others vying for control of his massive empire had them quickly murdered to commandeer power.
[6] Gleason Archer, *Daniel*. In F. E. Gaebelein (Ed.), *The Expositor's Bible Commentary, Volume 7: Daniel and the Minor Prophets* (Grand Rapids, MI: Zondervan Publishing House, 1986), 47.

EMPIRE #4. ROME: Legs of Iron—Feet of Iron and Clay, 10 horned beast with iron Teeth (Dan. 2:40; 7:7)

> Then there will be a *fourth kingdom as strong as iron*; inasmuch as *iron crushes and shatters all things*, so, like iron that breaks in pieces, it will crush and break all these in pieces. (Dan. 2:40)

> After this I kept looking in the night visions, and behold, a fourth beast, dreadful and terrifying and extremely strong; and it had *large iron teeth*. It devoured and crushed and trampled down the remainder with its feet; and it was different from all the beasts that were before it, and it had *ten horns*. (Dan. 7:7)

Daniel specifies this following kingdom as a single one ("it"), and he considers it more vicious than the earlier kingdoms. He connects the visions of chapters 2 and 7 by mentioning their ten iron toes and teeth (Dan. 7:7), as well as their ten toes and horns (Dan. 2:41-42). Since both empires are mentioned last in these visions, it only further links these two visions together.

The Roman Empire didn't exist when Daniel made this prediction in the sixth century BC. This is probably why Daniel can't even describe the beast itself, using language like "dreadful and terrifying and extremely strong," rather than giving it a name like the others (e.g. lion, bear, ram, etc.). At the same time, Daniel's descriptions surely match the Roman Empire, which "dominated the world from the defeat of Carthage in 146 B.C. to the division of the East and West empires in A.D. 395, approximately five hundred years."[7] Furthermore, both Josephus and 2 Esdras (12:10-51) believed the fourth empire was Rome. Actually, it wasn't until modern times that critics questioned this interpretation.[8]

Some critical scholars believe that the end of Daniel's four world kingdoms came with Antiochus in 167 BC, splitting Media-Persia into two successive kingdoms. But Daniel clearly speaks of Media-Persia as one empire—not two (Dan. 6:8, 15; 8:20). Other critical scholars argue that the fourth beast is the successor of Alexander the Great. However, Archer argues, "Such an identification of the fourth empire can hardly be reconciled with the

---

[7] Stephen R. Miller, *Daniel*. New American Commentary. Vol. 18. (Nashville, TN: Broadman, 1994), 95.

[8] Miller writes, "Only in modern times did the opinion that Greece was the fourth empire become widespread." Stephen R. Miller, *Daniel*. New American Commentary. Vol. 18. (Nashville, TN: Broadman, 1994), 95.

description of the fourth kingdom (cf. 7:7) as greater and stronger than the third. Could one segment of Alexander's empire be considered more extensive than his entire realm? Or could its power be considered more formidable than that of Alexander himself—Alexander who never lost a battle? This theory cannot be taken seriously."[9] Thus this fourth beast must be identified with the Roman Empire.

Why does Daniel give *three* visions, rather than just *one*?

God gave Daniel three successive visions about the future. But why? Was God trying to be needlessly confusing?

Undoubtedly, Daniel received three visions to convince him of the certainty of this event. Similarly, when Pharaoh asked Joseph why he received two dreams instead of one, Joseph told him, "As for the repeating of the dream to Pharaoh twice, *it means that the matter is determined by God, and God will quickly bring it about*" (Gen. 41:32). The repetition of these visions emphasized their certainty.

Moreover, these three visions offer different perspectives on world empires: one human and one divine. The vision of the daunting statue in Daniel 2 offers a human perspective on the empires, while the visions of the beasts in Daniel 7 and 8 offer God's perspective. While world empires might look impressive to humans (Dan. 2), they look like ravenous and savage beasts to God (Dan. 7, 8).

Was Daniel a prophet or a historian?

Daniel accurately predicted the world empires that would conquer Israel. How is this possible? Critics offer a simple answer: Daniel wasn't *foreseeing* future events; instead, he was *recording* past events. According to critical scholars, "Daniel" didn't write his book in 530 BC. Instead he wrote it in 167 BC to encourage Jewish patriots as they revolted against the tyranny of Antiochus Epiphanes IV—a vicious Greek dictator. Is it plausible that this book was really a forgery of the second century BC?

---

[9] Gleason Archer, *Daniel*. In F. E. Gaebelein (Ed.), *The Expositor's Bible Commentary, Volume 7: Daniel and the Minor Prophets* (Grand Rapids, MI: Zondervan Publishing House, 1986), 48.

Evidence for a sixth century composition of Daniel

Before we consider the evidence for an early dating of Daniel, we should remember that the biblical authors believed in the authenticity of Daniel. The author claimed to be writing during this time (Dan. 7:1; 12:4), and Jesus himself said, "You [will] see the abomination of desolation which was spoken of through Daniel the prophet" (Mt. 24:15). Here Jesus believed Daniel was a real and historical person, and he called him a prophet—not a historian. He also believed Daniel predicted his future Second Coming accurately (Mt. 26:64; c.f. Dan. 7:13-14).

Similarly, the prophet Ezekiel lived in roughly 575 BC, and he explained that Daniel was a real and historical figure (Ezek. 14:14, 20; 28:3). Of course, as we have already seen, even critics concede that Ezekiel dates to the sixth century. So, to deal with Ezekiel's reference to Daniel, they argue that Ezekiel was actually referring to an ancient Canaanite hero from pagan mythology![10]

Such a theory is absurd. In chapter 14, Ezekiel denounced both paganism and idolatry. Why would Ezekiel refer to this man as a hero of the Jewish faith, placing him alongside of Noah and Job (Ezek. 14:14), if he was actually a mythological Baal worshipper? Moreover, in Ezekiel 28:3 we read, "You are wiser than Daniel; there is no secret that is a match for you." Here Ezekiel gives us a clear reference to Daniel 1 and 2, where the prophet Daniel had wisdom in interpreting Nebuchadnezzar's dreams, when all of the false prophets were unable.

If we deny a sixth century dating of this book, we place ourselves in the rather awkward position of claiming that Daniel, Jesus, and Ezekiel were all mistaken. (Naturally, critics of the Bible see no problem in doing just this!) But were they mistaken? What is the evidence for a sixth century dating of Daniel?

First, early Jewish authors assume a sixth century dating for Daniel. Josephus—a first century Jewish and Roman historian—believed that fourth century Jews showed the book of Daniel to Alexander the Great, when he came to Jerusalem in 330 BC. After reading the prophecy of Daniel 8, Josephus records that Alexander had an uncharacteristically charitable attitude toward the Jewish people and "asked what favors they pleased of him... and he

---

[10] For example, see Walter Eichrodt, *Ezekiel: A Commentary* (Westminster Press: Philadelphia, 1970) 189; 391. Moshe Greenberg, *Ezekiel 1-20*. The Anchor Bible (New York: Bantam Doubleday Publishing, 1983), 257.

granted all they desired."[11] In addition to Josephus, the author of 1 Maccabees believed Daniel was a historical person in 167 BC (1 Mac. 2:59-61), as did the author of 1 Enoch in 150 BC (1 Enoch 14:18-22, citing Dan. 7:9-10).

Second, historical evidence supports a sixth century dating of Daniel. Throughout his book, Daniel offers firsthand knowledge of sixth century events:

> *Daniel differentiates Susa and Elam properly.* In Daniel 8:2, Daniel writes that he was "in the citadel of Susa, which is in the province of Elam." The Persian era assigned Susa to a new province in the sixth century. Later on, the territory of Elam shrunk, placing Susa in the province of Susiana. A second century author would have been out of date with this historical fact—yet a sixth century author would've known this detail.[12]

> *Daniel properly identifies Belshazzar (5:1).* Critics formerly held that Daniel invented the fact that Belshazzar ruled Persia in 539 BC. All non-biblical sources listed Nabonidus as the final king of Persia—not the unknown Belshazzar. Even by the time of Herodotus (450 BC), Greek historians had already forgotten the name of Belshazzar. However, in the last century, "thirty-seven archival texts dated from the first to the fourteenth year of Nabonidus now attest to Belshazzar's historicity."[13] These texts demonstrate that these two kings ruled at the same time. Nabonidus ruled in the south at Tema, while Belshazzar ruled the rest of the kingdom. A second century author would have needed to recover information about this historical figure apart from any known records.[14]

> *Daniel accurately described the methods of capital punishment for Babylonia and Persia.* Daniel knew that Babylonians killed people *by fire* (Dan. 3:11), but Persians killed people *by throwing them to lions* (Dan. 6:7). Miller writes, "Fire was sacred to the Zoroastrians of Persia," so they didn't use this for executions.[15]

---

[11] Josephus, *Antiquities*, 11.8.5.

[12] Gleason Archer, *A Survey of Old Testament Introduction: Revised and Expanded* (Chicago, IL: Moody, 2007), 380.

[13] Stephen R. Miller, *Daniel*. New American Commentary. Vol. 18. (Nashville, TN: Broadman, 1994), 147.

[14] Gleason Archer, *A Survey of Old Testament Introduction: Revised and Expanded* (Chicago, IL: Moody, 2007), 366.

[15] Stephen R. Miller, *Daniel*. New American Commentary. Vol. 18. (Nashville, TN: Broadman, 1994), 26.

Third, literary evidence supports an early dating of Daniel. Imagine if you read Elizabethan English alongside lyrics from a modern rap album. Surely you'd have no problem discerning which one was contemporary and which wasn't. Similarly, the Aramaic of Daniel 2-7 contains language from the sixth century—not the second. Yamauchi writes, "Discoveries, such as Adon's letter in Aramaic (sixth cent. BC), have confirmed the fact that the Aramaic of Ezra and of Daniel is basically the same as the Aramaic of the sixth-fifth centuries as we know it from contemporary evidence."[16] Archer concurs that Daniel uses *Imperial* Aramaic, which was common in the fifth century BC, not in later periods.[17]

Daniel's book does contain three Greek loan words (all of which refer to musical instruments, Dan. 3:5), and critics charge that this shows that Daniel wrote under Greek occupation in 167 BC. However, these words do not need to be Greek in origin. For example, an English document containing the word *piano* or *viola* would not need to be influenced by Italian culture. These loan words simply crept into multiple cultures at once. Greek culture likely influenced Persian culture—even before Greece conquered Persia. Therefore, this evidence doesn't carry much weight in discerning the dating of Daniel.

Moreover, scholar Gleason Archer flips this argument on its head by writing that we would actually expect *more* Greek words in Daniel, if he truly wrote it in 167 BC: "The presence of Greek words turns out to be one of the most compelling evidences of all that Daniel could not have been composed as late as the Greek period."[18] By 170 BC, the Greeks had occupied Palestine for a century and a half, and yet not one word of Greek is in the Hebrew sections of this book, flying directly in the face of a second century composition.

Why was Daniel placed with the Writings— rather than the Prophets?

Jewish Bibles placed Daniel with the Writings—not the Prophets. Why didn't the Jewish Bible place Daniel with the prophets, if he truly was a prophet?

---

[16] Edwin Yamauchi, *Greece and Babylon: Early Contacts Between the Aegean and the Near East* (Grand Rapids, MI: Baker, 1967), 91.
[17] Gleason Archer, *A Survey of Old Testament Introduction: Revised and Expanded* (Chicago, IL: Moody, 2007), 397.
[18] Gleason Archer, *A Survey of Old Testament Introduction: Revised and Expanded* (Chicago, IL: Moody, 2007), 396.

Daniel didn't hold the *profession* of a prophet in Israel. He served under pagan kings as a *statesman* and *royal official*. J. Barton Payne explains, "For though Christ spoke of Daniel's *function* as prophetic, his *position* was that of governmental official and inspired writer, rather than ministering prophet."[19] Jewish prophets held the title of prophet in Israel. Since Daniel never lived in Israel and served as a statesman in Babylon and Persia, this could explain why he wasn't placed with the other prophets. Of course, Jesus (a first century rabbi) believed that Daniel was a prophet—not a mere historian (Mt. 24:15).

Conclusion

Multiple lines of evidence point to a sixth century dating of Daniel, but critical scholars regularly reject an early dating. Why? They do not base this conclusion on the evidence, but rather on the *assumption* that the supernatural is impossible.

Yet this is really a *philosophical* objection to the dating of Daniel—not a *historical* one. If God exists, then predicting the accurate sequence of world empires would be no more difficult than knowing our shoe size or our favorite color. Critical historians merely *assume* that God does not exist in order to make supernatural predictions, but when we read their commentaries, do they ever offer any evidence for this assumption? For instance, in the introduction to a critical commentary on Daniel, do we ever see a chapter that philosophically argues that God cannot predict the future? Of course not. Why then should we treat their assumptions seriously?

Why should we trust the unjustified assumptions of a historian to guide our interpretation of Scripture? Philosophy of religion isn't their area of expertise. This would be like asking a *meteorologist* her professional opinion on *car transmissions*; or asking an *actor* his professional opinion on *politics*. While they might be insightful (and even accurate) in their views, they are out of their area of expertise! If we are supposed to take their claims seriously, they would need to offer evidence to support them—just like anyone else. Critical commentaries, however, abound with the assumption of anti-supernaturalism without offering any reasons to support it. If we are going to listen to their assertions and assumptions, then we need to hear their arguments.

---

[19] J.B. Payne, "Book of Daniel." Cited in Merrill C. Tenney, *The Zondervan Pictorial Bible Dictionary* (Grand Rapids: Zondervan Pub. House, 1963), 198.

It seems then that Daniel's predictions offer us two options: Either we deny the massive evidence for a sixth century composition, or we bend our knee to the existence of the God of the Bible. As Daniel himself said, "He changes times and seasons; he sets up kings and deposes them. He gives wisdom to the wise and knowledge to the discerning" (Dan. 2:21 NIV).

Discussion questions

1. How persuasive do you find these prophecies from Daniel? How do you think they compare to the other fulfilled predictions we surveyed so far? Are these more convincing or less convincing in your opinion?

2. If someone claimed that Daniel was written in 167 BC, what are three key points you could make to counter this claim?

3. At the end of the chapter, we read that "anti-supernaturalism" might explain why critical historians reject a sixth century dating of Daniel. Is this a fair assessment? Couldn't skeptics retort that Christians are also biased in *wanting* to believe in a sixth century dating because it supports their belief in God and the inspiration of the Bible? How might you respond?

Part Two: Competing Interpretations of the Future

Many books about biblical prophecy fill the shelves at bookstores, but how do we know if their interpretations are correct? Why do students of Scripture come to such different conclusions about God's plan for the future? Is this project completely hopeless?

If you have ever wondered about these questions, you should take your time working through the next section of this book. While this section might be technical and complicated at times, it's important to study in order to have a firm grasp of the issues. We shouldn't merely know *what* the Bible teaches, but *why* we hold our particular view and *how* our view compares to competing interpretations. If we cannot justify why we hold to our view, what makes us any better than a prophecy fanatic?

By studying several different views, we can see where we're biased in our own understanding, or perhaps recognize biases in the thinking of others. Therefore in these next several chapters, we will look at the major schools of thought concerning eschatology. Then, we will continue to the more specific details of God's plan.

Chapter 6. Interpreting Prophecy

When working on my undergraduate degree, I sat in a classroom filled with other 20-year-old college students. We read one of Walt Whitman's poems, and a girl in the class offered a very interesting interpretation: she thought the poem was about the Vietnam War. I remember objecting (politely, I hope) that the poem couldn't be about the Vietnam War—after all Whitman wrote the poem 100 years before that event ever occurred! Either Whitman was a prophet, or the young girl's interpretation was (dare I say it?) *wrong*.

One of the purposes of poetry is to speak to the reader in a multitude of ways, and that's part of its enjoyment. But should we interpret the Bible this way? Not at all. When we read the Bible, we do not want to import *our* meaning into the text; instead, we want to discover *God's* intended meaning. Like visiting a medical doctor to discover why we are sick, we don't want to bring our expertise to the table; we want the doctor's.

We all have our biases when we read our Bibles. To keep these biases from spoiling a proper interpretation, theologians study the subject of hermeneutics (pronounced her-muh-NOO-ticks). *Hermeneutics is the art and science of interpretation.* Put simply, we need rules to help guide us in understanding what the author intended when writing the text. When interpreting the Bible, we don't want to *see* what we *know*; instead, we want to *know* what we *see*. The study of hermeneutics guards us from turning the Bible into a collection of tea leaves at the bottom of a porcelain cup, creating a meaning about the future that was never intended.

RULE #1: Context, context, context!

In the movie *Fight Club* (1999), Tyler Durden (played by Brad Pitt) says, "The first rule of fight club is, *'You don't talk about fight club.'* The second rule of fight club is, *'You don't talk about fight club.'*" The same is true with the rules of hermeneutics: The first three rules are: (1) context, (2) context, and (3) context! This bears repeating, because interpreters most often ignore this vital rule.

Context can radically alter our interpretation. Imagine if someone told you, "I saw your wife kissing another man in bed this week." I'm sure this would immediately make your pulse rise. But what if you later discovered that your wife was actually kissing her elderly father on the forehead in his hospital bed? The context of this statement would mean the difference between adultery and empathy!

The same principle applies to interpreting Scripture. A number of years ago, a drunk man told a friend of mine that the Bible teaches, "There is no God," citing Psalm 14:1. This really bothered my friend, until someone showed him the context of this passage, which states, *"The fool has said in his heart*, 'There is no God.'" If my friend didn't check the context, he could have concluded that the Bible was an atheistic text![1]

If an interpreter believes that the context has changed, then he must shoulder the full burden of proof to explain why he thinks this is the case. Otherwise, we need to respect the context of a passage.

RULE #2: Assume a literal interpretation

In the science fiction film *Guardians of the Galaxy* (2014), the brilliant and bionic Rocket Raccoon states that his friend Drax comes from a species that understands language hyper-literally. Rocket says, "Metaphors go right over his head." Drax frowns and says, "Nothing goes over my head... My reflexes are excellent, and I would catch it!"

As this exchange demonstrates, we shouldn't interpret every statement literally. Symbolism, simile, and even sarcasm fill the pages of Scripture. If we took these statements literally, we would easily miss the author's intent. For instance, if someone said, "My pet dog kicked the bucket," she isn't talking about a literal bucket. This is an expression for death. Interpreting it literally would miss the meaning of the statement. Likewise, if I just finished awkwardly dancing on a wedding floor to rap music, and someone said, "Wow! That was the best dancing I've seen in a long time..." I would quickly (and painfully) discern that this was sarcasm. This "encouragement" wouldn't lead me to pursue a career in professional dancing!

While not all statements should be interpreted literally, we should assume a literal interpretation unless there is sufficient reason to interpret non-literally. In other words, the burden of proof rests on the person who holds to a non-literal reading. We should follow this maxim: "If the plain sense makes sense, seek no other sense, lest it result in nonsense."[2]

Without this basic rule, subjectivity poisons the meaning of the text. For instance, Matthew Henry interpreted the prophecy of Zechariah 14 to refer

---

[1] Other examples would include claiming that the Bible supports hedonism based on Luke 12:19, or smoking marijuana based on Genesis 1:29 and 1 Timothy 4:4.
[2] See Dwight Pentecost, *Things to Come,* 42.

to the Church. He writes that the "great mountain" is the "way of the Jews' conversion," and "the valley of the mountains is the gospel-church, to which there were added of the Jews daily such as should be saved, who fled to that valley as to their refuge."[3] Surely, nothing in the text itself would guide us toward this wild interpretation.

Just imagine if we ignored this principle when interpreting passages on soteriology (the study of salvation) or Christology (the study of Christ). We would quickly obscure key doctrines of the Christian faith. Similarly, we should hold this same principle consistently in every area of theology, including eschatology.

RULE #3: Learn to properly identify symbols

The greatest authors enjoy using symbolism, so it shouldn't surprise us to see Scripture using symbolism frequently. John writes that the Whore of Babylon is "drunk with the blood of the saints" (Rev. 17:6). What graphic imagery: A woman with blood dripping from her mouth, staggering from feasting on the bodies of believers! This captures something that the word "evil" simply couldn't.

But how can we identify symbolism without slipping carelessly into subjectivity? Several key principles help us to interpret symbols:

Does a literal reading lead to contradictions or nonsense? Imagine if someone said, "I'm freezing out here!" A literal interpretation would dictate that the person's body temperature had dropped below 32 degrees Fahrenheit. If the person was 32 degrees Fahrenheit, they'd be dead. While it might just seem like common sense, this shows that the literal meaning of the statement should be abandoned. Similarly, when the psalmist writes that God is a Rock (Ps. 78:35), we quickly identify that this cannot be the case, because God is a spiritual being (Jn. 4:24). Likewise, when Jesus said, "I am the door" (Jn. 10:7), common sense tells us that he was not made of wood with metal hinges.

What does the immediate context tell us about the symbol? We should prefer the explanation in the context, rather than looking elsewhere for its meaning. For instance, Daniel explains the meaning of his own symbols and visions (cf. Dan. 2:38). Likewise, the "great harlot who sits on many waters" might confuse us (Rev. 17:1), until we read verse 15, which explains that the

---

[3] Matthew Henry, *Matthew Henry's Commentary on the Whole Bible: Complete and Unabridged in One Volume* (Peabody: Hendrickson, 1994), 1593. While Henry's interpretation is surely dated, even modern interpreters still support this view. See Gary DeMar, *Last Days Madness* (Atlanta, GA: American Vision, 1999), 442.

"waters" are actually "nations." Most symbols can be interpreted by just reading the context.[4]

What does the rest of the Bible tell us about the symbol? The book of Revelation makes roughly 250 allusions to the OT.[5] In order to interpret symbols in the NT, we would be wise to steep ourselves in the OT Scriptures with which they were familiar. For instance in Revelation 12:14, we read, "Two wings of the great eagle were given to the [people], so that she could fly into the wilderness to her place." Because the book of Revelation does not explain this symbol, some interpreters have claimed that this must refer to helicopters saving the people during the Tribulation! When we turn to the OT, however, we discover this symbolism in Exodus 19:4 and Deuteronomy 32:11, where *God* rescues his people like an eagle.

Other times, we should appeal to the rest of the NT to interpret a given symbol. For instance, Revelation states that a sword protruded out of Jesus' mouth (Rev. 1:16). Obviously, we shouldn't interpret this passage as Jesus choking on a sword. Rather, this refers to him speaking the word of God, which "is living and active and sharper than any two-edged sword" (Heb. 4:12).

Many interpreters appeal to extra-biblical apocalyptic literature to discern symbols from the book of Revelation *before* appealing to the biblical sources. This is a mistake. While extra-biblical sources do offer insights into symbols, we shouldn't elevate these *over* allusions within the Bible itself. While we are certain that the book of Revelation does allude to the OT, we are not as certain in regards to extra-biblical sources; thus allusions to the biblical sources should carry greater value.

What does the historical or cultural context tell us about the symbol? Jesus promises believers a "white stone" (Rev. 2:17). This might confuse us until we study the city of ancient Pergamum, discovering that this culture historically used white stones in court to recognize guilt or acquittal.[6]

Does our interpretation eliminate the spirit of the symbol? John refers to a third of the ocean turning to blood (Rev. 8:8). Interpreters surely argue over

---

[4] For example, John tells us that the seven stars (Rev. 1:16) are the seven angels (Rev. 1:20); the seven lampstands (Rev. 1:13) are the seven churches (Rev. 1:20); the morning star (Rev. 2:28) is Christ (Rev. 22:16); the incense at the altar is the prayers of the saints (Rev. 5:8); the fallen star (Rev. 9:1) is the angel in the abyss (Rev. 9:11); the great city of Sodom and Egypt is Jerusalem (Rev. 11:8); the stars in the sky (Rev. 12:4) are fallen angels (Rev. 12:9); and the large red dragon (Rev. 12:3) is Satan (Rev. 12:9).
[5] Paul N. Benware, *Understanding End times Prophecy*, 31.
[6] Osborne notes that the image could be from the Pergamum games, where participants used the white stones as an admission ticket. Grant Osborne. *Revelation.* Baker Exegetical Commentary on the New Testament (Grand Rapids, MI: Baker Academic, 2002), 138-139.

whether this image should be understood literally or symbolically. However, all interpreters should agree that this passage predicts some sort of terrible judgment.

RULE #4: Historical backdrop

Millennia separate us from the biblical authors. To interpret accurately, we need to understand as much about their historical and cultural context as possible. Consider an often misinterpreted passage: Jesus tells the church in Laodicea, "I know your deeds, that you are neither cold nor hot; I wish that you were cold or hot. [16] So because you are lukewarm, and neither hot nor cold, I will spit you out of My mouth" (Rev. 3:15-16). Christian preachers often claim that Jesus was speaking about the "pew sitter," who neither wants to live radically for God (i.e. "hot") nor wants to walk away from God (i.e. "cold").

However, when we realize the historical background in Laodicea, we reach a more nuanced interpretation. Historically, Laodicea didn't have its own water supply. Instead, they imported "lukewarm" water from the springs of Denizli, which had an awful taste. The *hot springs* nearby Laodicea were known for their healing qualities (from Hierapolis), and the *cold springs* were known for their cold, pure drinking water (from Colossae).[7]

The hot water offered certain benefits to the Laodiceans (e.g. healing qualities, relaxation), and the cold water had benefits too (e.g. good to drink). But what about the lukewarm, sulfur water from Denizli? This would make the Laodiceans gag! This is why Jesus says, "I will spit [literally *vomit*] you out of My mouth" (Rev. 3:16). As you can see, in order to discover the author's intent, the historical and cultural background of their writing is often important.

RULE #5: Words can have multiple meanings

Rock singer Robert Plant famously sang, "There's a sign on the wall, but she wants to be sure, because *you know sometimes words have two meanings*." Many people today can sympathize with the girl in the song *Stairway to Heaven*. Words often have a broad range of meaning. For instance, when you hear the term "running," this could refer to running a race, running water, running a company, or running for office. In Scripture, the word "death" sometimes means *physical* death, while other times it means *spiritual* death. Likewise, the term "salvation" can refer to justification,

---

[7] Grant Osborne. *Revelation*, 205.

PROGRESSIVE REVELATION

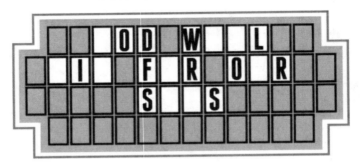

sanctification, or glorification. If we are too narrow in our understanding of a word's meaning, we can easily misinterpret a given text.

RULE #6: Recognize progressive revelation

God's *purposes* for humans have never changed, but his *methods* have. Consider a parent-child relationship. The parent always has the *purpose* of raising her child into an independent adult, but her *methods* may change. A young mother might instruct her toddler to grab his macaroni and cheese with his fingers and shovel it into his mouth. But when the child reaches grade school, she wouldn't allow this sort of behavior. The mother's *purpose* didn't change (i.e. raising the child into an independent adult), but her *methods* did (i.e. using fingers versus using a fork).

Similarly, the author of Hebrews states that God *formerly* worked through the prophets, but he worked *fully* in his Son (Heb. 1:1-2). This explains why many teachings are *partially concealed* in the OT, but are *fully revealed* in the NT. Consider the gameshow *The Wheel of Fortune*. On the show, contestants guess letters until they can "solve the puzzle."

At first, the message is *concealed*, but as the contestants guess more and more letters, the message is finally *revealed*.

PROGRESSIVE REVELATION

Once a contestant reaches the end of the game, the original letters don't suddenly morph into other letters. This would make the show incredibly frustrating to watch! Instead, the letters stay the same—even as more are revealed and our understanding increases. Similarly, God's revelation never contradicts previous revelation. Instead, he slowly revealed his plan of redemption throughout history until it was fulfilled in Christ (Rom. 16:25; 1 Cor. 2:7; 15:51; Eph. 3:3).

RULE #7: Understand the genre of the book

We interpret the front page of the newspaper differently than we interpret the comic section. Likewise, we interpret *poetry* differently than *history*. The Bible contains multiple genres: poetry, wisdom, apocalyptic, history, and many more. We need to carefully identify the genre of writing in order to properly interpret the text.

Consider an example: We read in the Proverbs, "A gentle answer turns away wrath, but a harsh word stirs up anger" (Prov. 15:1). Solomon wrote this passage in the genre of wisdom literature. Wisdom literature contains *general maxims*—not *universally binding laws*. Thus it is *generally true* that a "gentle answer turns away wrath," but it isn't *always* true. A skeptic might see this as an error in Scripture, but when we understand the genre of the Proverbs, we see this is unreasonable.

RULE #8: Mind the gaps

If you've ever been hiking in the mountains, you've seen this principle quite clearly. From your vantage point, the mountains often look close together. But as you hike miles closer to the first range of mountains, you discover that huge gaps of land exist in between. Similarly, biblical prophets often describe events in order, but they will not acknowledge the gaps of time in between the events.

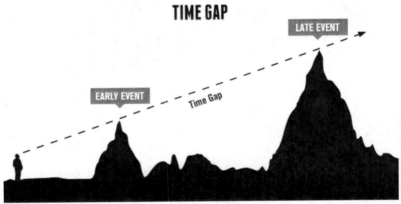

Some interpreters do not acknowledge gaps in biblical prophecy.[8] Yet Jesus himself taught this principle in Luke 4:18-20. Here Jesus read from Isaiah 61:1-2:

> The Spirit of the Lord GOD is upon me, because the LORD has anointed me to bring good news to the afflicted; He has sent me to bind up the brokenhearted, to proclaim liberty to captives and freedom to prisoners; to proclaim the favorable year of the LORD. (Isa. 61:1-2a)

Jesus claimed to fulfill this portion of the prophecy in Isaiah, telling the people, "Today this Scripture has been fulfilled in your hearing" (Lk. 4:21). However, he stopped mid-verse. If he had just finished the rest of the verse

---

[8] For instance, Amillennialist Sam Storms writes, "The appeal to the alleged gap between Isaiah 61:1-2a and 61:2b is invalid. Although our Lord in Luke 4 did not cite the entire passage, it may easily be demonstrated that the day of God's wrath as well as the day of redemption were inaugurated by our Lord's ministry (see Matt. 3:10-12; 23:37ff)." C. Samuel Storms, *Kingdom Come: The Amillennial Alternative* (Fearn, Scotland: Mentor, 2013), 83.

in Isaiah 61:2, he would've read, "To proclaim the favorable year of the LORD, *and the day of vengeance of our God.*" Clearly, in his First Coming, Jesus didn't bring "the day of vengeance" to humanity; he came to bring forgiveness (Jn. 3:17). Thus Jesus saw (at least) a two thousand year gap in between the events in this prophecy in Isaiah 61, which in Hebrew forms a couplet that should ordinarily hang together. While many gaps exist in biblical prophecy,[9] the interpreter shoulders the burden of proof to demonstrate a gap in biblical prophecy.

RULE #9: It's okay if you're seeing double

In an earlier chapter, we saw that the Jewish prophets would use *types* to predict the coming of Christ. Types serve as a foreshadowing or picture of future events. While theologians use the word "type" to describe this aspect of prophecy, perhaps the word "prototype" might be more helpful. Just as a prototype serves as the first version of the finished product, so also, types foreshadow future events.

---

[9] Some interpreters see a gap of time between ancient Rome and a future Roman Empire (Dan. 2:43-44; 7:7-8), skipping over the Church Age. Daniel sees a gap of time between Antiochus Epiphanes (Dan. 11:35) and the Antichrist (Dan. 11:36). Hosea sees Israel's exile and regathering separated by "many days" (Hos. 3:4-5). God leaves the Temple (Hos. 5:15) and there is a gap of time before he returns to them (Hos. 6:1). When Jesus first came into Jerusalem, he rode a donkey (Zech. 9:9; Mt. 21:5). But there is a gap between this event and his return in the very next verse (Zech. 9:10). God recognizes Jesus as the promised Messiah (Ps. 110:1), but at least 2,000 years will occur until he rules the Earth (Ps. 110:2, 5). Jesus' Olivet Discourse is unintelligible without seeing a gap of several thousand years from the destruction in AD 70 to a future world judgment (Mt. 24; Mk. 13; Lk. 21). Jesus fulfilled the first part of Isaiah 11 when the Spirit of God rested on him (Isa. 11:1-3), but he will not judge the Earth until his Second Coming—at least a couple of thousand years later (Isa. 11:4-5). Jesus was only incarnated *once*. When he returns a second time, he will not be born as a baby again (Dan. 7:13-14). But Isaiah predicts that this human baby will rule and judge the Earth. Again we see a gap of thousands of years in between these events—even though it splits up the very same verse (Isa. 9:6). Malachi predicts that the Lord (Jesus) would come into his Temple (Mal. 3:1), but then, he would come to destroy the Temple (Mal. 3:2). Daniel predicted that the Messiah would be cut off in AD 33 (Dan. 9:26), but then, he would return to judge later on.

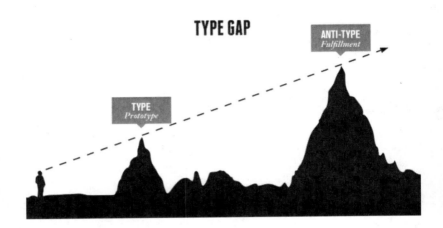

The OT prophets sometimes used types that were fulfilled in two separate waves: one in the *short term* and the other in the *long term*. For instance, Daniel made many predictions about how Antiochus Epiphanes IV would desolate the Jewish Temple. This godless ruler desecrated the Temple in 169 BC, when he sacrificed a pig to Zeus in the Holy of Holies. However, Jesus later taught that this "abomination of desolation" was still in the future (Mt. 24:15; cf. 2 Thess. 2:3). Thus Antiochus serves as the *first* fulfillment of Daniel's prophecy, but not the *final* one. Antiochus was a "prototype" of the Antichrist who is still to come. Similarly, God judged ancient Babylon (Isa. 13:1-3) as a foreshadowing (or type) of his judgment on the entire globe at the end of history (Isa. 13:4-16).

God most likely uses this method to build our confidence in prophecy. Pentecost writes, "It was the purpose of God to give the near and far view so that the fulfillment of the one should be the assurance of the fulfillment of the other."[10] When we see how God fulfilled the first prophecy (i.e. literally and historically), it helps us to understand how he'll fulfill the second part.

RULE #10: Don't confuse partial with complete

The OT prophets predicted the future messianic kingdom on many occasions. They failed, however, to foresee the Church Age—the time

---

[10] Dwight Pentecost, *Things to Come*, 47.

between the death of Christ and his return (Mt. 13:11; Rom. 16:25; Eph. 3:3-6).

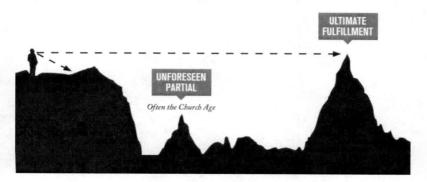

Sometimes prophecies are fulfilled in a moment of time (Lk. 4:21), but not always. For instance, when God predicted that Abraham's descendants would be a blessing to all of the nations of the Earth (Gen. 12:3), this was *partially* fulfilled through Jonah's preaching to the Ninevites. But it would be incorrect to think that Jonah's preaching was a complete fulfillment.

We might think of partial fulfillments like an empty glass. If you pour water into the glass, it is slowly *filled full* (or *fulfilled*). But just because half of the glass is filled, this isn't a complete filling—only a partial one. The Greek term for "fulfilled" (*plēroō*) carries this meaning. Matthew uses this term to refer to the filling of the fisherman's nets (Mt. 13:48), and John uses it to refer to Mary's perfume filling the house after anointing Jesus' feet (Jn. 12:3).

Conclusion

Many of these rules may just seem like common sense. Yet when studying eschatology, common sense seems to be in short supply. Indeed, common sense is often not that common! Moreover, while these interpretive rules may seem simple in *theory*, they become increasingly difficult to apply in *practice*. A man might think that he knows how to play football by watching it on television every week, as he drinks cold beer in his recliner at home, but we know that he doesn't really know how to play until he gets out onto the field himself. Likewise, we will need to remember these principles when we get our hands dirty throughout the following chapters, wading through the complexities of eschatology.

Discussion questions

1. We often hear the claim that everyone's interpretation is equally valid. Is there any truth to this claim? Do you believe that there really is a correct way to interpret the Bible, or are some interpretations better than others?

2. Which of the rules from the chapter do you find to be the most valuable in your experience of studying the Bible?

> RULE #1: Context, context, context
>
> RULE #2: Assume a literal interpretation
>
> RULE #3: Learn to properly identify symbols
>
> RULE #4: Historical backdrop
>
> RULE #5: Semantic range: words can have multiple meanings
>
> RULE #6: Recognize progressive revelation
>
> RULE #7: Understand the genre of the book
>
> RULE #8: Mind the gaps (Gap Prophecy)
>
> RULE #9: It's okay if you're seeing double (Type-Gap)
>
> RULE #10: Don't confuse partial with complete (Unforeseen Partial Fulfillment)

Have you seen readers break any of these rules before? If so, how? What were the effects of this?

3. Which of the rules from the chapter do you still have questions about? Feel free to discuss the validity of each.

4. How might our *interpretation* of a passage affect our *application* of a passage? Do you think it's possible that we might have *many* applications—even if there is only *one* correct interpretation?

Chapter 7. Revelation: Hindsight or Foresight?

Most Christians assume that the book of Revelation describes the distant future when it refers to Jesus' climactic return. But what if we're wrong? What if we're taking an entirely misguided approach? Some theologians believe that most of the NT's predictions of Jesus' return don't describe the *future*; instead, these predictions were largely fulfilled in the *past*.

Theologians call this perspective *Preterism*. The *preterite* in English is the past tense of a verb, and the Latin term *praeteritus* means "gone by" or "past." *Thus Preterism holds that most of the book of Revelation has already been fulfilled.* Preterist David Chilton explains, "The great majority of the Revelation is *history*: It has already happened… The Book of Revelation is not about the Second Coming of Christ. It is about the destruction of Israel and Christ's victory over His enemies."[1] Therefore, instead of looking in the *newspaper headlines* for the fulfillment of the book of Revelation, Preterism looks in *history books* to discover their fulfillment.

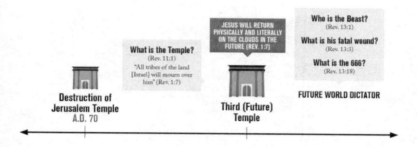

FUTURISM

JESUS WILL RETURN PHYSICALLY AND LITERALLY ON THE CLOUDS IN THE FUTURE (REV. 1:7)

What is the Temple? (Rev. 11:1)
"All tribes of the land [Israel] will mourn over him" (Rev. 1:7)

Who is the Beast? (Rev. 13:1)
What is his fatal wound? (Rev. 13:3)
What is the 666? (Rev. 13:18)

Destruction of Jerusalem Temple A.D. 70

Third (Future) Temple

FUTURE WORLD DICTATOR

---

[1] David Chilton, *The Days of Vengeance: An Exposition of the Book of Revelation* (Ft. Worth, TX: Dominion, 1987), 40, 43.

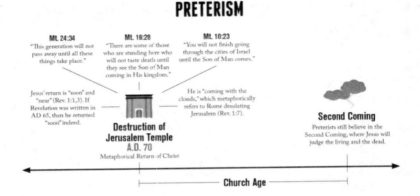

Hyper Preterism goes further, teaching that the Bible has absolutely nothing to say about the Second Coming of Christ or the end of history:[2]

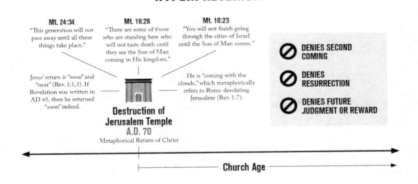

Of course, this view stands entirely at odds with core Christian teaching. Paul writes about false teachers like this "who have gone astray from the

---

[2] For an example of Hyper Preterism, see Don K. Preston, *Who Is This Babylon?* (Nashville, TN: Thomas Nelson, 2011.

truth *saying that the resurrection has already taken place*, and they upset the faith of some" (2 Tim. 2:18). He calls this perspective "ungodliness" and "gangrene" in the Christian community (2 Tim. 2:16-17). Surely Hyper Preterism stands outside of classical Christian teaching, denying the return of Christ and the resurrection of the dead.

Others, however, hold to a more moderate form of Preterism. They believe that the book of Revelation *generally* describes the destruction of Jerusalem in AD 70, and yet, they still affirm Jesus' return at the end of human history as well as the future resurrection of the dead.

Theologians call this Moderate or Partial Preterism, although adherents of this view often dislike this title, preferring to call their view simply "Preterism."[3] Thus when we refer to Preterism in this book, we are assuming this Moderate or Partial Preterism, rather than *Hyper* Preterism. To repeat, Preterism affirms the Second Coming of Christ and the general resurrection of the dead at the end of history—yet it believes that many passages in the NT do not refer to this event, but rather refer to a metaphorical coming of Christ in AD 70.

Futurism or Preterism?

Other interpreters (like myself) hold to *Futurism*, rather than *Preterism*, when interpreting the NT predictions about the future. As the term suggests, *Futurists* believe that the majority of prophecies describe the *future*—namely, the end of human history. Compare these views side by side:

Futurism versus Preterism		
Subject	**Futurism**	**Preterism**
Antichrist, Beast, Man of Lawlessness	*Future World Tyrant:* Persecutes Christians (2 Thess. 2:3; 1 Jn. 2:18; Rev. 13:1)	*Emperor Nero (AD 54-68):* Persecuted Christians (1 Jn. 2:18; Rev. 13:1)
The Temple	*Third Temple:* Will be built and then destroyed in the future (2 Thess. 2:4; Rev. 11:1-2; Mt. 24:15)	*Second Temple:* Destroyed in AD 70 (2 Thess. 2:4; Rev. 11:1-2; Mt. 24:15)
Apostasy:	Occurs throughout	Occurred before

---

[3] For example, see Preterist Dee Dee Warren's argument in her "Matthew 24 Podcasts," specifically "Episode 3: Perfuming the Hog of Hyperpreterist Mythology." Warren argues that the heretics deserve the qualification of *Hyper* Preterists—not those who hold the orthodox position.

Falling away from Christ	history but especially before Jesus returns (2 Thess. 2:3)	destruction of the Temple (2 Thess. 2:3)
Tribulation	Tribulation occurs throughout the Church Age (Jn. 16:33; Acts 14:22; Rev. 1:9) Yet "*the* tribulation" occurs at the end of history for a seven year period (Dan. 9:27; Mt. 24:21; Rev. 11:2-3; 12:6; 13:5)	Tribulation occurs throughout the Church Age (Jn. 16:33; Acts 14:22; Rev. 1:9) Yet "*the* tribulation" occurred during the destruction of Jerusalem for a seven year period (Dan. 9:27; Mt. 24:21; Rev. 11:2-3; 12:6; 13:5)
The "coming" of Christ	Occurs at the end of history, when Jesus returns to judge humanity (Mt. 24:3, 27, 30)	Occurred in AD 70 when Jesus metaphorically destroyed the Temple through the Roman army (Mt. 24:3, 27, 30). Jesus will also return at the end of history
Appearing on the clouds?	Jesus will return just as he left—on the clouds (Acts 1:9-11)	In the OT God often delivered judgment in a symbolic way through "clouds" (Ps. 104:3; Isa. 19:1)
Appearing like lightning?	Jesus will appear physically and bodily in a climactic way (Mt. 24:27)	In the OT, God came metaphorically to judge nations with "lightning" (Ex. 19:16; 20:18; Job 36:30; Ezek. 21:15, 28; Zech. 9:14). Jesus returned in AD 70 through the Roman armies

Which view makes the most sense of the book of Revelation? Many lines of evidence support Futurism. That is, the book of Revelation describes the *future* of human history—not the *past*.

The book of Revelation does not predate AD 70

The book of Revelation claims to be a book of "prophecy" about events in the future (Rev. 1:3; 22:7, 19). Therefore, in order for this book to be prophetic to the Preterist, it would need to be written *before* the destruction of Jerusalem in AD 70. If the book wasn't written before this time, then it would be a book of *history*—not *prophecy*. Thus if Revelation dates after AD 70, then Preterism is simply false. Preterist Ken Gentry admits this key fact:

> If the late-date of around A.D. 95-96 is accepted, a wholly different situation would prevail. The events in the mid to late 60s of the first century would be *absolutely excluded* as possible fulfillments. The prophecies within Revelation would be opened to an abundance of speculative scenarios, which could be extrapolated into the indefinite future. Revelation might… focus exclusively on the end of history, which would begin approaching thousands of years after John's time, either before, after, or during the tribulation or the millennium. The purpose of Revelation would then be to show early Christians that things will get worse, that history will be a time of constant and increased suffering for the Church.[4]

Likewise, Preterist R.C. Sproul writes,

> If the book was written after A.D. 70, then its contents manifestly do not refer to events surrounding the fall of Jerusalem—unless the book is a wholesale fraud, having been composed after the predicted events had already occurred… The burden for Preterists then is to demonstrate that Revelation was written *before* A.D. 70.[5]

On the other hand, if a person believes that the book of Revelation predicts the end of human history, it wouldn't matter when it was dated. For instance, Futurist Zane Hodges holds to the early date of Revelation,[6] but this doesn't affect his Futurist interpretation of Revelation at all. The dating of Revelation is *inconsequential* for the Futurist interpreter, but it is *essential* for the Preterist.

Surprisingly, many Preterists do not address this key issue. For instance, in his 700 page commentary on Revelation, Preterist David Chilton only

---

[4] Emphasis his. Kenneth L. Gentry, *The Beast of Revelation* (Tyler, TX: Dominion Press, 1994), 86.
[5] R. C. Sproul, *The Last Days According to Jesus* (Grand Rapids, MI: Baker, 1998), 140.
[6] Zane Hodges, *Power to Make War* (Dallas: Redencion Viva, 1995).

spends three and a half pages securing the early date for the book (whereas he spends *nine* pages interpreting the "666" of Revelation 13:18).[7]

Dating the book of Revelation: AD 65 or 95?

When should we date the book of Revelation? Tremendous evidence supports a late dating of AD 95 under the Roman Emperor Domitian, rather than AD 65 under the Roman Emperor Nero:

First, the early theologians of the Church held to the late date—not the early date. Irenaeus (AD 180) states that John wrote "at the end of the reign of Domitian."[8] Irenaeus was the disciple of Polycarp (who was the disciple of John, the author of Revelation). Irenaeus also lived in Smyrna where the book of Revelation circulated.[9] In his book *Against Heresies* (5:30), Irenaeus devotes an entire chapter to the number of the beast (Rev. 13:18), so the context clearly speaks of the end of history. Since Domitian died in AD 96, this would date the book of Revelation around AD 95.

Preterists argue that Irenaeus isn't a reliable authority, because he also claimed Jesus was 40 when he died.[10] If Irenaeus could be wrong about this, why would we trust him in the dating of Revelation? Gentry writes that this example "should demonstrate clearly that he could (he did at least once!) err on matters of historical detail—even when he claimed the authority of eyewitness accounts."[11]

However, Irenaeus primarily based this conclusion on a misinterpretation of John 8:57 ("You are not yet fifty years old"). In other words, this was an *interpretive* error—not a *historical* one. What student of Scripture cannot be guilty of interpreting the Bible erroneously from time to time?

Besides this error regarding Jesus' age, Irenaeus typically offers very reliable historical testimony. Even early date advocates will speak of Irenaeus' other historical testimony as typically "clear and weighty."[12] Moreover, in one breath, Preterist Hank Hanegraaff will *appeal* to the historical reliability of

---

[7] David Chilton, *The Days of Vengeance: An Exposition of the Book of Revelation* (Ft. Worth, TX: Dominion, 1987), 3-6.

[8] Irenaeus, *Against Heresies*, 5.30.3.

[9] Irenaeus, *Against Heresies*, 3.3.4.

[10] Irenaeus, *Against Heresies*, 2.22.5-6.

[11] Kenneth Gentry, *Before Jerusalem Fell: Dating the Book of Revelation* (Tyler, TX: Institute for Christian Economics, 1989), 64.

[12] Philip Schaff, *History of the Christian Church* (New York: C. Scribner's, 1907), 2:750-751.

Irenaeus when supporting the historicity of the NT documents,[13] but will *repeal* his trust in Irenaeus' reliability when dating the book of Revelation.[14] This sort of inconsistency could make your head spin!

In addition to Irenaeus, Victorinus (AD 304) wrote the earliest known commentary on Revelation, and he held to the late date,[15] as did the church historian Eusebius (AD 260-340).[16] Gentry argues that these sources don't add up as *separate* witnesses, but merely *repeat* the first witness: Irenaeus.[17] Yet, Gentry shoots himself in the foot when he also notes that the "church fathers did *not* accept necessarily Irenaeus's authority as conclusive" in other areas.[18] Gentry goes on to note that Eusebius didn't believe Irenaeus in two key areas: (1) Papias meeting John[19] and (2) the apostle John's authorship of Revelation.[20] He can't have it both ways.

In contrast to the evidence for the late date, the early date isn't affirmed until centuries later. Theologian Mark Hitchcock writes, "The first clear, accepted, unambiguous witness to the Neronic date is a one-line superscription in two Syriac versions of the New Testament in the sixth and seventh centuries."[21]

---

[13] Hanegraaff writes that Irenaeus sheds "significant light on the historical accuracy of the New Testament." Hank Hanegraaff, *Christianity in Crisis: 21st Century* (Nashville, TN: Thomas Nelson, 2009), 337. See also Hank Hanegraaff, *Has God Spoken?: Memorable Proofs of the Bible's Divine Inspiration* (Nashville, TN: Thomas Nelson, 2011), 193-194. See also Hank Hanegraaff, "20. Is The New Testament Canon Authoritative or Authoritarian?" in *The Bible Answer Book*. Vol. 2. (Nashville, TN: Thomas Nelson, 2006).

[14] Hanegraaff follows Gentry in challenging the "credibility" of Irenaeus, because "in the same volume [Irenaeus] contends that Jesus was crucified when he was about fifty years old." Hank Hanegraaff, *The Apocalypse Code* (Nashville, TN: Thomas Nelson, 2007), 153.

[15] Victorinus writes, "When John said these things he was in the island of Patmos, condemned to the labor of the mines by Caesar Domitian. There, he saw the Apocalypse; and when grown old, he thought that he should at length receive his quittance by suffering, Domitian being killed, all his judgments were discharged. And John being dismissed from the mines, thus subsequently delivered the same Apocalypse which he had received from God." Victorinus, *Apocalypse*, 10:11 [PL 5:333].

[16] Eusebius writes, "For [the name of the Antichrist] was seen, not long ago, but almost in our generation, *toward the end of the reign of Domitian*. He states these things concerning the Apocalypse in the work referred to." Eusebius, *Ecclesiastical History*, 5.8.5-7.

[17] Kenneth Gentry, *Before Jerusalem Fell: Dating the Book of Revelation* (Tyler, TX: Institute for Christian Economics, 1989), 66.

[18] Emphasis mine. Kenneth Gentry, *Before Jerusalem Fell: Dating the Book of Revelation* (Tyler, TX: Institute for Christian Economics, 1989), 62-63.

[19] Eusebius, *Ecclesiatical History*, 3:39.

[20] Eusebius, *Ecclesiatical History*, 3:24:17-18; 5:8:5-7; 7:25:7-8, 14.

[21] Mark Hitchcock, "A Defense of the Domitianic Date of the Book of Revelation." Dissertation for Dallas Theological Seminary (December, 2005), 74.

Second, if the early date is true, then John and Paul would have both served in Ephesus at the same time. At the end of 2 Timothy, Paul references 17 coworkers by name, but he never mentions the apostle John. Why wouldn't Paul tell the struggling and timid Timothy to get help from such a powerful Christian leader like John? Likewise, Jesus names several leaders in his letters to the seven churches of Revelation 2 and 3, but he never mentions Paul or Timothy when he speaks to the church of Ephesus (Rev. 2:1-7). This would be similar to writing a letter to the White House about American politics without mentioning the President. Of course, these are arguments from silence, but they are *conspicuous* silences. We would *expect* to read about these key Christians leaders if they were leading alongside one another.

Third, the late date makes sense of the church of Smyrna. Polycarp (AD 110) states that Smyrnaeans weren't believers during the time of Paul.[22] Jesus, however, speaks to an established church in Revelation 2:8-11, dating the book sometime after Paul's death (AD 67).

Fourth, the late date makes sense of John's banishment to Patmos (Rev. 1:9). Clement tells us that John came back from Patmos (due to a banishing?) after "the death of the tyrant."[23] If the early date for Revelation is true (AD 65), then why didn't Nero simply *execute* John, as he did with Peter and Paul? By contrast, the Roman emperor Domitian was far more likely to banish John, as he did with Flavia Domitilla in AD 95 to the island of Pandeteria. Blomberg writes, "John's brief exile on the island of Patmos (1:9) fits the mid-90s well, whereas there is no evidence of Christians being banished from their homelands by the government prior to this date."[24]

---

[22] Polycarp, *Letter to the Philippians*, 11.3.
[23] Clement of Alexandria, *Who is the Rich Man that Shall be Saved?* Section 42.
[24] Craig Blomberg, *From Pentecost to Patmos: an Introduction to Acts through Revelation* (Nashville, TN: B & H Academic, 2006), 510.

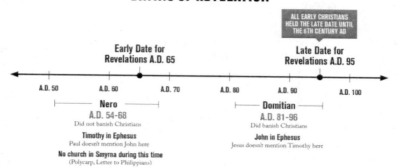

The early Christian theologians and leaders didn't hold to Preterism

Remember, under the Preterist view, Christians in the first century would have been keenly aware that the predictions in the book of Revelation had already been fulfilled at the destruction of Jerusalem in AD 70. Yet the early Christians didn't interpret Revelation in this way. They believed it referred to the end of human history—not the destruction of Jerusalem. Theologian Alan Johnson writes, "[Preterism] did not appear till 1614, when a Spanish Jesuit named Alcasar developed its main lines."[25]

The *Didache* (an early 2nd century document) holds that Jesus' teaching about the future called the Olivet Discourse (Mt. 24; Mk. 13; Lk. 21) is about "the last days."[26] It claims that the "false prophets"[27] and the "world deceiver"[28] (i.e. the Antichrist) haven't appeared. It also states, "Then shall appear the signs of the truth... the resurrection of the dead—yet not of all, but as it is

---

[25] Alan Johnson, *Revelation*. In F. E. Gaebelein (Ed.), *The Expositor's Bible Commentary, Volume 12: Hebrews through Revelation* (Grand Rapids, MI: Zondervan Publishing House, 1981), 409.
[26] *Didache*, 16:3.
[27] *Didache*, 16:3.
[28] *Didache*, 16:4.

said: 'The Lord shall come and all His saints with Him.' Then shall the world see the Lord coming upon the clouds of heaven."[29]

Papias (AD 60-130) was one of John's disciples (the author of Revelation). He writes, "There will be a millennium after the resurrection of the dead, when the kingdom of Christ will be set up in material form on this earth."[30]

The Epistle of Barnabas (2nd century) interprets the Temple of Daniel 9:27 as being fulfilled spiritually in the Church,[31] while the Preterist view holds that Daniel 9:27 refers to the destruction of the Temple in Jerusalem. The epistle states, "Ten kingdoms will reign over the earth, and after a little king will arise, who will subdue three of the kings with a single blow."[32]

The *Shepherd of Hermas* (an early 2nd century document) speaks of the Tribulation as a *future* event—not a *past* event: "Happy is he who endures the great tribulation that is coming."[33]

Justin Martyr (AD 150) writes, "He shall come from heaven with glory, when the man of apostasy, who speaks strange things against the Most High, shall venture to do unlawful deeds on the earth against us the Christians... *the rest of the prophecy shall be fulfilled at His Second Coming.*"[34] Elsewhere he writes, "But I and others, who are right-minded Christians on all points, are assured that there will be a resurrection of the dead, and a thousand years in Jerusalem, which will then be built, adorned, and enlarged, as the prophets Ezekiel and Isaiah and others declare."[35]

Irenaeus (AD 180) interpreted the events in Daniel 9:27 and 2 Thessalonians 2:3-5 in the *future* tense—not the *past*. He writes that the kingdom of Daniel 2 will be split up into ten parts, and then wait for the Antichrist to appear.[36] While Preterists believe that Emperor Nero was the Antichrist, Irenaeus states that the Antichrist has not appeared, writing, "It is therefore more certain, and less hazardous, to await the fulfillment of the prophecy."[37] He claims that we cannot know who the Antichrist is: "We will not, however,

---

[29] *Didache*, 16:6-7. Varner writes, "From the earliest commentators on the *Didache* down to current times, this expression of limited resurrection has been taken by many as indicating the chiliasm, or millennarianism, of the author." Though he adds we should avoid dogmatism on this issue, because the book ends so abruptly. William Varner, "The *Didache* 'Apocalypse' and Matthew 24." *Bibliotheca Sacra*. 165 (July-September, 2008), 318.
[30] Eusebius, *Church History*, 3.39.12.
[31] *The Epistle of Barnabas*, 16:9.
[32] *The Epistle of Barnabas*, 4:5.
[33] *Shepherd of Hermas*, Second Vision, Chapter Two.
[34] Justin Martyr, *Dialogue with Trypho*, Chapter 110.
[35] Justin Martyr, *Dialogue with Trypho*, Chapter 81.
[36] Irenaeus, *Against Heresies*, 5.30:1.
[37] Irenaeus, *Against Heresies*, 5.30:3.

incur the risk of pronouncing positively as to the name of Antichrist; for if it were necessary that his name should be distinctly revealed in this present time, it would have been announced by him who beheld the apocalyptic vision."[38]

Irenaeus believed in a future Temple in Jerusalem, and he claimed that the Antichrist will reign "for three years and six months, and sit in the temple at Jerusalem."[39] Irenaeus referred to the "first resurrection" (Rev. 20:6) as being fulfilled at the end of human history.[40] He writes, "All these and other words were unquestionably spoken in reference to the resurrection of the just, which takes place after the coming of Antichrist."[41] Crutchfield notes, "As a resident teacher in Ephesus in his declining years, John must be reckoned the cause of the uncommon fertility of millenarianism [a future thousand year reign of Christ] in Asia Minor. His views were championed by his immediate disciples Polycarp and Papias, who in turn influenced the eschatological views of other Church leaders until the Council of Nicea."[42]

Commodianus (AD 250) wrote that some will be "living again in the world for a thousand years" and "they, who make God of no account when the thousandth year is finished, shall perish by fire."[43]

Lactanius (AD 300) wrote that Christ "will Himself reign with them on the earth, and will build the holy city, and this kingdom of the righteous shall be for a thousand years."[44]

---

[38] Irenaeus, *Against Heresies*, 5.30:3.

[39] Irenaeus, *Against Heresies*, 5.30:4.

[40] Irenaeus, *Against Heresies*, 5.34:2.

[41] Irenaeus, *Against Heresies*, 5.35:1.

[42] Larry V. Crutchfield, "The Apostle John and Asia Minor as a Source of Premillennialism in the Early Church Fathers." *JETS* 31/4 (December, 1988), 427.

[43] Commodianus, *The Instructions of Commodianus: In Favor of Christian Discipline, Against the Gods of the Heathen*, "The Name of the Man of Gaza." 80.

[44] Lactanius, *The Divine Institutes*, 72 "Of Christ Descending from Heaven to the General Judgment, and of the Millennial Reign."

WERE THE EARLIEST CHRISTIANS PRETERISTS?

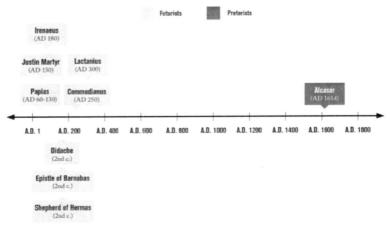

Surely, all of these early Christian leaders and theologians could be wrong. But here is the central question that confronts the Preterist interpreter: *If Preterism was so clear to the original historical audience, why didn't the earliest Christians adopt this view?*

What about Jesus claiming that he's coming "soon" and his return is "near" (Rev. 1:1, 3)?

If Jesus wouldn't return for at least two millennia, why would Revelation state that the events "must *soon* take place" (Rev. 1:1) and are "near" (Rev. 1:3). Preterists argue that these terms should be taken at face value: Jesus did come "soon," in AD 70 to destroy Jerusalem and the Temple.

However, these terms "soon" (*tachos*) and "near" (*eggus*) occur at the *beginning* of the book of Revelation, and also at the *end* (Rev. 22:6, 10). They form bookends (or what is called an *inclusio*) that makes the entire vision "soon" or "near." Can we really believe that the entire book of Revelation has already been fulfilled—including Jesus' Second Coming, the resurrection of the dead, and the New Heavens and Earth (Rev. 19-22)? Gentry consistently interprets Revelation in exactly this way. He sees Revelation 21 as a picture of "the gospel era, the church age... because of her heavenly source, divine blessing, redemptive promises, and future glory."[45] Thus we experience no more tears, death, mourning, crying, or pain "in principle" according to Gentry.[46]

Futurists reject such a bizarre interpretation. Instead, the term "soon" comes from the Greek *tachos* which is where we get our term *tachometer* (a device that measures the RPM's of car engines). This Greek word can also be rendered as "quickly" (Lk. 18:8; Acts 12:7). In other words, when the first domino falls, the rest will fall quickly after them. Benware writes, "These words are not to be understood as chronological indicators telling the reader *when* the Lord is returning. Rather, they are to be taken as qualitative indicators describing *how* the Lord Jesus will return. He will return 'suddenly.'"[47] Moreover, since God views time differently as an eternal being, these terms ("soon" and "near") could be relative to God's perspective of time. In the context of writing about the delay of Jesus' return, Peter writes, "With the Lord one day is like a thousand years, and a thousand years like one day" (2 Pet. 3:8; cf. Ps. 90:4).

What about Jesus appearing to "those who pierced him" (Rev. 1:7)?

At the beginning of Revelation, John writes, "[Jesus] is coming with the clouds, and every eye will see Him, *even those who pierced Him*; and all the tribes of the earth will mourn over Him" (Rev. 1:7). Gentry writes, "John's reference to Christ's piercing demands a first-century focus if the theme is to be relevant and true, for those who pierced him are now long since deceased."[48] Of course, Preterists acknowledge that Jesus never appeared literally on the clouds in AD 70, but they argue that the OT uses this language of "coming on the clouds" to symbolically refer to God's divine judgment (Isa. 19:1; Ps. 18:7-15; 104:3; Joel 2:1-2; Mic. 1:3-4). Thus this passage refers to all of the first century Jews "seeing Christ" when he invisibly judged Jerusalem. Moreover, when he writes that Jesus would

---

[45] Kenneth L. Gentry, *The Book of Revelation Made Easy: You Can Understand Bible Prophecy* (Powder Springs, GA: American Vision, 2008), 116-117.

[46] Kenneth L. Gentry, *The Book of Revelation Made Easy: You Can Understand Bible Prophecy* (Powder Springs, GA: American Vision, 2008), 118.

[47] Paul N. Benware, *Understanding End times Prophecy*, 172.

[48] Kenneth Gentry, "A Preterist View of Revelation." In S. N. Gundry & C. M. Pate (Eds.), *Four Views on the Book of Revelation* (Grand Rapids, MI: Zondervan, 1998), 48.

appear to "all the tribes of the earth," Preterists hold that this should not be translated *earth*, but *land* instead.[49]

However, this interpretation has serious problems. Just two verses earlier, John refers to Jesus as "the ruler of the kings of the *earth* (Greek *ge*)" (Rev. 1:5). John definitely uses this word to refer to the *entire globe*—not just *Israel*. In Revelation 3:10, he equates "those who dwell on the earth" with "the whole world." While "earth" (*ge*) can be translated as "land," there is no justification for that rendering in this context—especially when the rest of the book of Revelation is *global* in scope (Rev. 3:10; 6:10; 8:13; 11:10; 13:8, 12, 14; 14:6; 15:4; 17:2, 8). Interestingly, Chilton interprets Revelation 1:5 ("the kings of the earth") as referring to the *entire globe*, but interprets Revelation 1:7 ("all the tribes of the earth") to refer *only to Israel*.[50]

Furthermore, in Revelation 1:7, John quotes from Zechariah 12:10 ("every eye will see Him, even those who pierced Him; and all the tribes of the earth will mourn over Him"). Preterists interpret this passage to refer to Jesus' *destruction* of Jerusalem, but in context, Zechariah predicts the *protection* of Israel from the pagan nations. Zechariah 12:9 states, "I will set about to destroy all the nations that come against Jerusalem." Thus the Preterist interpretation directly contradicts Zechariah's prediction.

John claims that Jesus' return will be a *visible* event. He writes that "*every* eye will see Him" (Rev. 1:7), which matches Jesus' statement in Matthew 24:27 ("Just as the lightning comes from the east and flashes even to the west, so will the coming of the Son of Man be"). The angels even told the disciples that Jesus would return in the same way that he left Earth: "Jesus, who has been taken up from you into heaven, *will come in just the same way as you have watched Him go into heaven*" (Acts 1:11). Since Jesus left visibly *into* the clouds, we should expect him to return visibly *from* the clouds.

When John refers to "those who pierced him," this probably refers to the Jewish people in general—not those first-century people in particular. Only a relatively few people literally pierced Jesus on the Cross by driving the nails into his hands and feet. So a non-literal interpretation is warranted. It's interesting how Preterists take the time frame as *literal*, the city as *literal*, and the piercers as *literal*, but nothing else is taken literally.

---

[49] Gentry writes, "We should probably translate the Greek word *hē gē* as 'the land' rather than 'the earth' in the great majority of the cases where this word occurs in Revelation." Kenneth Gentry, "A Preterist View of Revelation." In S. N. Gundry & C. M. Pate (Eds.), *Four Views on the Book of Revelation* (Grand Rapids, MI: Zondervan, 1998), 48.

[50] David Chilton, *The Days of Vengeance: An Exposition of the Book of Revelation* (Ft. Worth, TX: Dominion, 1987), 63, 66.

Is the Temple of Revelation 11:2 the Temple of AD 70?

John writes of a Jewish temple in Jerusalem in Revelation 11:1-2. Because of this, Preterists argue that John must have been describing the Temple in Jerusalem in AD 70. Hanegraaff writes, "If the apostle John were indeed writing in AD 95, it seems incredible that he would make no mention whatsoever of the most apocalyptic event in Jewish history—the demolition of Jerusalem and the destruction of the temple at the hands of Titus."[51]

But this does not necessarily follow. Remember, when Daniel and Ezekiel wrote their books, the Jewish Temple lay in ruins. Yet both of these authors predicted a future temple (Ezek. 40-48; Dan. 9:24-27). Similarly, since John was writing "prophecy" (Rev. 1:3; 22:7, 19), we might very easily see him writing about a future temple as well. Moreover, since the seven (Gentile) churches of Revelation 2 and 3 existed several hundred miles from Jerusalem, he may have felt no need to write about the destruction of the Temple. While the destruction of Jerusalem in AD 70 was surely cataclysmic for Jerusalem Christians, these Gentile believers were far away from these events.

Doesn't a Futurist interpretation deny first-century readers any understanding or application?

Preterists argue that a Futurist interpretation ignores the original context in which John was writing. In John's day, Rome ruthlessly persecuted the Church, and these believers surely needed encouragement for their suffering. Thus if John was writing a book about the end of human history, wouldn't this neglect the needs of his original audience? J. Stuart Russell writes, "If the book were meant to unveil the secrets of distant times, must it not of necessity have been unintelligible to its first readers—and not only unintelligible, but even irrelevant and useless?"[52]

While this objection seems to carry some weight, we need to remember that Revelation *does* contain material for first-century churches. This is found in chapters 2 and 3. But once we reach chapter 4, John makes it clear that he is

---

[51] Hank Hanegraaff, *The Apocalypse Code* (Nashville, TN: Thomas Nelson, 2007), 153.
[52] J. Stuart Russell, *The Parousia* (Grand Rapids, MI: Baker Book House: [1887] 1993), 366. Cited in David Chilton, *The Days of Vengeance: An Exposition of the Book of Revelation* (Ft. Worth, TX: Dominion, 1987), 41.

directing his focus to the future. Just as chapters 2 and 3 can impact us *retrospectively*, chapters 4 through 22 impact us *prospectively*—even if we don't live during the time period in which these events take place.

Like the OT prophets before him, John wrote about events in the future, even as his audience was suffering in the present. For instance, as Israel suffered massive persecution, Jeremiah predicted a 70 year exile for a future generation (Jer. 25:11-12). While this did not exactly help Jeremiah's current audience, Daniel lived a century later, and he took great comfort from this prediction (Dan. 9:2-3). Likewise, Isaiah predicted the coming of King Cyrus to a generation 150 years later (Isa. 45:1). Those who read their Bibles quickly discover that many prophecies did not impact the current audience in the slightest, but these predictions had ramifications for future generations. Even on the Preterist view, *hundreds* of predictions in the OT didn't refer to Israel, but to the future Church.

Surely the people of John's day didn't understand everything in the book of Revelation, but why should we assume that they would? Even the prophets themselves didn't always know the meaning of their own prophecies. Peter writes, "This salvation was something *even the prophets wanted to know more about* when they prophesied about this gracious salvation prepared for you. *They wondered what time or situation* the Spirit of Christ within them was talking about when he told them in advance about Christ's suffering and his great glory afterward" (1 Pet. 1:10-11 NLT). Even the prophet Daniel explained that the content of his own prophecies brought him considerable confusion (Dan. 12:4, 9-10).

Conclusion

The Preterist interpretation of the book of Revelation fails on multiple fronts: (1) The book of Revelation is dated to AD 95—not AD 65; in order for Revelation to be a book of "prophecy" (Rev. 1:3), it cannot be describing *past* events in AD 70; (2) the earliest Christian theologians did not hold the Preterist view—even though they were closer to the events of the destruction of the Temple; and (3) the passages used to support a near fulfillment do not carry weight when considered closely. Since these predictions in the book of Revelation haven't been fulfilled, we should expect them to occur toward the end of human history.

Discussion questions

1. Briefly explain the difference between Moderate Preterism and Hyper Preterism.

2. What arguments do you find to be the most compelling from a Preterist reading of Revelation?

3. What arguments do you find to be the most compelling from a Futurist reading of Revelation?

4. Preterists argue that a Futurist reading will spoil the application of the book of Revelation. What application might Futurists take from the book of Revelation?

Chapter 8. Was Jesus a Preterist?

Jesus seems to have made several predictions about his Second Coming that needed to be fulfilled in the first century:

> You will not finish going through the cities of Israel *until the Son of Man comes.* (Mt. 10:23)
>
> There are some of those who are standing here who will not taste death *until they see the Son of Man coming in His kingdom.* (Mt. 16:28)
>
> This generation will not pass away *until all these things take place.* (Mt. 24:34)

These predictions stumble skeptics. Jesus seems to be claiming that he would return during the lifetime of his disciples, but because he never returned, skeptics assume that Jesus made false predictions.[1] Regarding Matthew 24:34, even C.S. Lewis wrote, "He was wrong. He clearly knew no more about the end of the world than anyone else. It is certainly the most embarrassing verse in the Bible."[2]

Preterism offers an intriguing answer to these difficulties: If Jesus believed that he would symbolically return to judge Jerusalem in AD 70, then all of these predictions were fulfilled. Thus Preterists argue that their view helps us in appealing to critics of Christianity.[3] Is this the case?

The Olivet Discourse

After fiercely rebuking the hypocritical religious authorities (Mt. 23), Jesus predicted that God would destroy the Temple. As he left the Temple, he gave a private teaching to his disciples on the Mount of Olives, which is why theologians call this the "Olivet Discourse." Preterists believe that Jesus fulfilled most of these predictions in AD 70, when he judged Jerusalem and the Temple via the armies of Rome. Matthew, Mark, and Luke all record Jesus' Olivet Discourse, while John does not. Some

---

[1] For example, see Bertrand Russell, *Why I Am Not a Christian: and Other Essays on Religion and Related Subjects* (New York: Simon & Schuster, 1967), 16. Tim Callahan, *Bible Prophecy: Failure or Fulfillment?* (Altadena, CA: Millennium, 1997), 185-189. Gerald Larue, "The Bible and the Prophets of Doom," *Skeptical Inquirer* (January/February, 1999), 29.

[2] C.S. Lewis, *The World's Last Night and Other Essays* (New York: Harcourt Brace & Company, 1973), 97-98.

[3] Gary DeMar, *Last Days Madness*, 46.

interpreters believe that John omitted it, because he would later write his
magnum opus—the book of Revelation.

Futurists believe that most of the Olivet Discourse relates to the end of
history—not to the fall of Jerusalem in AD 70. At the same time, they agree
that the first half of Luke's account refers to the destruction of Jerusalem in
AD 70, but after Luke 21:25, Jesus directs his predictions to the distant
future. While Luke's account and Matthew's account are certainly *similar* to
one another, they are not the *same*.

Comparing and Contrasting Matthew and Luke's account	
Luke 21	**Matthew 24**
Many are misled (v.8)	Many are misled (v.4) by false Christs (v.5)
Rumors of wars (v.9)	Rumors of wars are "not yet the end" (v.6)
Wars (v.10)	Wars (v.7)
Plagues, famines, great signs from heaven (v.11)[4]	Famines and earthquakes (v.7) called "birth pangs" (v.8)
Persecution in the synagogues (vv.12-16)	Persecution (v.9) and apostasy (v.10)
————	More false prophets (v.11)
————	Love will grow cold (v.12)
Divine protection for committed believers (vv.17-18)	Divine protection for committed believers (v.13)
Destruction of Jerusalem and the Temple (vv.20-24)	————
————	All nations hear the gospel "and then the end will come" (v.14)
————	Destruction of the Temple in Jerusalem (v.15)
Command to flee Jerusalem when *Judea is surrounded* (v.20)	Command to flee Judea after seeing the *Abomination of Desolation* (vv.16-20)
————	"A *great* tribulation such as has not occurred since the beginning of the world until now, nor ever will"

---

[4] This might refer to the fact that when the temple burned (AD 70), a bright star appeared
over the Jewish Temple (see Josephus, *Jewish War*, 6.5.1-3).

	(v.21)
————————————	"Unless those days had been cut short, no life would have been saved; but for the sake of the elect those days will be cut short" (v.22)
————————————	More false teaching predicting the Second Coming (vv.23-26)
Second Coming of Christ with signs in heaven (vv.25-27)	Second Coming of Christ with signs in heaven (vv.27-31)
Fig tree illustration (vv.29-31)	Fig tree illustration (vv.32-33)
"Truly I say to you, this generation will not pass away until all things take place" (v.32)	"Truly I say to you, this generation will not pass away until all these things take place" (v.34)
"Heaven and earth will pass away, but My words will not pass away" (v.33)	"Heaven and earth will pass away, but My words will not pass away" (v.35)

In their accounts of the Olivet Discourse, Luke emphasizes the destruction of the Temple in AD 70, but Matthew emphasizes the destruction of the Temple at the end of human history. Luke fails to mention three key components to Jesus' sermon: (1) no human would've survived these days unless God cut them short, (2) this was the greatest tribulation the world had ever seen or will see, and (3) the abomination of desolation would occur—only mentioning "its desolation."

These are significant omissions on Luke's behalf. Darrell Bock comments, "What do these differences mean? They indicate that Luke emphasizes a different element in Jesus' teaching at this point. He focuses on the nearer fulfillment in the judgment pattern described here, the fall of Jerusalem in AD 70, rather than the end (which he will introduce directly in 21:25)."[5]

The destruction of the Temple in AD 70 serves as a type (or foreshadowing) for the future destruction at Jesus' Second Coming. Since the Temple of AD 70 was destroyed in a literal way, the future Temple at the end of history will also be destroyed in the same way. Bock explains, "What happens to Jerusalem as AD 70 approaches will be like the real end, which brings the return. In these descriptions Jesus answers the disciples' short-term question about the temple, but he also sets up a long-term discussion about the end. The two events mirror each other in their

---

[5] Darrell Bock, *Luke: 9:51—24:53*. Vol. 2. (Grand Rapids, MI: Baker Academic, 1996), 1675.

terror."[6] Similarly, predictions about Jerusalem's *first* destruction by the Babylonians (6th century BC) are similar to her *second* destruction by the Romans (1st century AD). But these are not the same events. Instead, the fulfillment of the one offers confidence that the second will be fulfilled later in history.

Futurists see a gap somewhere in both accounts, but they aren't the only ones. Even some Preterists like Kenneth Gentry see a gap in Matthew 24 between verses 34 and 36. In fact, Gentry believes that verse 36 refers to Jesus' Second Coming at the end of human history.[7] Thus for most interpreters, the question isn't *whether* a gap exists in Jesus' teaching, but *where* it occurs.

Critique of the Preterist view of the Olivet Discourse

As we read through the Olivet Discourse from a Preterist interpretation, we discover many major interpretive problems and inconsistencies:

Matthew 23:38-39

> Behold, your house [the Temple] is being left to you desolate! [39]
> For I say to you, from now on you will not see Me until you say,
> 'Blessed is He who comes in the name of the Lord!' (Mt. 23:38-39)

On a Preterist view, when did the unbelieving Jewish nation ever bless the return of Christ? This prediction makes little or no sense for Preterism, but fits nicely within the Futurist view. Theologian Stanley Toussaint writes, "Jews would hardly call the horrible decimation of life in the destruction of their capital city a blessed coming of the Messiah. Rather, verse 39 describes Israel's future repentance when they will mourn because of their great sin (Zech. 12:10)."[8] On a Futurist view, this event will occur toward the end of human history (Zech. 12; Rom. 11:25-29).

Interestingly, Gentry has nothing to say about Matthew 23:39. In his commentary on Revelation he skips this passage, jumping from Matthew 23:38 to 24:1.[9] Other Preterists attempt to explain Jesus' statement by

---

[6] Darrell Bock, *Luke: 9:51—24:53*. Vol. 2., 1668.
[7] D. L. Turner, *Matthew* (Grand Rapids, MI: Baker Academic, 2008), 566.
[8] Stanley Toussaint, "A Critique of the Preterist View of the Olivet Discourse" *Bibliotheca Sacra* 161 (October-December, 2004), 472-473.
[9] Kenneth L. Gentry, *The Book of Revelation Made Easy: You Can Understand Bible Prophecy* (Powder Springs, GA: American Vision, 2008), 40.

arguing that the expression "until you say" is not a certainty in the future. Instead, this is an "indefinite possibility." R.T. France writes, "There is no promise that the condition will be fulfilled."[10] To support this interpretation, Preterist Gary DeMar cites four passages that demonstrate how this Greek word may not refer to a certain fulfillment (Mt. 5:26; 18:30; 18:34; Acts 23:12).[11]

While DeMar cites multiple passages to support his "indefinite possibility" reading, it's more interesting to note the passages he does *not* cite. Matthew uses the word "until" (*heos*) in several other predictions in his gospel (cf. Mt. 5:18; 17:9; 26:29):

> For truly I say to you, you will not finish going through the cities of Israel *until the Son of Man comes.* (Mt. 10:23)

> Truly I say to you, there are some of those who are standing here who will not taste death *until they see the Son of Man coming in His kingdom.* (Mt. 16:28)

> Truly I say to you, this generation will not pass away *until all these things take place.* (Mt. 24:34)

Do these passages look familiar? Preterists stake their view particularly on these three passages above. They claim that the preaching of the disciples (10:23), the coming of Christ (16:28), and the events of the destruction of Jerusalem (24:34) all needed to be fulfilled in the first century, during the lives of the disciples. But if Matthew's use of the word "until" only refers to an "indefinite possibility," then this would nullify the three most crucial passages that support the Preterist position!

Moreover, Jesus claims that the Jewish people need to say, "Blessed is He who comes in the name of the Lord!" (Mt. 23:39). DeMar holds that this refers to Jewish converts before AD 70. Thus these believing Jewish people could "bless" Christ's symbolic coming in AD 70, because this would mean that Jesus had fulfilled his promise to judge the hypocrisy of the Temple. But just three chapters earlier, we see what Jesus meant by having the crowds shouting such a praise. When Jesus came into the city of Jerusalem in Matthew 21:9, the crowds *literally* sang Psalm 118:26 and Jesus *literally* and *physically* entered the Temple—not *figuratively* or *symbolically* as Preterists contend.

---

[10] R. T. France, *Matthew: An Introduction and Commentary.* Vol. 1. (Downers Grove, IL: InterVarsity Press, 1985), 336.
[11] Gary DeMar, *Last Days Madness*, 61.

Matthew 24:1-3

> Jesus came out from the temple and was going away when His disciples came up to point out the temple buildings to Him. ² And He said to them, 'Do you not see all these things? Truly I say to you, not one stone here will be left upon another, which will not be torn down.' ³ As He was sitting on the Mount of Olives, the disciples came to Him privately, saying, 'Tell us, when will these things happen, and what will be the sign of Your coming, and of the end of the age?' (Mt. 24:1-3)

As the disciples looked at the Temple, Jesus predicted "not one stone here will be left upon another, which will not be torn down" (v.2). Preterists and Futurists agree that this refers to the Temple in AD 70. Josephus recorded, "It was so thoroughly laid even with the ground by those that dug it up to the foundation, that there was left nothing to make those that came [near] believe it had ever been inhabited."[12] Thus the destruction of the Temple in AD 70 fulfilled Jesus' prediction with precision.

The Jerusalem Temple stood as a massive monument to Israel's religious life. Josephus writes that the stones were 40 feet long, 18 feet deep, and 12 feet tall.[13] The Talmud records, "He who has not seen the Temple of Herod has not seen a beautiful thing."[14] Thus when Jesus predicted its destruction, this probably caused the disciples to think that Jesus was referring to the end of the world. Imagine if someone predicted that the Pentagon and White House would be burned to the ground. You'd probably assume that the world was ending!

But Preterists hold a different view: When Jesus referred to "the end of the age," he wasn't referring to the end of the *world*, but the end of the *old covenant*. These interpreters note that Paul used this expression ("the end of the age") in the present tense: "[These things] were written for our instruction, upon whom *the ends of the ages have come*" (1 Cor. 10:11). Maybe Jesus' prediction already came true in the destruction of the Temple?

While this interpretation might seem interesting, it doesn't fit with Matthew's use of the expression "the end of the age" (*ounteleias*). At the end of his gospel, Matthew writes that Jesus will be with the Church "until the end of the age" (Mt. 28:20; cf. Mt. 13:38-40; Lk. 20:35). Under a consistent Preterist view, this would mean that Jesus is no longer with us in fulfilling

---

[12] Josephus, *The Wars of the Jews*, 7:1:1.
[13] To be more accurate, he states that the dimensions were 25 cubits long, 12 cubit deep, and 8 cubits tall. A cubit is thought to be 18 inches long. Josephus, *Antiquities*, 15:392.
[14] *Baba Bathra*, 4a.

the Great Commission! Instead, his promise expired in the first century, and now, we're on our own.

Matthew 24:14

> This gospel of the kingdom shall be preached in the *whole world* as a testimony to *all the nations*, and then the end will come. (Mt. 24:14)

Jesus claimed that the gospel would reach all nations before his return. Clearly, this still hasn't happened—even in our day. Yet Preterists claim that Jesus was using hyperbolic language, referring to the spread of the gospel in the Roman Empire—not the entire globe.

While the NT authors did use the Greek term *oikoumene* ("whole world") to refer to the *known* world (Rom. 1:8; 10:18; 16:19; Col. 1:6, 23; Lk. 2:1), they also use it to describe the entire globe (Acts 17:31; Rom. 10:18; Rev. 12:9; Heb. 2:5). Thus the word can be understood either way. So was Jesus describing the *whole* world or just the *known* world?

The context makes this clear. Jesus says that the gospel will reach "*all* the nations" (*ethnesin*), and later in Matthew 28:19, he says, "Go... make disciples *of all the nations*" (*ethnesin*). Surely the Great Commission refers to the entire globe—not just the Roman Empire. Otherwise, we should fire the thousands of missionaries living in foreign countries today. Interestingly, DeMar neglects to connect Matthew's use of the *ethnesin* ("all the nations") with Matthew 28:19.[15]

Matthew 24:15-16

> When you see the abomination of desolation which was spoken of through Daniel the prophet, standing in the holy place (let the reader understand), [16] then those who are in Judea must flee to the mountains. (Mt. 24:15-16)

Preterists claim that this refers to the destruction of Jerusalem in AD 70. The Romans sieged Jerusalem for three years until they finally broke through the walls, killing the people and ravishing the city.

But a serious problem confronts this interpretation. Jesus tells the people to flee Judea *after* they see the abomination of desolation (i.e. the destruction of the Temple). Yet the Romans destroyed the Jewish Temple at the *end* of their three year siege—after all of the people were savagely murdered. Since this is the case, what use would it be to flee at this point? If anyone was still

---

[15] Gary DeMar, *Last Days Madness*, 87-89.

alive to see the destruction of the Temple, it would have only been after the wholesale slaughter of the city. This would be like telling the people of Hiroshima to flee the city when they see the mushroom cloud. It would've been too late to flee at this point. Everyone would've already been killed or sold into slavery at this time.

Matthew 24:21

> There will be a great tribulation, such as has not occurred since the beginning of the world until now, nor ever will. (Mt. 24:21)

Josephus estimated that the Romans killed 1.1 million Jews in AD 70,[16] and the descriptions of Jerusalem's destruction horrify us to read. Yet this surely wasn't the worst atrocity to ever occur on Earth (e.g. the Nazi Holocaust). To avoid this conclusion, DeMar argues that the language is "obviously proverbial and hyperbolic"[17] and Jesus was only referring to Jerusalem—not the entire globe.

Yet DeMar's interpretation cannot be held consistently, because he argued just a few verses earlier (v.14) that the entire world extends at least to the Roman Empire. If Jesus' expression "from the beginning of the *world*" is hyperbolic, it's odd to limit his expression simply to the city of Jerusalem in this passage.

Matthew 24:22

> Unless those days had been cut short, no life would have been saved; but for the sake of the elect those days will be cut short. (Mt. 24:22)

Jesus says that "no life would have been saved" unless this period of history was cut short. DeMar interprets this to mean that "God also restrained the Romans from venting their anger completely."[18] Thus "all life" refers "to those living in Judea."[19]

Futurists note that the NT uses the expression ("all life") ten times (Mt. 24:22; Mk. 13:20; Lk. 3:6; Jn. 17:2; Acts 2:17; Rom. 3:20; 1 Cor. 1:29; 15:39; Gal. 2:16; 1 Pet. 1:24), and "in every case except 1 Corinthians 15:39 the expression describes all humans. In that passage Paul was discussing the nature of the resurrection body: 'All flesh is not the same flesh, but there is

---

[16] Josephus, *The Wars of the Jews*, 6.9.3.
[17] He cites Ezekiel 5:9 to support this conclusion. Gary DeMar, *Last Days Madness*, 120.
[18] Gary DeMar, *Last Days Madness*, 122.
[19] Gary DeMar, *Last Days Madness*, 122.

one flesh of men, and another flesh of beasts.' Here he used the phrase in an even broader sense to designate all human and animal life."[20] Luke's account is even stronger than Matthew's. He writes, "It will come upon all those who dwell on the face of all the earth" (Lk. 21:35). This cannot merely refer to the destruction of the Temple in AD 70.

Matthew 24:27

> Just as the lightning comes from the east and flashes even to the west, so will the coming of the Son of Man be. (Mt. 24:27)

DeMar argues that God often revealed his presence through "lightning" (Ex. 19:16; 20:18; Job 36:30; Ezek. 21:15, 28; Zech. 9:14), but this isn't supposed to be interpreted literally. Moreover, he notes that even though "The LORD *came* from Sinai" (Deut. 33:2), this wasn't a visible coming. He writes, "Was God physically present? He was not. Did He come? Most certainly!" He then cites Jesus coming to judge the churches of Ephesus (Rev. 2:5), Pergamum (2:16), and Sardis (3:3). He asks, "Were any of these comings the Second Coming?"[21]

However, this interpretation seems to overlook a very important theological difference between God the Father and God the Son. God the Father is not a *physical* being (Jn. 4:24), but God the Son took on human flesh (Jn. 1:14). Jesus doesn't say that *God* will come on the clouds; he says *the Son of Man* will come. The angels told the disciples that Jesus would return to Earth bodily in the same way that he left bodily (Acts 1:9-11). All of this presupposes a literal and visible return of Christ—not a symbolic one.

As for DeMar's argument regarding Jesus "coming" to the churches in Revelation 2 and 3, this doesn't offer a very good parallel either. The word for "coming" in Matthew 24:27 is *parousia*—whereas the terms used for these churches is *erchomai* and *heko*. While the English translations render these visitations as the "coming" of Christ, the original Greek language uses two different terms, describing two different types of visitations.

Matthew 24:30

> The sign of the Son of Man will appear in the sky, and then all the tribes of the earth will mourn, and they will see the Son of Man

---

[20] Stanley Toussaint "A Critique of the Preterist View of the Olivet Discourse" *Bibliotheca Sacra* 161 (October—December, 2004), 481.
[21] Gary DeMar, *Last Days Madness,* 124.

coming on the clouds of the sky with power and great glory. (Mt. 24:30)

DeMar argues that in the OT God often delivered judgment in a symbolic way through "clouds" (Ps. 104:3; Isa. 19:1).[22] However, while the "cloud" motif often refers to God's judgment in the OT, the OT authors consistently use this symbol to explain God's judgment against *the enemies of Israel*—not *Israel* herself. For instance, Zechariah writes, "In that day I will set about to destroy all the nations that come *against* Jerusalem" (Zech. 12:9). In order for the Preterist reading to stand, Zechariah would have to be dead wrong (cf. Ezek. 38). Interestingly, DeMar takes Zechariah 12:10 as fulfilled in AD 70, but mentions nothing about verse 9.[23]

Matthew 24:31

He will send forth His angels (*angelous*) with a great trumpet and they will gather together His elect from the four winds. (Mt. 24:31)

DeMar interprets the angels to be *human* messengers, noting that the NT uses the same word (*angelous*) to describe John the Baptist (Mt. 11:10), the disciples (Lk. 9:52), and the Jericho spies (Jas. 2:25).[24] Thus he interprets the "angels" to refer to the spread of the gospel.

But just a few verses later, Jesus refers to these beings as "the angels *of heaven*" (Mt. 24:36), rather than human messengers. Moreover, this leads to the conclusion that world evangelism did not begin until after the destruction of Jerusalem in AD 70—a bizarre inference indeed.

Matthew 24:34

Truly I say to you, *this generation* will not pass away until all these things take place. (Mt. 24:34)

Preterists argue that Jesus was clearly claiming that his hearers ("*this* generation") would be alive when these events took place. DeMar states, "If you heard Jesus say that all these things would happen to 'this generation,' and in every other instance of its use 'this generation' meant the present generation, and you also heard Him speak of when 'you' see these things, what would you conclude?"[25] How could Jesus' prediction be true, unless

---

[22] Gary DeMar, *Last Days Madness*, 160-161.
[23] Gary DeMar, *Last Days Madness*, 167.
[24] Gary DeMar, *Last Days Madness*, 175.
[25] Gary DeMar, *Last Days Madness*, 58-59.

he returned in AD 70? This passage serves as a key to the Preterist interpretation of the Olivet Discourse.

However, Jesus didn't always use the term "you" to refer solely to his original audience. In the previous chapter, Jesus said, "Upon *you* may fall the guilt of all the righteous blood shed on earth, from the blood of righteous Abel to the blood of Zechariah, the son of Berechiah, whom *you murdered* between the temple and the altar" (Mt. 23:35). Of course, Jesus' audience had not personally murdered all of the prophets from the time of Abel. Yet Jesus used the term "you" to condemn them. Moreover, Jesus claimed that his hearers would sing, "Blessed is he who comes in the name of the Lord" when he returned to the Temple (Mt. 23:39). However, as the Roman armies stabbed and burned them to death, it's hard to imagine the unbelieving Pharisees blessing Christ's authority! He must have believed that a *future* generation would bless him at his climactic Second Coming (Zech. 12; Rom. 11:25-29).

Instead, when Jesus refers to "this generation," he is referring to those who will see "all these things," namely all of the events he had just predicted. Mark's parallel account states, "Even so, you too, *when you see these things happening*, recognize that He is near, right at the door. [30] Truly I say to you, *this generation* will not pass away until all *these things* take place" (Mk. 13:29-30). Since Jesus' audience hadn't seen all of the events, we should expect a future generation to witness "all these things."

What about the other statements from Jesus?

Preterists point to other key passages outside of the Olivet Discourse to support their view. For instance, Jesus said, "You will not finish going through the cities of Israel until the Son of Man comes" (Mt. 10:23). Futurists argue that this doesn't refer to the Second Coming, noting that Jesus uses the term *erchomai* ("comes"), rather than the term *parousia* (the normal term for the Second Coming). Thus Jesus may only be communicating that he will meet with his disciples before they finish their local mission.[26]

Likewise, when Jesus said, "There are some of those who are standing here who will not taste death until they see the Son of Man coming in His kingdom" (Mt. 16:28), this refers to the very next verse—namely, the

---

[26] Carson notes that there are at least seven different interpretations of this passage. Thus we should be cautious in being dogmatic on this difficult passage. D.A. Carson, *The Expositor's Bible Commentary with the New International Version*. Vol. 8. (Grand Rapids, MI: Zondervan, 1984), 250.

Transfiguration (Mt. 17:1). Peter and John travelled with Jesus to the Mount of Transfiguration, and both men associated Jesus' glory with the Transfiguration—not with the destruction of the Temple (2 Pet. 1:16-18; Jn. 1:14). Peter died before the destruction of the Temple, but he refers to the Transfiguration as the "coming" (Greek *parousia*) of Christ.[27]

Conclusion

Preterists want to offer an interpretation of Jesus' teaching which appeals to skeptical readers. But whatever they give with one hand, they take away with the other. When read carefully, a first century fulfillment of the Olivet Discourse creates more problems than it solves. Since Jesus' predictions have not been fulfilled yet, we should expect their fulfillment in the future.

Discussion questions

1. What were one or two of the arguments against Preterism from this chapter that you found most convincing?

2. What are some of the key mistakes that Preterists make in their interpretation? Were there any patterns you noticed that were recurring?

3. What might be some practical implications of holding either Preterism or Futurism? Do you think that either of these views could have practical application on our ability to serve Christ? What might these be?

---

[27] This is a foretaste of his ultimate coming in glory (Acts 1:11; Rev. 1:7). Note also that Jesus said, "There are *some* of those who are standing here..." This language fits better with the *three* disciples (Peter, James, and John) who saw him on the Transfiguration, rather than with the Resurrection, Ascension, Pentecost, or the Church Age. *All* of the disciples saw these other events. Finally, even according to the Preterist view, no one "saw" Jesus at his coming in AD 70, because it was an *invisible* coming. This wouldn't fit with the language of Matthew 16:28 either.

Chapter 9. Dispensationalism versus Covenantalism: The Role of Future Israel

God worked through the nation of Israel in the past in order to bring about his purposes in the world. Now he currently works through the Church—namely all those who believe in Christ. But will he ever return to Israel? Theologians differ in their answer to this question.

Covenantalists see the Church as *continuous* with the nation of Israel—very often stating that the Church began in the OT. Covenantalists call their view "replacement theology," "supercessionism," "fulfillment theology," "transference theology," or "absorptionism." Whatever we call it, under this view, God will not fulfill his promises with national Israel. Instead, the Church permanently replaces Israel in God's plan. For instance, Covenantalist Herman Ridderbos writes,

> The church, then, as the people of the New Covenant has taken the place of Israel, and national Israel is nothing other than the empty shell from which the pearl has been removed and which has lost its function in the history of redemption.[1]

Dispensationalists see the Church as radically *different* from the nation of Israel, believing that God started the Church in Acts 2 at Pentecost. At the same time, God will someday return to working through national Israel once again. Consider these different perspectives side by side:

Covenantalism versus Dispensationalism	
Covenantalism	**Dispensationalism**
Views salvation as more *continuous*. Generally *lumps* salvation history together.	Views salvation with more *differences* than the Covenantalist. Sometimes *splits* salvation history apart.
Read the Bible from *right* to *left*. They begin with the NT to interpret the OT.	Read the Bible from *left* to *right*. They begin with the OT to interpret the NT.
The Church inherits Israel's promises	*Israel* inherits Israel's promises. The

---

[1] Herman Ridderbos, *Paul: An Outline of His Theology* (trans. J. R. De Witt; Grand Rapids: Eerdmans, 1975), 354-55. Cited in Barry E. Horner, *Future Israel*, Introduction.

(Rom. 2:28-29; Phil. 3:3). Israel *forfeited* God's promises by rejecting and killing Jesus (Mt. 21:43; Lk. 17:20-21).	Church only inherits the "blessings" of the Abrahamic covenant (Gal. 3:6-9). Israel *could never forfeit* God's promises—no matter what they do.
Israel is *permanently* out of God's plan as a nation. God's promises to Israel were *conditional* on their faith.	Israel is *temporarily* out of God's plan as a nation. God's promises to Israel were *unconditional*.
The "holy land" is where Christians dwell, because they have the Holy Spirit in them. We are the Temple, and wherever we are, it is holy.	The "holy land" is still the literal land in Israel, which will be reclaimed by the Jews at the end of human history.
The promised OT kingdom is *spiritually* fulfilled in the Church (Mt. 13). OT promises of the Messiah reigning on a throne are fulfilled by Jesus reigning *spiritually* from heaven (Heb. 1:3).	The promised OT kingdom is *literally* fulfilled by the nation of Israel at the end of history. OT promises of the Messiah reigning on a throne are fulfilled by Jesus reigning *literally* on Earth (Mt. 19:28; Lk. 1:30-32).

DISPENSATIONALISM

Future Israel? Yes!

God made an unconditional promise to give David an eternal throne on Earth.

God made an unconditional promise to give the land to Abraham.

THE LATER JEWISH PROPHETS BELIEVED THESE PROMISES WERE UNCONDITIONAL.

Jesus, Paul, the author of Hebrews, and the book of Revelation all depict Israel's return at the end of history.

AGAINST ALL ODDS, THE NATION OF ISRAEL HAS BEEN REGATHERED IN THE 20TH CENTURY.

COVENANTALISM

Future Israel? No!

God made an unconditional promise to give the land to Abraham.
Fulfilled in Christians in New Heaven and Earth

God made an unconditional promise to give David an eternal throne on Earth.
Jesus sits on his throne in heaven, ruling in Christians' hearts

THE LATER JEWISH PROPHETS BELIEVED THESE PROMISES WERE UNCONDITIONAL.

Fulfilled in the Church

Jesus, Paul, the author of Hebrews, and the book of Revelation all depict Israel's return at the end of history.
Fulfilled in the Church of large number of Jewish conversions to Christ

AGAINST ALL ODDS, THE NATION OF ISRAEL HAS BEEN REGATHERED IN THE 20TH CENTURY.

Coincidence or mysterious providence of God

God clearly works differently in different periods. For instance, God walked in the presence of the first humans (Gen. 3:8), and he only gave them *one* commandment—not *many* (Gen. 2:16-17). He commanded theocracy, animal sacrifices, dietary laws, Sabbaths, holy days, and priests in the OT, but he has rendered all of these obsolete today (Rom. 13:1-7; Mt. 22:21; Jn.

18:36; Col. 2:16-17; Heb. 8). The question really isn't *if* there are differences in God's methods, but rather, *how many* differences have occurred.[2]

So the question remains: Will God return to the nation of Israel, or has the Church replaced Israel in God's plan? In this chapter, we will look at God's plan for the nation of Israel. Let's get started with the first Jewish man in history: Abraham.

Abraham's unconditional covenant

Modern people don't use the term "covenant" anymore, but we're familiar with the concept. A covenant is a *contract*. Today, we might make a contract over renting a house or agreeing to certain property lines.[3] Roughly 4,000 years ago, God (1) *stated* a covenant, (2) *signed* a covenant, and (3) gave a *symbol* for a covenant with Abraham.

(1) God STATED the covenant (Gen. 12:1-3)

God made at least three promises to Abraham: He would (1) give him the land of Israel, (2) make a great nation from his descendants, and (3) bring a blessing to the world through him (Gen. 12:1-3). These promises shocked Abraham so much that he interpreted them *figuratively*. How could he produce an heir with his elderly and aging wife (let alone a *nation* of people)? As a result, Abraham slept with his youthful housemaid (Hagar), giving birth to a boy named Ishmael. But God rebuked Abraham for doing this, telling him that he hadn't given Abraham *figurative* promises, but *literal* ones.

(2) God SIGNED the covenant (Gen. 15).

Abraham already had a "verbal contract" with God, and when God gives you his word on a matter, this should surely be good enough! Yet God went to even greater lengths to confirm this promise. Today, we sign contracts

---

[2] Some Dispensationalists see more differences (or "dispensations") in God's strategy, and some see less. We shouldn't squabble over the *number* of dispensations exactly, but instead, whether or not such categories even exist. Dispensationalist Roy Aldrich writes, "Titles for the dispensations may vary and there may even be legitimate disagreement over the number of dispensations." Roy Aldrich, "An Apologetic for Dispensationalism." *Bibliotheca Sacra.* (January, 1955), 47. Likewise, even an ardent Dispensationalist like Charles Ryrie has written that the number of dispensations is "in no way a major issue in the system." Charles Ryrie, *Dispensationalism* (Chicago: Moody, 1995), 38.

[3] We discover many examples of covenants throughout the Bible, including Abraham and Abimelech (Gen. 21:27), Laban and Jacob (Gen. 31:44ff), David and Jonathan (1 Sam. 18:3; 23:18), Solomon and Hiram (1 Kings 5:12), as well as husbands and wives (Mal. 2:14; Ezek. 16:8).

with ink, paper, and notaries present, but in the ancient Near East, they had a more gruesome method: They split animals in two, and both people would walk down the middle of the splayed animal parts. As their feet squished on the gory bodies beneath their feet, the two people would forge their contract. This method served as a grisly way of saying, "If one of us breaks this promise, then this is what will happen to the one who breaks it!" (cf. Jer. 34:18-20)

Yet God never asked Abraham to walk through the line of animals, thus signing the contract (Gen. 15:7-12, 17). God did this *all alone*. In fact, Abraham was asleep when God approached him (v.12). Therefore, Abraham wasn't a *participant* in the covenant; he was a *recipient* of it. This wasn't a *bilateral* agreement; it was a *unilateral* one (compare with Exodus 19:5). It was as if God was saying, "Abraham, I'm going to fulfill my end of the bargain, whether you're obedient or not." Moreover, God specifically stated that the land of Israel was included in this agreement (Gen. 15:18-20).

(3) God gave a SYMBOL for the covenant (Gen. 17).

God told Abraham that he would confirm his promise about the land, nation, and worldwide blessing (Gen. 17:3-8). To give a symbol of this promise, he told Abraham to circumcise himself and his male descendants (17:9-11).

Covenantalists sometimes argue that circumcision was a condition for God's covenant with Abraham. However, this wasn't a *condition* of the covenant, rather it served as a *declaration* of it. God tells Abraham that circumcision is "the *sign* of the covenant between Me and you" (Gen. 17:11). Today, the American Flag doesn't *secure* freedom for U.S. citizens; rather, it stands as a *symbol* (or sign) of our freedom. Evidently, individuals could forfeit the promise of the covenant for themselves, but no person could cancel the promise for the entirety of the nation. Walter Kaiser observes, "The conditionality was not attached to the *promise* but only to the *participants*."[4]

David's unconditional covenant

Abraham wasn't the only one to receive an unconditional covenant from God. King David received one as well. In the Davidic Covenant (2 Sam. 7:12-16), God made David a number of promises: (1) a house, (2) a kingdom for one of his descendants, (3) discipline for sin, but never

---

[4] Walter C. Kaiser, *The Promise-Plan of God: A Biblical Theology of the Old and New Testaments.* Grand Rapids, MI: Zondervan, 2008. 61.

rejection, and (4) eventually, an eternal throne. Since God's promise to David was unconditional, we should expect a literal kingdom to exist in the future for the ultimate heir of David: Jesus Christ.

The Jewish prophets believed in Israel's covenants

Covenantalists argue that God fulfilled his covenants to Israel during the time of Joshua (Josh. 21:43-45) or maybe King Solomon (1 Kings 4:21).[5] Yet the Bible serves as its own best interpreter in this regard. When we read through the rest of the OT, we find that the later Jewish prophets understood these promises to be *eternal*—not *temporary*. Ron Rhodes writes, "Every Old Testament prophet except Jonah speaks of a permanent return to the land of Israel by the Jews."[6]

Jeremiah compares the certainty of Israel's covenants with the sun, moon, and the stars: "Only if these decrees vanish from my sight... will the descendants of Israel ever cease to be a nation before me... Only if the heavens above can be measured and the foundations of the earth below be searched out will I reject all the descendants of Israel because of all they have done" (Jer. 31:36-37 NIV; cf. 24:6; 32:40; 33:20-21; 33:24-26).

Isaiah stated that the Jewish people would "possess the land *forever*" (Isa. 60:21). Elsewhere he writes, "Though the mountains be shaken and the hills be removed, yet my unfailing love for you will not be shaken nor my covenant of peace be removed" (Isa. 54:10 NIV).

Ezekiel assumed that Israel would have her land at the end of human history (Ezek. 11:17; 36:22-38; 37:1-14; 39:28-29).[7]

The *Psalmist* believed that the Abrahamic Covenant was an "*everlasting* covenant" (Ps. 105:10-11).

Zechariah foresaw that the Jewish people would occupy their land at the end of human history (Zech. 9-14). Moreover, he compares the *future* return of

---

[5] See Kim Riddlebarger, *A Case for Amillennialism: Understanding the End Times*: Expanded Edition (Grand Rapids, MI: Baker Books, 2013), 60. Gary DeMar, *Last Days Madness*, 398.

[6] Ron Rhodes, *The 8 Great Debates of Bible Prophecy* (Eugene, OR: Harvest House, 2014), 41.

[7] Townsend writes, "In terms of the fulfillment of the land promise it should be noted that the geographic boundaries during Ezekiel's glorious restoration are the same literal seas, rivers, and towns mentioned both before and after the conquest in Numbers 34 and Joshua 15. Clearly the Abrahamic promise of the land will extend to the age pictured in Ezekiel 40-48." Jeffrey Townsend, "Fulfillment of the Land Promise in the OT." *Bibliotheca Sacra* (October-December, 1985), 326.

the Messiah to be similar to a *past* literal event: "Just as you fled before the earthquake in the days of Uzziah king of Judah. Then the LORD, my God, will come, and all the holy ones with Him!" (Zech. 14:5). This literal, historical past event (recorded in Amos 1:1) implies a literal, historical future event.

Covenantalists often respond by saying that the Jewish people forfeited these promises because of disobedience. And yet, many of these passages that confirm the promises to Israel occurred during the worst forms of disobedience in Israel's history, including child sacrifice (Jer. 32:35), prostitution (1 Kin. 14:24), and large-scale idolatry. Yet even during these horrific times, the prophets still declared that God would be faithful to his promises.

If God makes a promise, does it matter who the recipients are? Would this affect God's ability to keep his unconditional promise in any way? Covenantalist Gary Burge writes, "Possession of the land is tied to obedience to the covenant."[8] But why would we ever think that Israel could lose her divine promises because of *disobedience*, but Christians will keep their divine promises because of *grace?* We shouldn't have a double standard in interpreting God's promises to his people—one standard will do just fine.

Jesus believed in Israel's covenants

Immediately before Jesus ascended into heaven, his disciples asked him, "Lord, is it at this time you are restoring the kingdom to Israel?" (Acts 1:6) If the Church replaced Israel, Jesus would have said, "Restoring the kingdom… *to Israel?* Don't you realize that we're in a *spiritual* kingdom now? The Church has replaced Israel!" But instead, Jesus said, "It is not for you to know the times or dates the Father has set by his own authority" (Acts 1:7 NIV). Jesus didn't question *if* Israel would return, but rather *when* they would return.[9]

He told his disciples, "In the regeneration when the Son of Man will sit on His glorious throne, you also shall sit upon twelve thrones, *judging the twelve tribes of Israel*" (Mt. 19:28). Furthermore, earlier in his Olivet Discourse, Jesus said that the Jewish people would be "led captive into all the nations; and

---

[8] Gary Burge, *Whose Land? Whose Promise?* (Cleveland, Ohio: Pilgrim, 2003), 163. Cited in Barry E. Horner, *Future Israel*, 53.

[9] Covenantalist Stephen Sizer answers this passage by claiming, "There are as many mistakes in this question as there are words." Stephen Sizer, *Christian Zionism: Road Map to Armageddon* (Leicester: InterVarsity, 2004), 168-169. Storms answers this passage by claiming that the kingdom of God (Acts 1:3) refers to the coming of the Holy Spirit at Pentecost (Acts 1:8). C. Samuel Storms, *Kingdom Come*, 283-285.

Jerusalem will be trampled under foot by the Gentiles *until the times of the Gentiles are fulfilled*" (Lk. 21:24). According to Jesus, the Jewish people will *temporarily* lose control of Jerusalem, but will *ultimately* regain the city. Bock writes, "Why describe this period this way unless there is an intended contrast between Israel and the Gentiles?"[10]

Paul believed in Israel's covenants

Paul argued that the Mosaic Covenant does not invalidate the covenant made to Abraham: "The Law, which came four hundred and thirty years later, *does not invalidate a covenant* previously ratified by God, so as to nullify the promise. [18] For if the inheritance is based on law, it is no longer based on a promise; but God has granted it to Abraham by means of a promise" (Gal. 3:17-18). Paul's argument in Galatians 3 rests on the fact that the Law could not invalidate this previous promise to Abraham. In other words, you can't sign a contract and then add conditions to it later.

Remember, the Abrahamic Covenant didn't just promise the land to the Jewish people. It also promised the Messiah as well ("In you all the families of the earth will be blessed"). Therefore, if the promises about the land were conditional on obedience, does this mean that the promise about the Messiah coming through Abraham was also conditional in the same covenant? Could the Jewish people have disobeyed so badly that God would've revoked his promise about the Messiah? Of course not! God doesn't keep one part of his promise and not another.

Paul does *not* say that the ethnic Jews *had* the promises or covenants; he says that they *still* have them, writing in the present tense (Rom. 9:3-5). Later in Romans 11, he addresses the role of ethnic Israel before the end of human history. In this context, he asks the question, "God has not rejected His people, has He?" and he answers this question by saying, "By no means!" (Rom. 11:1 NIV) This statement "expresses 'abhorrence' at this incredible possibility."[11] Later in the chapter, Paul goes on to rebuke the Gentiles for believing that they had replaced the Jews in God's plan (Rom. 11:11-24). Then we read:

> For I do not want you, brethren, to be uninformed of this mystery—so that you will not be wise in your own estimation— that a partial hardening has happened to Israel until the fullness of the Gentiles has come in; [26] *and so all Israel will be saved*; just as it is

---

[10] Darrell Bock, *Luke: 9:51—24:53*. Vol. 2., 1681.
[11] R.Jewett & R.D. Kotansky, *Romans: A Commentary* (Minneapolis, MN: Fortress Press. 2006), 653.

written, 'The Deliverer will come from Zion, He will remove ungodliness from Jacob." [27] 'This is My covenant with them, when I take away their sins.' [28] From the standpoint of the gospel they are enemies for your sake, but from the standpoint of God's choice they are beloved for the sake of the fathers; [29] for the gifts and the calling of God are irrevocable. (Rom. 11:25-29)

Who is Israel (v.25)? Some Covenantalists deny that Paul means to describe ethnic Israel,[12] yet most admit that "the reference to 'all Israel' in Romans 11:26 must refer to ethnic Israel, the broader group."[13] Out of the 148 times the OT uses the expression "all Israel," it *always* refers to ethnic Israel. In Romans 11:1, Paul uses the term "Israel" of his own ethnic identity ("I too am an Israelite"), and he calls unbelieving Israel "enemies" of the gospel (v.28), which can hardly be used to describe Christians! In fact, "throughout Romans 'Israel' means ethnic or national Israel, in contrast to the Gentile nations."[14]

How long will the hardening last (v.25-26)? It's certainly possible to render *houtōs* ("*and so* all Israel will be saved") to mean "in this way" (ESV) as Hoekema does.[15] But Paul's use of the word "until" in verse 25 refers to a *sequential event*—not an *overlapping process*.[16] Douglas Moo sees this language as that of "temporal reference."[17] Thus the NEB ("when that has happened") and the JB ("then after this") translate this passage correctly. After the Gentiles come to faith, the hardening will be lifted. This will occur after all nations hear about Christ (Mt. 24:14); otherwise, the "fullness of the Gentiles" would not yet have been completed.

---

[12] For instance, John Calvin writes, "I extend the word Israel to include all the people of God in this sense." John Calvin, *The Epistle of Paul the Apostle to the Romans* (Edinburgh, St Andrews Press, 1961), 255. Likewise, Augustine held that "Israel" referred to as "the predestined elect, drawn into a unity out of Jews and Gentiles." Cited in Peter Gorday, *Principles Of Patristic Exegesis: Romans 9–11 in Origen, John Chrysostom, and Augustine* (New York: E. Mellen Press, 1983), 171, 333.

[13] Kim Riddlebarger, *A Case for Amillennialism*, 212.

[14] John Stott, *The Message of Romans: God's Good News for the World* (Leicester, England: InterVarsity Press, 2001), 303.

[15] Hoekema prefers this reading for the purpose of relating Israel's salvation to the Gentile salvation—namely, Israel will be saved *in the same way that the Gentiles were saved*. They will be made jealous of the Gentiles knowing Christ, and they will come to faith in this way. Anthony Hoekema, *The Bible and the Future*, (Grand Rapids, MI: Eerdmans, 1979), 145.

[16] John Walvoord, "Eschatological Problems IX: Israel's Restoration." *Bibliotheca Sacra* (October-December, 1945), 415.

[17] Douglas Moo, *The Epistle to the Romans* (Grand Rapids, MI: Eerdmans, 1996), 720.

The "mystery" revealed here is the *timing* of Israel's mass salvation. Paul's Jewish readers assumed that the nation would accept Jesus as their Messiah at the First Coming, but as it turns out, they wouldn't accept him in this way until his Second Coming.

When Paul writes that "all Israel will be saved," does this refer to the nation of Israel or simply a large number of Jewish people (v.26)? Covenantalists typically interpret "all Israel" to refer to a large number of Jewish people meeting Christ before the Second Coming.[18] Yet Paul must be referring to the nation of Israel—not just individual Jewish people. "All Israel" stands in opposition to the small remnant mentioned earlier in the chapter (Rom. 11:5). Paul described, "They are not all Israel who are descended from Israel" (Rom. 9:6). Whatever Paul means by "all Israel," it must stand in contrast to the small and partial rescuing of the Jews mentioned earlier.

Unless we believe that every Israelite on Earth will come to Christ during this time, then we must concede Paul is thinking in terms of the *nation*—not just another *remnant*. Since Paul has been thinking in terms of *nations* throughout Romans 9-11, the expression "all Israel" must refer to the *nation* of Israel.[19]

When will Israel be saved (v.26)? Paul quotes from Isaiah 59:20-21 in verse 27 ("The Deliverer will come from Zion, He will remove ungodliness from Jacob. This is My covenant with them, when I take away their sins"). Covenantalists often argue that this refers to the First Coming of Christ.[20] This would fit their view better, because it wouldn't place the salvation of Israel alongside the return of Christ at the end of history.

In contrast to this view, however, Paul consistently uses the *future* tense to describe this event—not the *past* tense. Moreover, read the context of Isaiah 59 for yourself: Isaiah states that the Redeemer will come with "vengeance"

---

[18] Kim Riddlebarger, *A Case for Amillennialism*, 215.

[19] Dispensationalists don't necessarily believe that this means every single Jewish person on Earth will come to Christ in the future. Yet they do believe that Paul must be thinking of something more than just another "remnant" in the future. Walvoord writes, "The release, such as it is, will undoubtedly occasion a great turning to Christ among Israel after the rapture of the church, *but by no means is the entire nation won to Christ.*" Emphasis mine. John Walvoord, "Eschatological Problems VIII: Israel's Blindness." *Bibliotheca Sacra* (July-September, 1945), 289.

[20] John Stott writes, "This was, in Isaiah's original, a reference to Christ's First Coming." John Stott, *The Message of Romans: God's Good News for the World* (Leicester, England: InterVarsity Press, 2001), 303. Hoekema also takes this view. See Anthony Hoekema, *The Bible and the Future* (Grand Rapids, MI: Eerdmans, 1979), 146.

(Isa. 59:17) and "He will repay his enemies for their evil deeds" (Isa. 59:18 NLT). Does this sound like the First Coming or the Second?

Zechariah predicts that the people of Jerusalem will mourn over crucifying Jesus (Zech. 12:10-12), and "in that day a fountain will be opened for the house of David and for the inhabitants of Jerusalem, for sin and for impurity" (Zech. 13:1). Paul could be reflecting on his own conversion to Christ: When Jesus appeared to him on the Damascus road, he bent his knee to him. Similarly, Jesus' Second Coming will have the same effect on the nation of Israel.

What covenant is this referring to (v.27)? He could be thinking of the covenant made through the work of the Suffering Servant (Isa. 42:6), the promise to "restore the land" (Isa. 49:8), or the Davidic covenant (Isa. 55:3). He is most likely referring to the New Covenant of Jeremiah 31. God promised to make this covenant with Israel despite "*all* that they [had] done" (Jer. 31:17). Clearly, Paul believes that these OT covenants were still in effect.

What does Paul mean by "the gifts and the calling of God are irrevocable" (v.29)? Paul quotes multiple OT passages to make his case for Israel's salvation: He gets his concept of a remnant from 1 Kings 19:18 (v.4); he gets the concept of Israel's blindness from Isaiah 29:10 and Psalm 69:22 (vv.8-10); finally, he gets the concept of the holy root from Leviticus 23:10 and Numbers 15:17-21 (v.16). Thus when Paul writes that "the gifts and the calling of God are irrevocable" (v.29), he must have the covenants to Israel in mind from the OT. In Greek, the order of words shows us emphasis. In verse 29, the word "irrevocable" (*ametamelatos*) starts Paul's sentence, showing emphasis. "In other words," Paul writes, "do *not* ever say that God will revoke his promises to Israel!"

Covenantalists argue that the NT authors should have written more on this topic, if they truly believed in a restoration of the nation of Israel at the end of history. However, arguments from silence are only compelling if we would *expect* to read more on the topic. The NT authors were first century Jewish men who assumed that the restoration of Israel was in order (Acts 1:6). They felt no need to write more on the topic. As Jewish believers, they simply *assumed* it. Moreover, when the NT authors were writing their letters, the Jewish people were still in their land, and they were still a nation. Therefore, we shouldn't expect the NT to say more about a topic that wasn't even an issue when they were writing.

The author of Hebrews believed in Israel's covenants

The author of Hebrews states that the Mosaic Covenant has been fulfilled through Christ (Heb. 8:13), but only because it was a *temporary* covenant. God never stated that the Mosaic Covenant would be eternal; thus it was fulfilled by Christ. By contrast, he states that the Abrahamic Covenant was based on God's promise: "When God made the promise to Abraham, since He could swear by no one greater, He swore by Himself" (Heb. 6:13). He states the Abrahamic Covenant still stands in effect based on the "unchangeableness of [God's] purpose, interposed with an oath" (Heb. 6:17) and the fact that "it is impossible for God to lie" (Heb. 6:18).

The Book of Revelation supports Israel's covenants

Revelation 7 states that a contingent of Jewish believers will exist at the end of history. John records 144,000 Jews appearing during this time, going to great lengths to number them and even record their twelve tribes.[21] Covenantalists believe that this figure symbolizes the Church. Yet John records the Church immediately afterward, referring to "a great multitude" in heaven. Consider these two groups side-by-side below:

Differences between the 144,000 and the Church (Rev. 7)	
144,000	**The Church**
They are "from every tribe of the sons of *Israel*" (v.4)	They are from "every *nation* and all *tribes* and *peoples* and *tongues*" (v.9).
They are "sealed" (v.4). This means that they are still alive on Earth.	They are "standing before the throne" in heaven (v.9). This means they are dead.
They are *specifically numbered* 144,000 (v.4).	They are an *innumerable* group of people ("a great multitude which no one could count"—v.9).

---

[21] Some commentators take a symbolic interpretation of the 144,000. These numbers are: (1) too symmetrical to be literal, (2) part of a symbolic context, and (3) harken back to a symbolic OT event in Ezekiel 9:4-5. Yet even if the *number* (144,000) serves as a symbol for a large number of Jews, this would still not invalidate the *ethnicity* of these believers. Similarly, John describes *seven* churches in chapters 2 and 3, and the gospels contain *twelve* apostles. These numbers may carry some sort of symbolic significance. Yet this would not be grounds for thinking that these churches or people did not exist, or for changing their identities as churches or apostles. Likewise, even if the *number* is symbolic, this says nothing about the *ethnicity* of these Jewish believers.

Revelation sometimes uses two separate symbols to refer to the same person or event. For instance, Revelation describes Jesus as both a "lion" (Rev. 5:5) and a "lamb" (Rev. 5:6). Here both symbols refer to Jesus, and the author gives signifiers to make this clear.[22] But in Revelation 7, the 144,000 and the great multitude radically differ from one another in ethnicity, location, and number. So, theoretically, these different symbols could both refer to the Church, but nothing in the text signifies such an interpretation.[23]

Covenantalists hold an inconsistent hermeneutic regarding the First and Second Coming of Christ

Covenantalists hold that the predictions about Christ's First Coming should be interpreted *literally*, but those predicting his Second Coming should be understood *metaphorically*. For instance, Micah predicted that the Messiah would be born in the city of Bethlehem (Mic. 5:2). Naturally, Covenantalists interpret this at face value, but when Micah continues to write, "[The Messiah] will return *to the sons of Israel*," they interpret this symbolically to refer to the Church—not national Israel (Mic. 5:3; cf. Zech. 9:9-10).[24]

---

[22] For instance, the *Lion* (Rev. 5:5) must refer to Jesus because he is the only one worthy to break the seals (Rev. 5:2), and Jesus was from the tribe of Judah and the line of David. Likewise, the *Lamb* (5:6) must refer to Jesus because he was the only one slain for the sins of the Earth (Jn. 1:29), and he is the only one worthy of worship (5:8-13). By contrast, we do not have these sorts of signifiers for thinking that the 144,000 is equivalent with the great multitude. Moreover, these visions are separate—not offering interpretation of one another. Yates accurately notes, "Verses 9-17 are not a follow-up interpretation of verses 1-8. Instead verses 13-17 interpret the distinct vision of verses 9-12 but not verses 1-8, for none of the elements in verses 1-8 are referred to in the interpretation in verses 13-17." Richard Yates, "The Identity of the Tribulation Saints." *Bibliotheca Sacra*. 163 (January-March, 2006), 82.

[23] Amillennialists hold that the 144,000 refers to the *militant* Church (i.e. the Church on Earth), while the innumerable multitude refers to the *triumphant* Church (i.e. the Church in Heaven). C. Samuel Storms, *Kingdom Come*, 219.

[24] Regarding Micah 5:4, theologian Bruce Waltke writes, "The reigning Messiah will stand (i.e. endure forever; cf. Ps. 33:11; Is. 14:24) and shepherd his flock, providing for their every need, including spiritual food, and protecting them (Jn. 10; Heb. 13:20; 1 Pet. 5:4). Through faith he will rule in the strength of the Lord, not through human engineering and manipulation (cf. 5:10—15). His subjects will live securely for, conquering Satan (Mt. 12:22—29; Rom. 16:20), he will extend his kingdom to the ends of the earth (4:3—4; Mt. 28:18—20; Jn. 17:2). Christ gives his elect people eternal life and no one can snatch them from his hands (Jn. 10:28)." Bruce Waltke, *New Bible Commentary: 21ˢᵗ Century Edition* (InterVarsity Press: Leicester UK, 1997) 829.

The angel Gabriel told Mary that she would conceive and give birth to Jesus (Lk. 1:31), and God fulfilled the first portion of this prediction *literally*. But in the very next breath, Gabriel predicted that Jesus would sit on "the throne of His father *David*; and He will reign over the *house of Jacob* forever" (Lk. 1:32-33). According to Covenantalists, this statement should be interpreted *symbolically*. Jesus will reign *spiritually* from heaven, rather than *literally* on Earth.

Finally, and most surprisingly, Covenantalists believe that the *judgments* for Israel are literal, but the *blessings* are metaphorical, applying them to the Church. For instance, Jeremiah writes, "Just as I brought all this great disaster on this people [*judgment*], so I am going to bring on them all the good that I am promising them [*blessing*]" (Jer. 32:42). How odd to interpret Israel's *judgments literally* while taking her *blessings figuratively!*

Covenantalists effectively render vast portions of Scripture meaningless

If we neglect the return of national Israel, we effectively eliminate vast sections of OT prophecy (Isa. 2:1-4; 10:20-23; 11:1-16; 13; 19:16-25; 24; 25:6-12; 26:11-21; 33:10-24; 34:16-35:10; 42:10-17; 43:14-21; 51:1-52:12; 54; 60-62; 65:17-25; 66:7-24; Jer. 30; 31:1-14, 35-40; 32:36-44; 33; 50:17-20; Ezek. 36-48; Joel 2:18-27; 3:17-21; Amos 9:11-15; Micah 7:7-20; Zeph. 3:8-20; Zech. 8-14). Aldrich writes, "Our [Covenantalist] brethren seldom or never preach on prophecy and ignore large portions of the Bible in their ministries. Perhaps this is because they have no clear, positive system of Eschatology."[25] Even Covenantalist Loraine Boettner agrees, "A whole continent of prophecies [are left] unexplained, many of which then become quite meaningless."[26]

Could Israel remove God's curse and judgment?

If we asked a Covenantalist if God cursed Israel by destroying the Temple and scattering the Jewish people, they would surely agree. According to the Law (Deut. 28; Lev. 26), God would bless the nation for obeying him, and curse the nation for disobedience. Since Israel rejected Christ, God rejected Israel and placed her under divine judgment.

---

[25] Roy Aldrich, "An Apologetic for Dispensationalism." *Bibliotheca Sacra* (January, 1955), 52.
[26] Loraine Boettner, *The Millennium* (Philadelphia, PA: Presbyterian and Reformed, 1958), 119. Cited in Paul N. Benware, *Understanding End times Prophecy*, 29.

But this raises a serious theological problem for the Covenantalist. The modern nation of Israel is largely atheistic and still stands in rejection of Jesus as the Messiah. Yet they regathered themselves into their land despite their lack of repentance. Does this mean that God placed Israel under a curse, but they willfully lifted the curse two millennia later? Is it theologically possible to "uncurse" what God has cursed—especially when no national repentance has occurred in the nation to this day?

How could Covenantalism dominate Christian circles for so long?

In the early centuries after Christ, Christians and Jews warred violently. Justin Martyr (AD 150) notes that Bar Cochba had Christians tortured and killed if they would not renounce Christ.[27] This and other factors led to extreme anti-Semitism in the Christian community.[28]

As a result, Jewish converts to Christ had to renounce their Jewish ethnicity and culture to enter the Christian community.[29] Ignatius stated that if anyone celebrated the Passover with the Jewish people, "he is a partaker with those that killed the Lord and His apostles."[30] Rausch notes the irony that "Jesus and the apostles always observed the Passover."[31] Ambrose of Milan "orchestrated and celebrated a burning of a synagogue."[32] Jerome "had as much contempt for Judeo-Christians as did the Jews themselves," calling the Jews "carnal," "lewd," and "materialistic."[33] Chrysostom stated that while the Jews are "unfit for work, they are fit for killing."[34] Martin Luther stated,

> The blind Jews are truly stupid fools... One should toss out these lazy rogues by the seat of their pants... Eject them forever from this country. For, as we have heard, God's anger with them is so intense that gentle mercy will only tend to make them worse and

---

[27] Justin Martyr, *First Apology*, 31.

[28] See David A. Rausch, *A Legacy of Hatred: Why Christians Must Not Forget the Holocaust* (Chicago, IL: Moody Press, 1984), 16-30.

[29] David A. Rausch, *A Legacy of Hatred*, 25.

[30] Ignatius, *Letter to the Philippians*, 14.

[31] David A. Rausch, *A Legacy of Hatred*, 20.

[32] Barry E. Horner, *Future Israel: Why Christian Anti-Judaism Must Be Challenged* (Nashville, TN: B&H Academic Publishing, 2007), 20.

[33] Barry E. Horner, *Future Israel*, 21.

[34] Chrysostom, *Homily One*, 2:6.

worse, while sharp mercy will reform them but little. Therefore, in any case, away with them![35]

Likewise, John Calvin wrote, "[The Jews'] rotten and unbending stiff-neckedness deserves that they be oppressed unendingly and without measure or end and that they die in their misery without the pity of anyone."[36] Even today, some Covenantalist interpreters seem to blame Jewish persecution on the Jewish people themselves! For instance, in 2001 R.C.H. Lenski wrote,

> Read their long history. The sum of that history is not the fact that the Jews innocently suffered these centuries of woe; *it is that they have ever brought these woes upon themselves anew*. Ever they keep acting as an irritant among the nations... They crucified their own Christ; to this day their hatred of the crucified stamps them more than anything else as 'Jews'; *their segregation is of their own choosing*. The more they retain the character of 'Jews,' the more does this appear; and during the long centuries this their character made them the irritant they have been.[37]

So we see from this Christian interpreter that the problem with anti-Semitic persecution is not primarily with the *persecutors*—but with the *persecuted!* If only the Jewish people surrendered their ethnic identity, they wouldn't have been persecuted so badly. How odd that statements like these could still be made by Christian theologians today! Would we ever use this line of reasoning in any other area of life? If a woman was being beaten by her husband, would we blame *her* or would we blame *her husband?* Compare this with Paul, who told the Gentile Christians in Rome, "Do not be arrogant toward the branches [the Jewish people]; but if you are arrogant, remember that it is not you who supports the root, but the root supports you" (Rom. 11:18).

With anti-Semitism of this kind raging in the Church, Christians (then and now) have found it increasingly difficult to believe that God would return to work through the Jewish people. Dwight Pentecost states, "This

---

[35] Martin Luther (Franklin Sherman, ed.), *From Luther's Works, Volume 47: The Christian in Society IV* (Philadelphia: Fortress Press, 1971), 268-293.

[36] Excerpt from "Ad Quaelstiones et Objecta Juaei Cuiusdam Responsio," by John Calvin; *The Jew in Christian Theology*, Gerhard Falk, McFarland and Company, Inc., Jefferson, NC and London, 1931.

[37] Emphasis mine. R. C. H. Lenski, *The Interpretation of St. Paul's Epistle to the Romans* (Peabody, Massachusetts: Hendrickson, 2001), 691. Cited in Barry E. Horner, *Future Israel*, 91.

antagonism ultimately led to the rejection of the millennium because it was 'Jewish.'"[38]

The nation of Israel has been restored against all odds

Before Israel became a nation again in 1948, many theologians expected such an event. In preaching on Ezekiel 37 in 1887, Charles Spurgeon said, "If there be anything clear and plain, the literal sense and meaning of this passage—a meaning not to be spirited or spiritualized away—must be evident that both the two and the ten tribes of Israel are to be restored to their own land, and that a king is to rule over them."[39] Likewise in 1870, Horatius Bonar wrote, "I am one of those who believe in Israel's restoration and conversion; who receive it as a future certainty, that all Israel shall be gathered, and that all Israel shall be saved… I believe that the sons of Abraham are to re-inherit Palestine."[40]

Other interpreters were not so optimistic about Israel's regathering. In 1939, theologian Louis Berkhof wrote,

> This literalism lands [Dispensationalists] in all kinds of absurdities, for it involves the future restoration of all the former historical conditions of Israel's life… The altered situation would make it necessary for all the nations to visit Jerusalem from year to year, in order to celebrate the feast of tabernacles.[41]

Much to Berkhof's chagrin, Israel became a nation *less than ten years after writing this!* Covenantalist Kim Riddlebarger comments, "When Berkhof completed his venerable *Systematic Theology* in 1939, the restoration of Israel looked like an impossibility. Berkhof could not have foreseen the events of World War II, the Holocaust, and the formation of the state of Israel in 1948 and surely overstated his case."[42] While Dr. Berkhof could not foresee this event, the Bible did all along. Riddlebarger takes a different stance than Berkhof when he speaks frankly of the remarkable nature of Israel's modern regathering:

---

[38] J. Dwight Pentecost, *Things to Come*, 379.
[39] C. H. Spurgeon, *The C. H. Spurgeon Collection, Metropolitan Tabernacle Pulpit, I*, no. 34. 1887. Albany, Oregon: Ages Software, 1998. XXXIV, 1887, no. 2036: 545. Cited in Barry E. Horner, *Future Israel*, 12.
[40] H. Bonar, "The Jew," *The Quarterly Journal of Prophecy* (July, 1870): 214-215. Cited in Barry E. Horner, *Future Israel*, 10.
[41] Louis Berkhof, *Systematic Theology* (Grand Rapids, MI: William Eerdmans Publishing Company, 1939), 712.
[42] Kim Riddlebarger, *A Case for Amillennialism*, 286.

Even if the land promise of the Abrahamic covenant has already been fulfilled, it is quite remarkable that the Jews have returned *en masse* to their ancient homeland. This is a fact that cannot be easily dismissed… Israel is a nation again. The Jews as a people are largely gathered together in one place. [We] need to offer a cogent explanation for this amazing historical development.[43]

He concludes that the modern reforming of Israel "falls within the mysterious providence of God," probably to lead many Jews to Christ at once. But he writes that "this is not connected to the fulfillment of the Abrahamic covenant."[44] Other interpreters (like myself) believe that the restoration of Israel is not mysterious at all. Instead, God had predicted this throughout the Bible—from one end to the other. The only mystery here is how so many theologians and interpreters could ignore such clear fulfilled prophecies in our day.

Discussion questions

1. After reading this chapter, do you believe there are good biblical reasons for thinking that Israel will return in God's plan? Which reasons did you find to be the most convincing? Which were the least convincing? Why?

2. What might be some ramifications of God removing his unconditional promises to Israel? How might this affect our theology or hermeneutics?

3. How much significance should we place on Israel's restoration in the 20th century? How much should this historical fact affect our study of Scripture?

---

[43] Kim Riddlebarger, *A Case for Amillennialism*, 286-287.
[44] Kim Riddlebarger, *A Case for Amillennialism*, 287.

Part Three: The Mystery of the Millennium

We've established, so far, a basic case for why we should hold to a Futurist and Dispensationalist view regarding eschatology. These categories will help guide us as we work through another important subject: The Millennial Kingdom.

The Latin prefix *mille* means "thousand." We use this Latin root when we refer to a "millimeter" or "millisecond." The Latin word *annus* means "year," which is where the English word "annual" derives. Thus when theologians refer to the "millennium," they are describing their view of the thousand year reign of Christ. How should we understand the Millennium? Theologians fall into three major categories: *Pre*millennialism, *A*millennialism, and *Post*millennialism. We will evaluate each view in the following chapters.

Chapter 10. Premillennialism

Premillennialism teaches that Jesus will return *before* a literal Millennium of time where he will reign on Earth (hence *Pre*-millennialism). When Jesus returns, he will fulfill the prophecies of reigning on a physical throne in Israel, and at this time, Satan will be bound. After Jesus reigns throughout the Millennium, Satan will be let loose, and humanity will openly rebel once again. But this time, Christ will quell the rebellion and initiate the eternal and sinless reign of the New Heavens and Earth. Since multiple lines of evidence support a future Israel, *Dispensational Premillennialists* argue that Christ will return to initiate his kingdom in Israel for a thousand years. *Historical Premillennialists* hold the same view—except the Church replaces Israel in their view:

Millennial Views			
VIEW	*Premillennial*	*Amillennial*	*Postmillennial*
The Millennium	**A literal 1,000 year period**	A figurative number	A figurative number
Christ's reign	**Reigns literally in a kingdom on Earth after his Second Coming**	Reigns spiritually on a heavenly throne or reigns spiritually in the hearts of believers	Reigns spiritually in the hearts of believers, as the gospel transforms the nations of the Earth
Israel	**Christ reigns in Israel over a regathered Israel**	The Church replaces the promises given to national Israel	The Church replaces the promises given to national Israel
View of Human History	**Believes human history will get progressively *worse*, as the gospel reaches all nations**	Believes human history will get progressively *worse*, as the gospel reaches all nations	Believes that human history will get progressively *better*. The nations will eventually be transformed by Christ's reign in society

Will Jesus come back to reign on Earth for a thousand years before the New Heavens and Earth arrive? Amillennial and Postmillennial theologians raise a number of objections that we should consider closely.

PREMILLENIALISM

First Coming

Second Coming
Satan bound

Final Judgment

Apostasy
Tribulation
Antichrist
Armageddon

Satan released
*Battle of Gog
and Magog*

**New Heavens
and Earth**

Church Age
Spread of the gospel

Millenium
*Christ reigns on Earth
Resurrection of believers to reign with Christ
Temple restored*

DIFFERENCE FROM
AMILLENIALSIM &
POSTMILLENIALISM

Did Jesus claim that he would reject the nation of Israel?

While God made covenants with Israel, Amillennialists argue that Israel nullified these promises by crucifying their Messiah, rather than accepting him. According to the Amillennialist, once you crucify the Messiah, all bets are off. After all, Jesus taught, "The kingdom of God will be taken away from you and given to a people, producing the fruit of it" (Mt. 21:43).

However, Jesus was speaking to the Jewish leaders in *earshot*—not those at the *end of human history*. This isn't a *permanent curse* on Israel, but a *temporary* one. Jesus didn't want the Pharisees to be content with the *future blessings* of the covenant (at the end of history). He wanted them to seek the *current blessings* (in the Church Age).

When Jesus says that the kingdom will be taken away from you, he is referring to that contemporary generation. But when he says that it will be "given to a people, producing the fruit of it," he is either referring to the Gentiles or perhaps to Israel at the end of history. Thomas notes, "In the NT the singular noun *ethnos* [i.e. "people"], when unqualified by other words such as 'nation against nation' (Matt 24:7; Mark 13:8; Luke 21:10) and 'every nation of humankind' (Acts 17:26), usually refers to Israel."[1] This interpretation would fit with Jesus' woes against "this generation" in Matthew 23:36.

Does the NT reinterpret ethnic Israel as the Church?

Amillennialists argue that Paul reinterpreted the physical kingdom of the OT as a spiritual kingdom: the Church.[2] Paul wrote, "He is not a Jew who is one outwardly, nor is circumcision that which is outward in the flesh. 29 But he is a Jew who is one inwardly; and circumcision is that which is of the heart, by the Spirit, not by the letter" (Rom. 2:28-29). Furthermore, they show that Paul believed *all* Christians are "the *true* circumcision" (Phil. 3:3),[3] and "it is those who are of faith who are sons of Abraham" (Gal. 3:7; cf. Mt. 3:9). According to theologian Sam Storms, "If you are 'in Christ' through faith and thus belong to him, then you too 'are Abraham's offspring' or 'seed' and thus you too are an heir of the covenant promises!"[4] Based on these passages above, these theologians believe that Christians inherit the promises given to Abraham and to Israel. Did the Church inherit all of Israel's promises?

Not necessarily. These passages deal with God's *present* plan through the Church Age—not his *future* plan in the Millennium. Take Romans 2:28 for example ("He is a Jew who is one inwardly"). Paul cannot be saying that Christians spiritually inherit the promises to Israel. At this point in the book of Romans, Paul hasn't even explained *how* to become a Christian. Instead, he makes the argument that keeping the moral law takes precedence over rituals like circumcision. At this point in the letter, he doesn't even claim that these Gentiles are Christians. Thus it would be a mistake to conclude that Paul is nullifying the covenants to the Jewish people based on this passage.

What about Galatians 3:7? Here Paul writes that "it is those who are of faith who are sons of Abraham." Amillennialists note that here Paul quotes the Abrahamic Covenant (Gal. 3:8), and states that all Christians have inherited

---

[1] Robert Thomas, *Perspectives on Israel and the Church: 4 Views* (Nashville, TN: B&H Publishing Group), 72.
[2] See Oral Robertson, *The Israel of God* (Phillipsburg, NJ, 2000), 44.
[3] Horner notes that Paul's use of "we" might only refer to himself and Timothy, who were both circumcised—not all believers. He sees the same contrast of "we" (Jews) and "you" (Gentiles) in Galatians 2:15-3:3.
[4] C. Samuel Storms, *Kingdom Come*, 190.

this. Venema writes that "it is expressly stated that this promise has been fulfilled in Christ."[5]

Even so, notice which part of the Abrahamic Covenant Paul cites: "All nations will be blessed through you" (Gal. 3:8; cf. Gen. 12:3), and notice which portions he does not cite (i.e. the fulfillment of the land or national promises). Paul selectively quotes the portion that has been *literally* fulfilled: Abraham's descendant (Jesus) has blessed the Gentile nations through the gospel. As you might expect, if this part was *literally* fulfilled, then we should expect the other portions of the Abrahamic Covenant to be *literally* fulfilled as well.

Did the NT authors spiritualize OT prophecies?

Joel predicted that in the future God would pour out his Holy Spirit on his people (Joel 2:28-29). Yet as we keep reading, we see that he also predicted, "I will display wonders in the sky and on the earth, blood, fire and columns of smoke. [31] The sun will be turned into darkness and the moon into blood" (Joel 2:30-31). We might think that this passage hasn't been fulfilled yet, because we haven't ever seen such cataclysmic events. But the apostle Peter quoted this passage in its entirety in his speech to the Pharisees (Acts 2:17-21). Was Peter spiritualizing Joel's predictions?

The context serves as the key to unlocking Peter's citation. Peter's speech focused on evangelism—not eschatology. To make his evangelistic case, Peter observed that God had poured out his Spirit on the people (Acts 2:4-12), just as he promised in Joel. He quotes the entire passage about the Second Coming of Christ to reinforce the fact that the risen Jesus will return to judge humanity. So Peter quotes all the way to Joel 2:32 in order to show how people under judgment might be forgiven: "Everyone who calls on the name of the Lord will be saved" (Acts 2:21). If the first portion of Joel's prediction has been fulfilled (i.e. the gift of the Holy Spirit), then the final portion will as well (i.e. being forgiven by Christ before judgment day). Since this is clearly an *evangelistic* sermon, this makes better sense of the context. Peter isn't spiritualizing the Millennial Kingdom of Christ; instead, he is using prophecy as an apologetic for evangelistic purposes.

---

[5] Cornelius Venema, *The Promise of the Future* (Castleton, NY: Hamilton Printing Co., 2009), 283.

Doesn't Paul teach that the division between Jews and Gentiles has been abolished (Eph. 2:14-15)?

Amillennial interpreters criticize the fact that God would have separate promises for the Jewish people, because Paul wrote that Jesus "made both groups [Jews and Gentiles] into one and broke down the barrier of the dividing wall, 15 by abolishing in His flesh the enmity, which is the Law of commandments contained in ordinances, so that in Himself He might make the two into one new man, thus establishing peace" (Eph. 2:14-15).[6]

Of course, before Christ, Gentiles were "strangers to the covenants of promise" (Eph. 2:12), and now they are included in God's plan. But does this mean that our equality therefore eliminates any diversity between the groups? Not at all. When Paul writes, "There is neither male nor female; for you are all one in Christ Jesus" (Gal. 3:28), he does not mean that men and women lose their gender. He means that we are equal—even though we are diverse. Similarly, God has included the Gentiles in his plan of salvation by breaking down the *Mosaic Covenant* ("the Law of commandments contained in ordinances"), but the *Abrahamic Covenant* still stands.

How does 1 Corinthians 15:22-26 fit with Premillennialism?

In Christ all will be made alive. 23 But *each in his own order. Christ the first fruits*, after that *those who are Christ's at His coming*, 24 *then* comes the end, when He hands over the kingdom to the God and Father, when He has abolished all rule and all authority and power. 25 For He must reign until He has put all His enemies under His feet. 26 The last enemy that will be abolished is death. (1 Cor. 15:22b-26)

Amillennialists argue that this passage shows that death will end immediately after the return of Christ, leaving no room for a millennium. Venema points to passages where the NT uses the term "then" (*epeita, eita*), and he notes that this term is "used to express events in the closest temporal connection, without any protracted period of time intervening (Luke 8:12, Mark 4:17, John 20:27)."[7] Storms writes, "How can these two prophesied events (Isa. 25:7-9) find their fulfillment at the close of a 1,000-

---

[6] C. Samuel Storms, *Kingdom Come*, 184.
[7] Cornelius Venema, *The Promise of the Future* (Castleton, NY: Hamilton Printing Co., 2009), 250.

year [post-Second Coming] millennial kingdom when Paul has so clearly stated that they find their fulfillment at the second coming of Christ?"[8]

Premillennialists argue that a gap of time exists in between these events. For one, Paul specifies the resurrection of different *groups*. He writes that Christ will bring people to life "each in his own *order*" (1 Cor. 15:23). This Greek term (*tagmata*) is "a clearly defined group" or "a stage in a sequence."[9] If Paul believed that everyone would be raised all at once (as Amillennialism teaches), then this statement would carry no meaning.

Secondly, Paul specifies the resurrection at different *times*. Throughout this section, he uses the term "then" (*eita*) to distinguish the separate events that will occur. Just as a large gap of time occurred between Jesus' resurrection ("Christ the first fruits") and his Second Coming ("after that those who are Christ's at His coming"), so there is also a gap between his Second Coming and the New Heavens and Earth ("then comes the end").[10]

Why is the length of 1,000 years only mentioned in Revelation 20?

Those critical of Premillennialism argue that the doctrine of the Millennium is based on only one passage: Revelation 20. How can we be so certain about the Millennial Kingdom, when we only find the length of the Millennium in one chapter of Scripture? Postmillennialist Kenneth Gentry writes, "If a literal earthly Millennium is such an important and glorious era in redemptive history (as premillennialists argue), then it is odd that reference to the thousand years should appear in only one passage in all of Scripture."[11]

It's true that the Bible only mentions the *length* of this era in one chapter of Scripture, but the Bible speaks of the *concept* of a future kingdom repeatedly (Isa. 2:1-4; 10:20-23; 11:1-16; 13; 19:16-25; 24; 25:6-12; 26:11-21; 33:10-24; 34:16-35:10; 42:10-17; 43:14-21; 51:1-52:12; 54; 60-62; 65:17-25; 66:7-24; Jer. 30; 31:1-14, 35-40; 32:36-44; 33; 50:17-20; Ezek. 36-48; Joel 2:18-27;

---

[8] C. Samuel Storms, *Kingdom Come*, 152.

[9] Arndt, W. (et al.), *A Greek-English Lexicon of the New Testament and Other Early Christian Literature*, 3rd ed. (Chicago: University of Chicago Press, 2000), 987.

[10] Historical Premillennialist George Ladd notes, "An unidentified interval falls between Christ's resurrection and his Parousia [Second Coming], and a second unidentified interval falls between the Parousia and the *telos* [the end], when Christ completes the subjugation of his enemies." George Eldon Ladd (et al.), *The Meaning of the Millennium: Four Views* (Downers Grove, IL: InterVarsity, 1977), 39.

[11] Kenneth Gentry, "Postmillennialism." Darrell Bock (General Editor). *Three Views on the Millennium and Beyond* (Grand Rapids, MI. Zondervan, 1999), 51.

3:17-21; Amos 9:11-15; Micah 7:7-20; Zeph. 3:8-20; Zech. 8-14; Mt. 19:28; Lk. 21:24; Acts 1:6-7; Rom. 9:3-5; 11:25-29; Gal. 3:17-18; Heb. 6:13-18). Thus it would be a mistake to claim that the Millennium is based on a solitary passage. Similarly, while the Bible only predicts the *date* of Jesus' death in one solitary passage (Dan. 9:24-27), countless passages predict the *event* of the First Coming of Christ.

Moreover, while the thousand-year period only occurs in Revelation 20, we should note that it appears in that chapter no less than *six times*. Robert Thomas observes, "It is doubtful that any symbolic number, if there be such, is ever repeated that many times."[12] We might also ask: How many times does Scripture need to teach something for us to believe it?

Throughout Revelation, John demonstrates that he can use specific numbers (Rev. 5:11; 7:1; 14:1; 9:16), numbers for short periods of time (Rev. 12:12), and even incalculable numbers (Rev. 7:9). Surely, John couldn't *see* one thousand years transpiring in a vision; he must have been *told* this figure.

How can immortal believers live in the presence of mortal people?

Amillennialists find it bizarre that immortal believers would live alongside mortal ones during the Millennium. Hoekema writes, "Do not glorified resurrection bodies call for life on a new earth, from which all remnants of sin and of the curse have been banished?"[13] Likewise Berkhof writes,

> It is impossible to understand how a part of the old earth and of sinful humanity can exist alongside a part of the new earth and of a humanity that is glorified. How can perfect saints in glorified bodies have communion with sinners in the flesh? How can glorified sinners live in this sin-laden atmosphere and amid scenes of death and decay?[14]

And yet, while this might seem strange to us, it has already happened multiple times. For one, Jesus rose from the dead and walked among sinful people in his immortal, resurrected body. Moreover, a number of believers rose from the dead in Jerusalem, walking among the people at that time as well (Mt. 27:53). Finally, Moses and Elijah appeared alongside Jesus at the

---

[12] Robert L. Thomas, *Revelation 8-22: An Exegetical Commentary* (Chicago: Moody, 1995), 408.
[13] Anthony Hoekema, *The Bible and the Future* (Grand Rapids, MI: Eerdmans, 1979), 185.
[14] Louis Berkhof, *Systematic Theology* (Grand Rapids, MI: William Eerdmans Publishing Company, 1938), 715.

Mount of Transfiguration. While it might seem strange to think of immortal believers standing alongside fallen and corruptible humans, for those who believe in the Bible, it has already happened on several occasions.

Why is there another fall at the end of the Millennium?

At the end of the Millennium, Satan will leave his maximum security prison to deceive the nations once again (Rev. 20:7-8). Amillennialists believe that this picture of the future is bizarre: Why would God allow another fall of humanity toward the end of human history? Storms writes, "It is difficult to understand how anyone would *not* come to saving faith while standing for a lifetime in Christ's glorified presence."[15] Riddlebarger calls this "one of the most serious weaknesses of premillennialism."[16]

But of course, *resurrected believers* will not rebel at this time—only those *mortal people* who will procreate during the Millennium. It shouldn't surprise us to see fallen people rebelling against Christ in this setting. The first humans rebelled against God—even though they were directly in his presence (Gen. 3:8). Judas (and many of the religious leaders) rebelled against Christ when he first came to Earth, and even after Jesus rose from the dead, some of his disciples who saw him "were doubtful" (Mt. 28:17). Even Peter saw Jesus glorified at the Transfiguration, but he still denied Christ. Why should it surprise us to see history repeating itself in the future?

God's purposes take time. God's creation of the world took *billions* of years; his work through the nation of Israel took 2,000 years; he plans on working through the Church for at least 2,000 years; and even Jesus' ministry took around three decades to get started (Lk. 3:23). It often baffles us that God would work through such slow processes, but this is his pattern in history.

When humanity falls for the second time under the reign of Christ, God will show our utter sinfulness for what it really is. Even with the perfect King reigning on Earth, humans will *still* rebel and *still* try to thwart God's leadership. When people sin today, they often blame it on their culture, education, or upbringing. But in this day, God will show without a doubt that our problem isn't with others; it's with our own sinful and rebellious hearts.

---

[15] C. Samuel Storms, *Kingdom Come*, 156.
[16] Kim Riddlebarger, *A Case for Amillennialism*, 230.

Why does Isaiah blend the Millennium with the New Heavens and Earth?

Premillennialists hold that the end of the book of Isaiah refers to the Millennium—not the New Heavens and Earth (cf. Isaiah 65:20). And yet in the middle of these two chapters, God states that he has created the "new heavens and a new earth" (Isa. 65:17; cf. 66:22). Amillennialists note that this demonstrates that the Millennium doesn't exist; instead history will move directly into the New Heavens and Earth.[17]

Other translations, however, render Isaiah 65:17 in the future tense. For instance, the NIV renders this as "I *will* create new heavens and a new earth," making the New Heavens and Earth future to the Millennium. Moreover, Garland writes, "The prophets did not make distinctions between the millennium and the eternal state when describing the period of messianic blessing,"[18] sometimes blending the events together. Theologian Wayne Grudem adds that OT prophets often didn't make distinctions between future events "just as these prophecies do not distinguish between the first and second comings of Christ."[19]

The difficulty of Ezekiel's future Temple (Ezek. 40-48)

After describing the regathering of Israel (Ezek. 37) and God judging the nations at the end of human history (Ezek. 38-39), Ezekiel spends nine chapters describing (in painstaking detail!) a future Temple at this time (Ezek. 40-48). Premillennialists believe that this refers to a *literal* temple, while Amillennialists believe this is a *symbolic* temple that actually refers to the Church. As we will see, both Premillennialists and Amillennialists have difficulty interpreting the temple sacrifices in Ezekiel 40-48.

How do Premillennialists interpret the future Temple?

Amillennialists believe it is blasphemous to hold to animal sacrifices in the Millennium, because the author of Hebrews clearly states that "where there is forgiveness of these things, *there is no longer any offering for sin*" (Heb. 10:18).

---

[17] Anthony Hoekema, *The Bible and the Future* (Grand Rapids, MI: Eerdmans, 1979), 202.
[18] David E. Garland (et al.), *Jeremiah-Ezekiel* (Grand Rapids, MI: Zondervan, 2010), 870.
[19] Wayne Grudem, *Systematic Theology* (Grand Rapids, MI. Zondervan Publishing House, 1994), 1127.

Storms writes, "It would be an egregious expression of the worst imaginable *redemptive regression* to suggest that God would ever sanction the rebuilding of the Temple."[20] Ezekiel uses the term atonement five times—three of which refer to atoning for *inanimate objects* (Ezek. 43:20, 26; 45:20) and two of which refer to atoning for *people* (Ezek. 45:15, 17). Do these sacrifices replace the work of the Cross in this time period?

Premillennialists do not think so. The sacrifices in Ezekiel's Temple will *memorialize* Jesus' sacrifice *in the Millennium*, just as the Lord's Supper *memorializes* his sacrifice during the *Church Age*. Just like the old sacrifices pointed *forward* to Christ (Heb. 10:4), these future sacrifices will point *backward* to him. Regarding the Lord's Supper, Paul writes, "As often as you eat this bread and drink the cup, you proclaim the Lord's death *until He comes*" (1 Cor. 11:26). Notice that Paul writes that we will practice communion until... *when?* We practice it *until Christ returns*. Therefore, we should expect a change in communion at this time.

Even in the old covenant, the festivals and sacrifices didn't *produce* salvation for the people; instead, they served as "memorials" of Yahweh's redemption (Ex. 30:16; Lev. 2:2, 9; 5:12; 6:15; 24:7; Num. 5:15, 18, 26).[21] God gave the law and sacrificial system *after* Israel already had an unconditional covenant with him. Hullinger writes, "Sacrifices were not intended as a means of procuring the salvific favor of God but to deal with those things that disrupted fellowship with Him and with fellow members of the community."[22]

These future sacrifices will not pay for sin—even as the past sacrifices never paid for it. Ezekiel mentions that the Temple will make "atonement" (Ezek. 43:20, 26; 45:15, 17, 20), but Leviticus states that the OT sacrifices "make atonement" as well (Lev. 4:20, 26, 31, 35). The Bible uses the same language in each instance, but we know from the author of Hebrews that the old sacrifices didn't actually pay for sin (Heb. 10:4). Like the Levitical sacrifices, these point to the ultimate sacrifice of Jesus.

---

[20] C. Samuel Storms, *Kingdom Come*, 21.

[21] Archer writes, "So it is with these burnt offerings. They will have no atoning efficacy—atonement has been accomplished by Calvary—but they will serve as elements in that form of *holy communion* that will be instituted during the Millennium... It is therefore only to be expected that after the Second Coming some different elements should be appointed for the Kingdom Age, and very naturally also, elements reminiscent of those God appointed for His ancient people in Moses' time." Gleason Archer (et al.), *Three Views on the Rapture: Pre-, Mid-, or Post-Tribulation?* (Grand Rapids, MI: Zondervan, 1996), 110.

[22] Jerry Hullinger, "The Function of the Millennial Sacrifices in Ezekiel's Temple: Part 1." *Bibliotheca Sacra.* 167 (January-March, 2010), 42.

Additionally, Ezekiel's picture of animal sacrifices changes drastically from those found in Leviticus. The Ark of the Covenant, the manna, Aaron's rod, the Tables of the Law, the Cherubim, the mercy-seat, the golden candlestick, the showbread, the veil, the Holy of Holies, and the high priest *all disappear in these visions.*[23] Moreover, in Ezekiel's prophecy, the future prince[24] offers the sacrifices (Ezek. 45:16-17), rather than the priests. These differences demonstrate that this future sacrificial system radically differs from the old one.

How do Amillennialists interpret the future temple?

While Premillennialists have difficulty interpreting Ezekiel's future temple, Amillennialists have an even harder time. These interpreters offer various interpretations: (1) Ezekiel's temple refers to the Church, (2) Ezekiel's temple refers to worship in heaven, (3) Ezekiel's temple refers to the temple during Jesus' day, or (4) Ezekiel's temple was a false prediction.

INTERPRETATION #1: Ezekiel's temple refers to the Church

Most Amillennialists understand Ezekiel's future temple to refer to the Church.[25] After all, Paul called the Church the "temple of God" (1 Cor. 3:16; cf. 6:19). According to one Amillennialist, the features of Ezekiel's temple are "an impressionistic literary cartoon with an intentional ideological aim."[26]

However, Ezekiel writes 260 verses of Scripture and hundreds of descriptions of the dimensions, furnishings, and measurements of this future temple. Why does he spill so much ink if it's merely symbolic for the

---

[23] David E. Garland (et al.), *Jeremiah-Ezekiel* (Grand Rapids, MI: Zondervan, 2010), 873.
[24] The prince is not Christ, because he has sons (Ezek. 46:16), but he is a new figure that did not exist in the old system of priests. He is probably just a future ruler that has delegated authority under Christ (Lk. 19:17).
[25] Amillennialist Iain Duguid writes, "There on the cross the radical focus on sacrifice of Ezekiel's temple found its full expression, as the new temple itself was made a complete sacrifice for sin, by which God's people were cleansed once and for all... Since the church is Christ's body, it is also the new temple. This means that we too as the church are called to share the radical focus on sacrifice of Ezekiel's temple... Reflecting the order of Ezekiel's temple, we too are called to recognize the difference between the holy and the profane, to separate ourselves from the sin that so easily besets us (Heb. 12:1) and the ties that improperly bind us to unbelievers, who keep us apart from God (2 Cor. 6:14-7:1)." Iain Duguid, *The NIV Application Commentary: Ezekiel*, 481-482.
[26] Daniel Block, *The Book of Ezekiel: 25-48*, 701.

Church? God told Ezekiel that he wrote these details for the purpose of the temple actually being built: "Make known to them the design of the house, its structure, its exits, its entrances, all its designs, all its statutes, and all its laws. And write it in their sight, *so that they may observe its whole design and all its statutes and do them*" (Ezek. 43:11).

OT scholar Richard Hess notes that Ezekiel offers more description of his temple than any other OT author.[27] Moreover, he notes that later Jewish interpreters held that Ezekiel's temple was very literal: "Wherever it can be checked—among Samaritans and Second Temple mainstream Jews and in the separatist Jewish community of Qumran—the vision of Ezekiel was understood as intending a real, physical temple in the centuries after the prophet wrote."[28]

Amillennialists argue that the Bible offers similar descriptions of Solomon's Temple, which Jesus spiritually fulfilled (Jn. 2:19-21). For example, Iain Duguid writes, "If this statement [about Jesus fulfilling the OT Temple] is true of the literal temple of the Old Testament, how much more for the symbolic temple of Ezekiel's vision: Christ is the meaning for which Ezekiel's vision exists."[29] Of course, God gave the Temple as a symbol for Jesus. But do we need to state the obvious? *Jesus spiritually fulfilled a literal Temple!* Ezekiel's temple surely has a symbolic meaning, but it will be literal as well.

Ezekiel surely had the ability to signify if he was utilizing symbolism in his visions. In chapter 37, for example, he sees a vision of dried bones, yet he clearly explains the vision as symbolic for the nation of Israel. By contrast, his vision of the temple gets no such symbolic interpretation—only chapter after chapter of meticulous detail. Furthermore, Ezekiel saw a vision of Solomon's Temple in chapter 8, and his vision of a temple at the end of human history "is a mirror image of chapters 8-11."[30] If Ezekiel saw a

---

[27] Richard Hess, "Chapter Two: The Future Written in the Past: The Old Testament and the Millennium." Craig Blomberg and Sung Wook Chung, *A Case for Historic Premillennialism: An Alternative to "Left Behind" Eschatology* (Grand Rapids, MI: Baker Academic, 2009), 31.

[28] Richard Hess, "Chapter Two: The Future Written in the Past: The Old Testament and the Millennium." Craig Blomberg and Sung Wook Chung, *A Case for Historic Premillennialism: An Alternative to "Left Behind" Eschatology* (Grand Rapids, MI: Baker Academic, 2009), 32-33.

[29] Iain Duguid, *The NIV Application Commentary: Ezekiel*, 482.

[30] Richard Hess, "Chapter Two: The Future Written in the Past: The Old Testament and the Millennium." Craig Blomberg and Sung Wook Chung, *A Case for Historic Premillennialism: An Alternative to "Left Behind" Eschatology* (Grand Rapids, MI: Baker Academic, 2009), 33.

vision of a *literal* temple in the beginning of the book, to be consistent, the vision of a future temple needs to be *literal* as well.

The prophet Ezekiel wasn't the only one to mention a rebuilt temple at the end of human history: four other OT prophets mention a temple as well. *Isaiah* writes, "Burnt offerings and their sacrifices will be acceptable on My altar" (Isa. 56:7). He also mentions "grain offerings" during this time (Isa. 66:20). *Jeremiah* writes, "The Levitical priests shall never lack a man before Me to offer burnt offerings, to burn grain offerings and to prepare sacrifices continually" (Jer. 33:18). *Zechariah* writes that the Messiah will rebuild a temple in the messianic age (Zech. 6:12),[31] and he refers to "all who sacrifice" (Zech. 14:21). After the coming of the Messiah (Mal. 3:2), *Malachi* writes, "The offering of Judah and Jerusalem will be pleasing to the Lord as in the days of old and as in former years" (Mal. 3:3-4).

In addition to the Jewish prophets, the NT authors foresaw a future temple. Jesus stated, "When you see the abomination of desolation which was spoken of through Daniel the prophet, *standing in the holy place*" (Mt. 24:15). Paul writes that the man of lawlessness "opposes and exalts himself above every so-called god or object of worship, so that he takes his seat *in the temple of God*" (2 Thess. 2:4). Likewise, John writes that he was told to "measure the temple" at this time period (Rev. 11:1).

We cannot merely spiritualize Ezekiel's prophecies about the temple, because many other prophets and apostles predict this as well.

INTERPRETATION #2: Ezekiel's temple refers to worship in heaven.

Hoekema argues that Ezekiel's vision refers to our worship in the New Heavens and Earth: "The details about temple and sacrifices are to be understood not literally but figuratively. The closing chapters of the book of Revelation, in fact, echo Ezekiel's vision... What we have in Ezekiel 40 to 48, therefore, is not a description of the millennium but a picture of the final state on the new earth, in terms of the religious symbolism in which Ezekiel and his readers were familiar."[32] This interpretation, however, is surely precluded by the fact that Revelation states there will be "no temple" in heaven "for the Lord God the Almighty and the Lamb are its temple" (Rev. 21:22). How can we equate nine chapters of specific details for rebuilding a temple with John writing that there is "no temple" in heaven?

---

[31] Of course, this cannot refer to Zerubbabel's Temple which was already being worked on in Zechariah 4:9-10.

[32] Anthony Hoekema, *The Bible and the Future* (Grand Rapids, MI: Eerdmans, 1979), 205.

INTERPRETATION #3: Ezekiel's temple refers to the temple during Jesus' day

Postmillennialist Gary DeMar holds that Ezekiel's vision refers to the temple standing in Jesus' day (called the Second Temple). He writes, "This passage is simply a visionary expression of the faithful remnant that returned after the exile and the glorious future they would have."[33]

Such a view doesn't hold water. Ezekiel's temple differs from the Second Temple in its architecture and design, as well as in its worship practices.[34] Amillennialist Daniel Block writes, "Not only were the returnees but a handful of Judeans; the land was never divided among the tribes, no figure like Ezekiel's *nasi* emerged in the community, the reconstructed temple fell far short of Ezekiel's plan, and most seriously of all, the *kabod* of Yahweh failed to return (cf. Hag. 2:3-9)."[35] More importantly, Jesus didn't view the second Temple as pure and undefiled, as Ezekiel did. He cleared the Second Temple with a whip and called the people hypocrites (Jn. 2:16). Since we will have no temple in heaven (Rev. 21:22), when will this temple be rebuilt? It must be a future temple to our own day and age.[36]

INTERPRETATION #4: Ezekiel's temple was a false prediction

Some Amillennialists believe that Ezekiel's future temple will never exist, making it a false prediction. For instance, commentator Leslie Allen (of Fuller Theological Seminary) writes, "To resort to dispensationalism and postpone them to a literal fulfillment in a yet future time strikes the author as a desperate expedient that sincerely attempts *to preserve belief in an inerrant prophecy*. The canon of scriptures, Jewish and Christian, *took unfulfillment in its*

---

[33] Gary DeMar, *Last Days Madness,* 96.

[34] David Garland writes, "The historical temples of Solomon, Zerubbabel, and Herod do not share the design and dimensions of the temple described in Ezekiel 40-42. The worship procedure, though Mosaic in nature, has not been followed in history in exactly the manner described in these chapters... The geographical dimensions and tribal allotments of the land have not been followed up to the present day. Geographical changes will be necessary prior to the fulfillment of chs. 45, 47-48." David E. Garland (et al.), *Jeremiah-Ezekiel* (Grand Rapids, MI: Zondervan, 2010), 868.

[35] Daniel Block, *The Book of Ezekiel: 25-48,* 502.

[36] Hess agrees, "It seems best to describe the time of the restored temple as millennial or as the millennium. It will be an ideal time in which many of the prophecies that occur elsewhere in the OT will find their fulfillment." Richard Hess, "Chapter Two: The Future Written in the Past: The Old Testament and the Millennium." Craig Blomberg and Sung Wook Chung, *A Case for Historic Premillennialism: An Alternative to "Left Behind" Eschatology* (Grand Rapids, MI: Baker Academic, 2009), 34-35.

stride."[37] How does this fit with Ezekiel's own statement about his prophecies: "The days are near when *every* vision will be fulfilled" (Ezek. 12:23 NIV)? A certain irony confronts us here: In trying to uphold what the Bible teaches about the Cross, these interpreters need to deny Ezekiel's prediction altogether.

Conclusions

The Premillennial view faces difficulties on many levels because it actually attempts to struggle with the OT prophecies about the Millennium. It would surely be a lot easier to whitewash these prophecies by simply saying that they predict the Church in some vague and general sense. But if we are to take these prophecies of the future seriously, it's better to *struggle* with them, rather than simply *spiritualizing* them.

Discussion questions

1. With a pen and paper, could you draw a timeline of the Premillennial view versus the Amillennial view?

2. What are the biggest *weaknesses* you see regarding Premillennialism? What are the biggest *strengths* you see regarding the Premillennial view? Do you find the Amillennial or Postmillennial answers more persuasive or less persuasive than the Premillennial view?

3. In your opinion, which view best explains the phenomenon of Ezekiel's temple in chapters 40-48? The Premillennial view or the Amillennial view?

4. Is this subject worth studying, or is it a meaningless or trivial discussion? What is at stake in this theological debate?

---

[37] Emphasis mine. Leslie C. Allen, *Word Biblical Commentary (vol. 29): Ezekiel 20-48* (Dallas: Word, Incorporated, 2002), 214.

Chapter 11. Amillennialism

The term *Amillennial* literally means "no millennium." Amillennialists don't like this name, because they *do* believe in a millennial kingdom, but just a *spiritual* one.[1] Under this view, Jesus will not reign on Earth. Instead, we are currently in the kingdom of God—whereby Jesus reigns in heaven over glorified believers and on Earth in the hearts of those who follow him. Premillennialists (like myself) agree that the Church serves as the "kingdom" here on Earth right now, but this doesn't negate a future physical kingdom.

While God made promises to Israel about having land (Gen. 12:1; 15:18; 17:8), a physical king (2 Sam. 7:11-16), and an Earthly kingdom (Gen. 12:2), Amillennialists argue that the Jewish people abandoned their Messiah. Once you kill the son of God, they argue, these promises are nullified. While God married Israel, they argue that by killing the Messiah, God wrote Israel a certificate of divorce (Isa. 50:1; Jer. 3:8). Instead of reigning on Earth for a thousand years, Amillennialists state that history will move directly into the New Heavens and Earth at the return of Christ. Hoekema writes, "The Old Testament says nothing about such a millennial reign. Passages commonly interpreted as describing the millennium actually describe the new earth."[2]

We might define this view by comparison with the others:

Millennial Views			
VIEW	*Premillennial*	*Amillennial*	*Postmillennial*
The Millennium	A literal 1,000 year period	**A figurative number**	A figurative number
Christ's reign	Reigns literally in a kingdom on Earth after his Second Coming	**Reigns spiritually on a heavenly throne or reigns spiritually in the hearts of believers**	Reigns spiritually in the hearts of believers, as the gospel transforms the nations of the Earth

---

[1] Some theologians of this persuasion prefer to call their view a "realized millennium." For brevity, however, most theologians like Hoekema retain the term Amillennialism. Anthony Hoekema, *The Bible and the Future* (Grand Rapids, MI: Eerdmans, 1979), 173.

[2] Anthony Hoekema, *The Bible and the Future* (Grand Rapids, MI: Eerdmans, 1979), 201.

Israel	Christ reigns in Israel over a regathered Israel	**The Church replaces the promises given to national Israel**	The Church replaces the promises given to national Israel
View of Human History	Believes human history will get progressively *worse*, as the gospel reaches all nations	**Believes human history will get progressively *worse*, as the gospel reaches all nations**	Believes that human history will get progressively *better*. The nations will eventually be transformed by Christ's reign in society

AMILLENIALISM

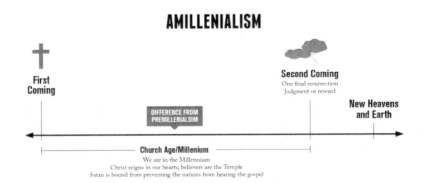

By far, most Christians believe in Amillennialism. Benware admits, "If all Christendom could be gathered together and a vote taken on which of the three millennial views was favored, amillennialism would easily win. Amillennialism is clearly the majority view."[3] But while Amillennialism is the majority view, we shouldn't determine our theology by taking a vote. For the Christian, Scripture serves as the final authority, and many serious

---

[3] Paul N. Benware, *Understanding End Times Prophecy*, 121.

problems confront the Amillennial view. (Since many Amillennial and Postmillennial beliefs overlap one another, we will consider views from both schools where appropriate.)

Amillennialists hold that Satan is currently bound (Rev. 20:2-3)

> And he laid hold of the dragon, the serpent of old, who is the devil and Satan, and bound him for a thousand years; [3] and he threw him into the abyss, and shut it and sealed it over him, so that he would not deceive the nations any longer, until the thousand years were completed; after these things he must be released for a short time. (Rev. 20:2-3)

Under Amillennialism (and Postmillennialism), we are *currently* in the millennial kingdom. Thus when John writes that "[Jesus] laid hold of the dragon, the serpent of old, who is the devil and Satan, and bound him for a thousand years" (Rev. 20:2), this must mean that Satan is *currently* bound. These interpreters often line up the restrainer of 2 Thessalonians 2 with the confinement of Satan in the abyss. Under this view, when the restrainer is taken away (2 Thess. 2:7), this is the same as the opening of the abyss and the releasing of Satan at the end of the Church Age.[4] Amillennialists typically offer four arguments for the view that Satan is currently bound:

ARGUMENT #1: Amillennialists argue that the sealing of the abyss doesn't mean absolute confinement.

To explain this argument, an Amillennialist once quipped, "Satan is chained in the abyss… but he has a very *long* chain!" G.K. Beale writes, "'Sealing' may connote an absolute incarceration, but could just as well connote the general idea of 'authority over,' which is its primary meaning also in Dan. 6:17 and Matt. 27:66."[5]

But neither verse supports Beale's case. Daniel 6:17 refers to the king "sealing" Daniel in the lion's den with his signet ring, and he could not escape. Likewise, Matthew 27:66 refers to the guards that set a royal seal over the tomb of Jesus. Of course, God's power opened the tomb, but that was not the intent of the Roman guards when they set a "seal" on the tomb

---

[4] G.K. Beale, *The Book of Revelation* (Grand Rapids, MI. William B. Eerdmans Publishing Company, 1999), 989.
[5] G.K. Beale, *The Book of Revelation* (Grand Rapids, MI. William B. Eerdmans Publishing Company, 1999), 985-986.

of a dead person. Paul uses this same word (*sphragizō*) to describe how
believers are "sealed" in their relationship with Christ (2 Cor. 1:22; Eph.
1:13; 4:30). Moreover, even if it could be shown that "sealing" is not
absolute, the Amillennial interpreter would also need to show that the
"binding" and "shutting" are not absolute either.

Postmillennialist Kenneth Gentry writes that the "binding increasingly
constricts Satan" throughout the Church Age.[6] However, this doesn't do
justice to the language in Revelation 20, which states that Satan is bound,
shut out, and sealed in an abyss (Rev. 20:2-3). This language may be
symbolic, *but symbolic of what?* For instance, if I said, "I'm as hungry as a
horse," this shouldn't be taken *literally* (i.e. I have the appetite of a 900
pound animal), but it should be taken *seriously* (i.e. I'm famished). Likewise,
what does John mean by these serious symbols ("bound him" "shut it"
"sealed it")? Revelation 9:14 states that the angels were "bound" to the river
Euphrates, which doesn't merely restrict the *power* or *influence* of the angels,
but also their *location*.

Most importantly, when we read the rest of the Bible, we find absolutely no
evidence that Satan is bound. Indeed, the Bible repeatedly states that Satan
is currently alive and well on Earth—not in an abyss (Acts 5:3; 1 Cor. 5:5;
7:5; 1 Tim. 1:20; 2 Cor. 2:11; 4:3-4; 11:14; 12:7; Eph. 2:1-3; Heb. 2:8; 1
Thess. 2:18; 1 Tim. 4:1; 2 Tim. 2:24-26; 1 Pet. 5:8; 1 Jn. 3:8-10; 5:19-20).
Why do we read so much about Satan in the NT *only to find that he is
immediately bound?* It seems more reasonable to assume that God has given us
so much information on Satan, so that we can face him in battle (Eph. 6:10-
18).

ARGUMENT #2: Amillennialists argue that Satan's binding only relates to the spread of the gospel to the nations—not an absolute binding.

Amillennialists claim that Satan is still active, but Christ bound him from
deceiving the nations ("bound him... so that he would not deceive the
nations any longer"). For instance, Riddlebarger writes, "It does not mean
that all satanic operations cease during the millennial age, as many
opponents of amillennialism mistakenly assume."[7] Later he argues, "Christ's

[6] Gentry, Kenneth. "Postmillennialism." Darrell Bock (General Editor), *Three Views on the Millennium and Beyond*, 52.
[7] Kim Riddlebarger, *A Case for Amillennialism*, 237.

work of restraining the devil's ability to 'deceive' is *not a complete curtailment* of all of the devil's activities but *only a restraint on his deceiving activities.*"[8]

However, why would John use such emphatic language ("bound him…" "shut it…" "sealed it…"), if Satan is actually entering the hearts of believers (Acts 5:3; 2 Tim. 2:24-26), scheming against believers (2 Cor. 2:11), thwarting Paul's ministry (1 Tim. 2:18), looking to destroy believers (1 Pet. 5:8), blinding the eyes of non-Christians (2 Cor. 4:4), and controlling the entire world (1 Jn. 5:19-20)? Can we really say that Satan has been bound, when he currently "deceives the whole world" (Rev. 12:9) and "all the nations were deceived" by Babylon's sorcery (Rev. 18:23)? Moreover, can we really say that the spread of the gospel has been unopposed in closed countries by Satan? Such a view stretches our credulity.

ARGUMENT #3: Amillennialists argue that Jesus bound Satan at the Cross.

Jesus asked, "How can anyone enter the strong man's house and carry off his property, unless he first *binds* the strong man?" (Mt. 12:29). Here Jesus uses the same Greek word for "binding" (*deo*) as we see in Revelation 20:2 (cf. Mk. 3:27). Based on this word association, Amillennialists hold that Satan was bound at the Cross. Moreover, Jesus said he was "watching Satan fall from heaven like lightning" (Lk. 10:18).

Yet it's a mistake to build our doctrines on *word association*. As we saw in our earlier chapter on hermeneutics, words can have different meanings in different contexts (e.g. "running"). While Matthew 12 and Revelation 20 both use the same word for "binding" Satan (*deo*), they use this term in different contexts. Matthew 12 uses it before the Cross; Revelation 20 uses it at the end of history.

ARGUMENT #4: Amillennialists argue that Jesus defeated Satan at the Cross.

Jesus predicted that "the ruler of this world will be cast out" (Jn. 12:31). By dying on the Cross, "[God] disarmed the rulers and authorities, He made a public display of them, having triumphed over them through Him" (Col. 2:14-15; cf. Col. 1:13; Acts 26:18). Thus Amillennialists argue that Satan *has* been defeated—by the Cross.

---

[8] Emphasis mine. G.K. Beale, *The Book of Revelation* (Grand Rapids, MI. William B. Eerdmans Publishing Company, 1999), 986.

Certainly, these passages teach that Jesus triumphed over Satan at the Cross, but in what sense? Christ "disarmed" Satan, but this stops short of saying that Jesus bound him. Premillennialists hold that Jesus disarmed Satan's primary weapon: his accusations against God's character. Satan would like us to believe that God is selfish and controlling, but after the Cross, these accusations have forever lost their force. Likewise, while Satan "will be cast out" (Jn. 12:31), Jesus never states *when* this will occur. Neither side of this debate can claim this passage to support their view, because Jesus never tells us when it will be fulfilled. Amillennialists simply read too much into these passages to support their view.

Amillennialists believe the "first resurrection" is spiritual—not physical (Rev. 20:4-5)

> I saw the souls of those who had been beheaded because of their testimony of Jesus and because of the word of God, and those who had not worshiped the beast or his image, and had not received the mark on their forehead and on their hand; and *they came to life and reigned with Christ for a thousand years.* [5] The rest of the dead did not come to life until the thousand years were completed. This is the first resurrection. (Rev. 20:4-5)

Premillennialists believe that this passage gives warrant for at least *two* resurrections: one at the *beginning* of the Millennium and one at the *end*. However, Amillennialists (and Postmillennialists) contend that this refers to our *spiritual* resurrection when we come to Christ. They appeal to John 5:24-25, where Jesus says that we obtain eternal life at the moment of conversion ("he has passed out of death into life"). Thus Gentry writes, "According to John the 'first resurrection' secures the participation of the saints (both dead and living) in the rule of Christ (Rev. 20:4-6). This refers to the spiritual resurrection of those born again by God's grace."[9] Riddlebarger explains that this can either mean (1) the believer's conversion to Christ or (2) their death when they go to reign with Christ in heaven. Thus "the first resurrection is spiritual and not bodily and occurs before, not after, the second advent."[10] By contrast, Premillennialists argue that the "first resurrection" must refer to the physical resurrection in the future for a number of key reasons.

---

[9] Gentry, Kenneth. "Postmillennialism." Darrell Bock (General Editor), *Three Views on the Millennium and Beyond*, 53.
[10] Kim Riddlebarger, *A Case for Amillennialism*, 243.

Grammatically, John uses the same language to refer to both resurrections. If the first resurrection is spiritual in verse 4 ("they came to life and reigned with Christ for a thousand years"), then wouldn't the resurrection of the rest of the dead also be spiritual ("The rest of the dead did not come to life until the thousand years were completed")?

Lexically, the words used here refer to a physical resurrection—not a spiritual regeneration. The "first resurrection" (*protos anastasis*) literally means "to stand up again." John uses this word (*anastasis*) only twice in Revelation, in verses 5 and 6 of chapter 20, but there is no precedent in the NT for using *anastasis* to refer to anything but a physical resurrection. Even Beale admits, "*Anastasis* appears forty-one times in the NT and refers to physical resurrection except in Luke 2:34 and John 11:25."[11] However, when read in context, even John 11:25 refers to a physical resurrection ("I am the resurrection [*anastasis*] and the life"),[12] and Luke 2:34 doesn't refer to a spiritual resurrection either ("This Child is appointed for the *fall and rise* [*anastasis*] of many in Israel").

Contextually, the passage teaches that it is the martyrs who are raised here—not all believers. John tells us that the Christian martyrs (not all believers) are those who are raised ("...the souls of those who had been beheaded because of their testimony of Jesus..."). Clearly, the people must have been believers *before* they were beheaded for following Christ! Thomas rightly observes, "People who have died for Christ can hardly experience a spiritual resurrection. They are already spiritually alive."[13] Moreover, the fact that they were beheaded shows that they were *physical* bodies—not *spiritual* souls.

---

[11] G.K. Beale, *The Book of Revelation* (Grand Rapids, MI. William B. Eerdmans Publishing Company, 1999), 1004.

[12] In John 11:24-25, despite the death of her brother Lazarus, Jesus promised Martha that Lazarus would rise again. Martha turned to Jesus and said, "I know that he will rise again in the resurrection (*anastasis*) on the last day." Jesus replied, "I am the resurrection (*anastasis*) and the life; he who believes in Me shall live even if he dies, and everyone who lives and believes in Me shall never die." To illustrate what he meant, Jesus called Lazarus from his tomb and restored his physical life. This, too, would support a physical resurrection—not a spiritual one.

[13] Robert L. Thomas, *Revelation 8-22: An Exegetical Commentary* (Chicago: Moody, 1995), 415.

Amillennialists argue that the thrones of believers are in heaven—not on Earth (Rev. 20:4)

> I saw thrones, and they sat on them, and judgment was given to them. (Rev. 20:4)

Riddlebarger argues that Jesus' throne is in heaven, and this is where believers will reign as well (citing Rev. 3:21). Thus, for Riddlebarger "the answer is simple: the thrones are in heaven."[14] Yet Revelation 5:10 promises that the believers in heaven will eventually reign "upon the *earth*." Moreover, John states that he saw "an angel coming down *from heaven*" (Rev. 20:1). Grudem comments, "If the angel came down from heaven, then he carries out his activity on the earth, and the entire scene is set on the earth."[15]

Amillennialists believe that Revelation 20 is a recap of chapter 12

Amillennialists do not interpret the events of Revelation 20 as occurring chronologically after the return of Christ in Revelation 19. Instead, they take chapter 20 as a recap of chapter 12. Riddlebarger shows these similarities between the two chapters:[16]

Parallels between Revelation 12 and 20	
Revelation 12:7-11	**Revelation 20:1-6**
Heavenly scene (v.7)	Heavenly scene (v.1)
Angelic battle against Satan and his host (vv. 7-8)	Presupposed angelic battle with Satan (v. 2)
Satan cast to earth (v. 9)	Satan cast into the abyss (v. 3)
The angels' evil opponent called "the great dragon, … that ancient serpent called the devil or Satan, who leads the whole world astray" (v. 9)	The angels' evil opponent called "the dragon, that ancient serpent, who is the devil, or Satan," restrained from "deceiving the nations anymore" (vv. 2-3), to be released later "to deceive the nations in the four corners of the

---

[14] Kim Riddlebarger, *A Case for Amillennialism*, 241.
[15] Wayne Grudem, *Systematic Theology* (Grand Rapids, MI. Zondervan Publishing House, 1994), 1118.
[16] Kim Riddlebarger, *A Case for Amillennialism*, 229.

	the earth" (vv. 3, 7-8)
Satan "is filled with fury, because he knows that his time is short" (v. 12)	Satan to be "set free for a short time" after his imprisonment (v. 3)
Satan's fall, resulting in the kingdom of Christ and his saints (v. 10)	Satan's fall, resulting in the kingdom of Christ and his saints (v. 4)
The saints' kingship, based not only on the fall of Satan and Christ's victory but also on the saints' faithfulness even to death in holding to "the word of their testimony" (v. 11)	The saints' kingship, based not only on the fall of Satan but also on their faithfulness even to death because of their "testimony for Jesus and because of the word of God" (v. 4)

While some *similarities* exist between Revelation 12 and 20, many *differences* exist between these two passages as well:

Differences between Revelation 12 and 20	
Revelation 12	**Revelation 20**
Satan hurled *from heaven* (Rev. 12:8-9)	Satan hurled *from Earth*—into the abyss (Rev. 20:1-3)
Satan *released* to persecute God's people (Rev. 13:14; 18:23)	Satan *confined* from deceiving God's people
Described as a "*short*" time" (Rev. 12:9, 12)	Described as a *thousand* years (Rev. 20:2-7)
Satan is very active on Earth (Rev. 2:10, 13; 12:17; 16:13; 18:23)	Satan is held from deceiving the nations (Rev. 20:2)

Amillennialists focus on the similarities between Revelation 12 and 20, but often fail to see the similarities between Revelation 20 and repeated OT predictions. Over and over, the OT predicts a similar pattern: Many nations will try to attack Israel, God will intervene, he will judge the nations, and finally, he will inaugurate a kingdom on Earth.

> *David* predicted that the nations of the Earth would gather against Israel and the Messiah (Ps. 2:1-3), but the Messiah would protect the nation and destroy these invading armies (Ps. 2:9).

> *Isaiah* predicted that "the Lord has a day of vengeance, a year of recompense for the cause of Zion" (Isa. 34:8; cf. 63:6). Then God will set up his kingdom in Israel (Isa. 56-66).

Joel predicted that God would gather the nations to battle Israel in "the valley of Jehoshaphat" (Joel 3:2, 12). He will rescue the people of Israel in this battle (Joel 3:1, 17). After this battle, the nation will live in peace and harmony (Joel 3:18-21).

Zechariah predicted that "all the nations of the earth will be gathered against [Israel]" (Zech. 12:3), but God will supernaturally protect Israel from her enemies (Zech. 12:4-9). After God protects Israel, people will come to Christ in great numbers (Zech. 12:10-13:9). God will judge the surrounding nations by returning to the Mount of Olives with his holy ones (Zech. 14:3-5). The sky will be darkened (Zech. 14:6-8). After this, God will rule and protect the nation (Zech. 14:9-15), and Israel will be a light to the nations (Zech. 14:16-21).

Daniel predicted that "there will be a time of distress such as never occurred since there was a nation until that time; and at that time your people, everyone who is found written in the book, will be rescued" (Dan. 12:1).

Malachi predicted that God would protect the nation of Israel and destroy the nations surrounding her (Mal. 4:1-5).

Ezekiel writes that Israel will be regathered (Ezek. 37). The enemies of Israel will attack her, and then God will protect her, judging the nations (Ezek. 38-39). Afterward God will bring about a time of peace and security (Ezek. 40-48).

One prophet after another predicts this sequence, and when we come to the book of Revelation, *we find the exact same sequence.* Jesus returns (Rev. 19:11-14), judges the nations (Rev. 19:15-20:5), and creates a kingdom on Earth (Rev. 20:6). But instead of interpreting Revelation through this repeated OT pattern, Amillennialists read this chapter through the grid of chapter 12.

Amillennialists hold that Isaiah 65:20 refers to the New Heaven and New Earth[17]

> No longer will there be in it an infant who lives but a few days, or an old man who does not live out his days; for *the youth will die at the age of one hundred* and *the one who does not reach the age of one hundred will be thought accursed.* (Isa. 65:20)

Amillennialists have a very difficult time interpreting this passage. Remember, under Amillennialism, we're either in the *Church Age* or in the *New Heaven and Earth.* They have no category for a Millennium where death and sin still exist. But how can Isaiah be describing heaven here, if death still occurs? Moreover, how can people still be bearing children (Isa. 65:20, 23), when Jesus taught that we will not have marriage or children in heaven (Mt. 22:30)? It's interesting to read Amillennial interpreters on this passage.

Some interpreters refuse to interpret this verse.[18] Like the strange uncle at Christmas dinner, they ignore this passage altogether. Goldingay says nothing except that "long life replaces early death."[19] Even in his 300 page book defending Amillennialism, Riddlebarger quotes this passage, but never interprets it.[20]

Some interpreters claim that this verse refers to eternal life. Hoekema writes, "I conclude that Isaiah in verse 20 of chapter 65 is picturing in figurative terms the fact that *the inhabitants of the new earth will live incalculably long lives...* It is not implied that there will be anyone on the new earth who will fail to attain a hundred years."[21] Likewise, Venema writes, "Perhaps the language used is simply a way of figuratively or poetically affirming the incalculably long lives that the inhabitants of the new earth will live."[22] Storms writes, "His point isn't to assert that people will actually die or that

---

[17] Other passages speak of an age greater than our current one, but less serene than the New Heavens and Earth: Isaiah writes of the lion and the lamb being at peace with one another—even around little infants (Isa. 11:6-9). Surely this has not happened yet. However, he continues to write that it will be "in *that* day" that the Messiah will gather the nation of Israel. Moreover, Solomon predicts a day of peace, when God "will deliver the needy when he cries for help" (Ps. 72:12). He will save the lives of the needy (Ps. 72:13), and he will rescue the marginalized from "oppression and violence" (Ps. 72:14). Zechariah predicts an age where God will reign on Earth, where there will still be rebellion as well (Zech. 14:5-17).

[18] John L. McKenzie, *Second Isaiah* (Garden City, NY: Doubleday, 1968).

[19] John Goldingay, *Isaiah* (Peabody, MA: Hendrickson, 2001), 369.

[20] Kim Riddlebarger, *A Case for Amillennialism*, 86.

[21] Emphasis mine. Anthony Hoekema, *The Bible and the Future*, 202-203.

[22] Cornelius Venema, *The Promise of the Future* (Castleton, NY: Hamilton Printing Co., 2009), 293.

women will continue to give birth. Rather, he has taken two very concrete and painful experiences from the common life of people in his own day to illustrate what to them, then, was an almost unimaginable and inexpressible glory to come."[23] Thus, according to these interpreters, when Isaiah writes, "The youth will *die* at the age of one hundred" we should understand this to refer to *eternal life!* Undoubtedly, Isaiah was quite capable of describing the abolition of death altogether (Isa. 25:8), but he chose not to describe this here.

Some interpreters believe that this verse refers to the Church Age.
Instead of squeezing Isaiah 65:20 into the New Heaven and Earth, Kenneth Gentry moves in the other direction, interpreting this era to refer to the Church Age. He acknowledges that "no orthodox Christian believes that in the eternal order anyone will give birth to children, experience sin, grow old, die, and endure the curse." So he concludes that "Isaiah is prophesying the coming of Christ's new covenant kingdom, the gospel era, the church age."[24] Likewise, Chilton writes, "Isaiah is clearly making a statement about *this* age, *before* the end of the world, showing what future generations can expect as the Gospel permeates the world, restores the earth to Paradise, and brings to fruition the goals of the Kingdom... The 'new heavens and earth' promised to the Church comprise the age of the Gospel's triumph."[25] Such a reading is surely bizarre. Isaiah cannot be predicting the Church Age, because Christian babies still die today, and Christians still die before the age of 100.

Some interpreters claim that this verse shouldn't be in the Bible.
Atkins calls it a "late gloss" on the original text, because the thought is "unaccountably labored and obscure."[26]

Why not just bite the bullet and admit that there will be a golden age between the Church Age and New Heaven and Earth, where Jesus will reign, but people will still be able to die?

---

[23] C. Samuel Storms, *Kingdom Come*, 36.
[24] Kenneth L. Gentry, *The Book of Revelation Made Easy: You Can Understand Bible Prophecy* (Powder Springs, GA: American Vision, 2008), 115-116.
[25] David Chilton, *The Days of Vengeance: An Exposition of the Book of Revelation* (Ft. Worth, TX: Dominion, 1987), 539, 543.
[26] Glenn Atkin's, *The Interpreter's Bible.* George Buttrick, ed. (Vol. V. Nashville, TN: Abingdon, 1956), 755.

Amillennialism offers a largely negative position on prophecy

If Christ doesn't return to reign on Earth in the Millennium, vast swathes of Scripture remain unintelligible. If you read Amillennial commentaries, you quickly notice that they spend more time criticizing the Premillennial view than they do explaining these OT prophecies themselves. Walvoord writes,

> The current millennial debate is singular for its negative quality. While premillennialism has had poor handling by many of its own adherents, it has at least aimed at being constructive, offering a definite system of interpretation and providing a positive voice. While amillennialism has attracted many scholars and has produced many works on the millennial issue in the last two decades, *for the most part their approach has been one of ridicule and attack on premillennialism* rather than an ordered presentation of their own system of beliefs.[27]

The Amillennial view offers a much simpler explanation of prophecy: Jesus will return, judge the world, raise the dead, and inaugurate the New Heavens and Earth. To the Amillennialist, that's it. That's all. When Premillennialists offer a more complicated view, they usually poke holes in these interpretations for being too complex or confusing, but a *complicated* interpretation is surely better than *no* interpretation at all!

The Amillennial view purges the complexity of biblical prophecy, offering too reductionistic of an approach. Whenever Israel appears at the end of human history, Amillennialists pull out their "Church Brush" and paint over it. Whenever tension occurs between the Millennium and New Heavens and Earth, they collapse these concepts together. When Ezekiel spends nine chapters explaining the complexities of a future temple, they resolve this by calling this the Church. While this makes it "easy" to interpret prophecy, it also robs these predictions of their content in the process.

Amillennialists read the Bible from right to left, rather than left to right

Amillennialists do not begin from the beginning of the Bible and work *forward* through prophecy. Instead, they begin at the *end* of the Bible with the person of Christ and work *backward*. Amillennialists often argue for a

---

[27] Emphasis mine. John F. Walvoord, *The Millennial Kingdom* (Findlay, OH: Dunham Pub., 1959), 12-13.

"Christocentric" interpretation of OT prophecy, rather than a grammatical-historical hermeneutic. As Riddlebarger writes, "The New Testament should explain the Old. This is one of the most basic principles of Bible study. The New Testament must be seen as the final authority and interpreter of the Old Testament."[28] Amillennialist Sam Storms writes, "The Old Testament must always be read in light of the New."[29]

This perspective, however, purges meaning from these OT authors. While the NT authors should be able to *add* information that the OT doesn't contain, can we really say that they can *contradict* or *override* OT promises? Paul writes, "*All* Scripture is inspired by God" (2 Tim. 3:16). Truth is truth—no matter where we find it in our Bible. As Ryrie states, "It is true that progressive revelation brings additional light, but does it completely reverse to the point of contradiction what has been previously revealed?"[30] This view doesn't just say that the OT authors were *ignorant* on certain details about the future, but that they were *wrong* about the future.

Conclusion

Premillennialism certainly offers a more complicated view of biblical prophecy: multiple views of the Tribulation, the Second Coming, the Millennium, another temple, multiple resurrections, multiple judgments, multiple battles of Gog and Magog, and then, finally, the New Heavens and New Earth. However, the *simpler* explanation is not necessarily the *true* explanation.

Consider a rabbi living in 200 BC who believed that there was *one* coming of the Messiah. As it turned out, there wasn't *one* coming, but *two* comings of Christ. Prophecy is messy, and let's take it at face value in all its complexity, following the text where it leads us. Premillennial interpreters (like myself) would prefer to *struggle* with these prophecies, rather than *spiritualize* or *oversimplify* them.

Discussion questions

1. Amillennialists believe that Satan is only bound from deceiving the nations—not in general. Do you agree that this perspective adequately explains the rest of the NT teaching regarding the activity of Satan?

---

[28] Kim Riddlebarger, *A Case for Amillennialism*, 50.
[29] C. Samuel Storms, *Kingdom Come*, 178.
[30] Charles Ryrie, *Dispensationalism* (Chicago: Moody, 1995), 84.

2. Read through Revelation 20:1-5. Can you clearly explain how an Amillennial interpreter would understand this passage? What are the Premillennial responses to this interpretation?

3. How might Premillennialism and Amillennialism affect believers in other areas of their faith? What is practically at stake in this debate?

Chapter 12. Postmillennialism

Postmillennialism (also called "Progressive Millennialism") holds that Jesus will return at the *end* of the Millennium (hence *Post*-millennialism). Theologians such as Charles Hodge,[1] B.B. Warfield,[2] Loraine Boettner,[3] R. J. Rushdoony,[4] Greg Bahnsen,[5] Kenneth Gentry,[6] Gary DeMar,[7] and Gary North[8] hold to this view.

Postmillennialism teaches that Jesus *currently* reigns in the hearts of believers from heaven. When Revelation 19 describes Jesus conquering the nations with a sword on a horse, Postmillennialists believe that this refers to the Church "conquering" the world with the gospel. They see Jesus' sword (Rev. 19:15) as the word of God (Heb. 4:12), which "conquers" the nations teaching them to obey God.[9] As the gospel spreads, Postmillennialists believe that Christian teaching will infiltrate and "Christianize" society. Thus, according to the Postmillennialist, history will eventually become better and better until Jesus returns.

Postmillennialists hold different views on whether or not the Millennium is *literal* or *symbolic*.[10] We can see this view in contrast to the others below:

---

[1] Charles Hodge, *Systematic Theology* (Vol. 3), (Oak Harbor, WA: Logos Research Systems, Inc., 1997),

[2] B. B. Warfield, "The Gospel and the Second Coming," *The Bible Magazine*, III, 1915. 300-309.

[3] Loraine Boettner, *The Millennium* (Phillipsburg, NJ: Presbyterian and Reformed Publishing Company, 1957).

[4] Rousas John Rushdoony, *God's Plan for Victory: The Meaning of Post Millennialism* (Fairfax, VA: Thoburn Pr., 1977). Rushdoony also founded the Chalcedon Foundation in 1965.

[5] Greg L. Bahnsen, *Victory in Jesus: The Bright Hope of Postmillenialism* (Texarkana, AR: Covenant Media, 1999).

[6] Kenneth Gentry, *He Shall Have Dominion* (Tyler, TX: Institute for Christian Economics, 1992).

[7] See his ministry: *www.postmillennialism.com*

[8] Gary North, *Theonomy: An Informed Response* (Tyler, TX: Institute for Christian Economics, 1991).

[9] David Chilton, *The Days of Vengeance* (Fort Worth: Dominion, 1987), 485.

[10] Riddlebarger writes, "Postmillennialists are divided as to whether the period of time is a literal one thousand years and whether the millennial age begins abruptly or gradually." Kim Riddlebarger, *A Case for Amillennialism*, 38.

Millennial Views			
VIEW	*Premillennial*	*Amillennial*	*Postmillennial*
The Millennium	A literal 1,000 year period	A figurative number	**A figurative number**
Christ's reign	Reigns literally in a kingdom on Earth after his Second Coming	Reigns spiritually on a heavenly throne or reigns spiritually in the hearts of believers	**Reigns spiritually in the hearts of believers, as the gospel transforms the nations of the Earth**
Israel	Christ reigns in Israel over a regathered Israel	The Church replaces the promises given to national Israel	**The Church replaces the promises given to national Israel**
View of Human History	Believes human history will get progressively *worse*, as the gospel reaches all nations	Believes human history will get progressively *worse*, as the gospel reaches all nations	**Believes that human history will get progressively *better*. The nations will eventually be transformed by Christ's reign in society**

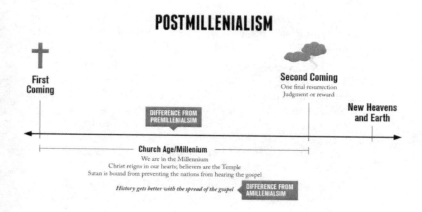

As you can see, Postmillennialism offers a similar view to Amillennialism in many ways. Yet it differs from Amillennialism in its view of history getting better—not worse—as the Church "Christianizes" society. Many of the theological problems that face Amillennialism also confront Postmillennialism, but in addition, other specific problems challenge the Postmillennialist view.

Postmillennialism is a relatively recent view

Unitarian minister Daniel Whitby fully articulated this view for the first time (1638-1726). Postmillennialist Kenneth Gentry argues that Athanasius, Augustine, and John Calvin held to Postmillennialism, but others have criticized his historical reconstruction:

> *Athanasius*. Robert Strimple writes, "The documentation cited for Athanasius in Gentry's earlier book, *He Shall Have Dominion*, consists entirely of statements by Athanasius showing that 'the great progress of the gospel is expected.' On the basis of *that* criterion virtually every Christian theologian could be claimed as a postmillennialist!"[11]

> *Augustine*. Augustine should be classified as Amillennial—not Postmillennial. Walvoord writes, "Augustine (354-430) also

---

[11] Robert Strimple, "Amillennialism." Bock, Darrell (General Editor). *Three Views on the Millennium and Beyond*. Grand Rapids, MI. Zondervan. 1999. 68.

believed in the coming of Christ after the millennium and could for this reason be classified as postmillennial. His view of the millennium, however, was so removed from a literal kingdom on earth that it is virtually a denial of it, and he is better considered as an amillennialist."[12]

John Calvin. Gentry argues that Calvin held to Postmillennial theology, citing Calvin's *Institutes* (1:12).[13] However, upon closer inspection, Calvin fits better with Amillennialism. Strimple cites the Second Helvetic Confession (1566),[14] which represents Calvin's teaching (article 11): "We further condemn Jewish dreams that *there will be a golden age on earth before the Day of Judgment*, and that the pious, having subdued all their godless enemies, will possess all the kingdoms of the earth."

Historical arguments do not hold much weight. In the end, Scripture is the final authority. Nonetheless, it's worth noting that Postmillennialism arrived late on the theological scene.

Postmillennialism holds that history will become better—not worse

While the world may not seem to be getting better, Postmillennialists argue that God will bring about world peace (eventually) through the spread of the gospel. Postmillennialist John Dick wrote, "However improbable it may seem that the whole world should be Christianized, we know that God is able to perform what he has promised.... A future generation will witness the rapidity of its progress; and long before the end of time."[15]

How does this compare with Scripture? Jesus uses lurid language to describe the decay of human society and suffering toward the end of human history. He states that there will be an increase in wars (Mt. 24:6-7), plagues (Mt. 24:7), famines (Mt. 24:7), persecution (Mt. 24:9), false religion (Mt. 24:4-5, 11), and lawlessness (Mt. 24:12). Paul writes that in the "last days" people will continue to become more and more selfish, greedy, and evil (2 Tim. 3:1-5). To avoid these clear biblical teachings, Postmillennialists hold

---

[12] Walvoord, John F. *The Millennial Kingdom* (Findlay, OH: Dunham Pub., 1959), 8.

[13] Kenneth Gentry, "Postmillennialism." Darrell Bock (General Editor). *Three Views on the Millennium and Beyond* (Grand Rapids, MI. Zondervan, 1999), 17.

[14] Robert Strimple, "Amillennialism." Darrell Bock (General Editor). *Three Views on the Millennium and Beyond* (Grand Rapids, MI. Zondervan, 1999), 68.

[15] John Dick, *Lectures on Theology* (New York: Robert Carter, 1852), 156. Cited in Kim Riddlebarger, *A Case for Amillennialism*, 138.

to Preterism. Under their view, these passages do not predict the future; they merely predict the era before AD 70. Thus if Preterism is false, then so is Postmillennialism.

Additionally, human history shows no sign of becoming less evil, even as the gospel has spread (Mt. 24:14). This past century, we saw the gospel reach more people than ever before, *yet at exactly the same time*, we saw more bloodshed than any other time in history. As theologian Craig Blaising asks, "After almost two thousand years, should we not be able to see this progress?"[16]

Paul states that believers will suffer until Christ returns (Rom. 8:19-23). We are conquerors *in* suffering—not when we get *out* of suffering (Rom. 8:35-37). Postmillennialism seems to obscure this key biblical teaching.

Postmillennialism holds that we should reinstate theonomy

Theonomy comes from the Greek roots *theos* meaning "God" and *nomos* meaning "law." Theonomy (also called "Reconstructionism") holds that we should institute God's laws in human society. Gentry explains, "The judicial-political outlook of Reconstructionism includes the application of those justice-defining directives contained in the OT legislation, when properly interpreted, adapted to new covenant conditions, and relevantly applied."[17] Postmillennialist Gary North writes,

> Postmillennialism's view of the future makes Christians morally responsible before God for discovering and applying a Bible-based judicial and ethical blueprint—a blueprint that should and eventually will govern the institutions of this world. This means that the world is required by God to be run in terms of His revealed law. It also means that God will positively bless societies and institutions in terms of their faithfulness to His revealed law. This is a crucial and long-neglected aspect of the biblical doctrine of sanctification—the progressive sanctification of institutions in history—which neither the premillennialists nor the amillennialists are willing to accept.[18]

---

[16] Craig Blaising, "Premillennialism." Darrell Bock (General Editor). *Three Views on the Millennium and Beyond* (Grand Rapids, MI. Zondervan, 1999), 75.
[17] Kenneth Gentry, "Postmillennialism." Darrell Bock (General Editor). *Three Views on the Millennium and Beyond* (Grand Rapids, MI. Zondervan, 1999), 19.
[18] Kenneth Gentry, *Before Jerusalem Fell: Dating the Book of Revelation* (Tyler, TX: Institute for Christian Economics, 1989), xiii.

Are we supposed to sanctify human government? Where do we see such a teaching in Scripture? Sanctification is for Christians—not non-Christians (1 Thess. 4:3; Phil. 1:6). In fact, the NT contains no prescriptions whatsoever for ruling a secular society. As Christians, our faith may influence our decision-making as citizens, but we are repeatedly told to submit to government—not to take it over (Rom. 13:1-7), as Jesus modeled for us (Jn. 6:15; 18:36-37). Theonomy wasn't the practice of the apostles or the early church—nor should it be for us as Christians today. Consider just three examples:

> **False teaching.** Israel executed false teachers for leading people astray (Deut. 13:5; 18:20; Lev. 19:26; Ex. 22:18). However, in the NT, Peter did not stone Simon the magician to death. Instead he preached the gospel to him (Acts 8:9-13). Later, when Simon the magician made drastic doctrinal errors, Peter did not order capital punishment, but instead he only rebuked him for his false beliefs (Acts 8:18-23). Likewise, Paul came across a "Jewish false prophet" named Bar-Jesus. And yet, instead of stoning the man to death, Paul rebuked him (Acts 13:10) and temporarily blinded him (Acts 13:11).

> **Circumcision.** In the OT law, Gentiles needed to be circumcised to be allowed into the community of God (Gen. 17:14). However, when Jewish Christians argued for the necessity of circumcision (Acts 15:1, 5), the early Christian leaders determined that Gentiles did *not* need circumcision (Acts 15:23-29).

> **Adultery.** In 1 Corinthians 5, a man slept with his stepmother. Yet Paul didn't call for his *execution*, as the OT law prescribed (Lev. 20:10). Instead, he called for *removal from fellowship*.

If the OT law is still in effect, why such a massive change in the early church? God gave the Law to Israel (Ex. 20:2), which was a physical nation-state, but the Church is not a nation-state. Thus it strikes Premillennialists (like myself) as bizarre to reinstitute OT civil laws in a secular society.

Postmillennialism has little to no biblical support

Amillennialist Robert Strimple argues that very few NT passages support Postmillennialism.[19] In addition to its lack of biblical evidence, it offers bizarre interpretations of key passages. For instance, Postmillenialists argue that Psalm 2:7 ("You are My Son, today I have begotten you") refers to

---

[19] Craig Blaising, "Premillennialism." Darrell Bock (General Editor). *Three Views on the Millennium and Beyond* (Grand Rapids, MI. Zondervan, 1999), 69.

Jesus' spiritual kingdom on Earth, because Peter interpreted this passage to refer to Jesus' resurrection (Acts 13:33). Thus Gentry writes, "The word 'today' suggests a formal moment at which the title becomes associated with the new Ruler. Rather than occurring at Christ's Second Advent, as many assume, the NT relates it once again to the first century—at the exaltation of Christ, beginning with his resurrection."[20]

But if Psalm 2 refers to the Church Age, then consider David's further prediction, "You will rule them with an iron scepter; *you will dash them to pieces like pottery*" (Ps. 2:9 NIV). Under a Postmillennial view, this prediction refers to the *peaceful spread of the gospel!* Regarding Psalm 2:9, Gentry writes, "This he does by his mighty Word and under his controlling providence."[21]

Conclusion

Postmillennialism contains many similarities with Amillennialism. It holds that Satan is currently bound, we are *currently* in the Millennium, and the Church has replaced Israel. However, in contrast to the other perspectives, it holds that history will get better as the Church Christianizes the world. While the Church will surely reach the world with the gospel (Mt. 24:14), this is not the basis of our Christian hope. Our hope lies in Christ when he returns to establish his kingdom on Earth (Titus 2:13).

Discussion questions

1. How does Postmillennialism differ from Amillennialism?

2. What is practically at stake in holding to Postmillennialism versus Premillennialism?

3. What do you think of the concept of theonomy as described by Postmillennialism? How do you think we should integrate our Christian convictions in the political arena?

---

[20] Kenneth Gentry, "Postmillennialism." Darrell Bock (General Editor). *Three Views on the Millennium and Beyond* (Grand Rapids, MI. Zondervan, 1999), 34.
[21] Kenneth Gentry, "Postmillennialism." Darrell Bock (General Editor). *Three Views on the Millennium and Beyond* (Grand Rapids, MI. Zondervan, 1999), 35.

Part Four: Interpreting the Future

Before we could look at the Bible's view of the future, we needed to survey the various views and weigh their credibility. Now that we've made a case for a Futurist (versus Preterist), Dispensational (versus Covenantal), and Premillennial (versus Postmillennial or Amillennial) view, we're ready to dive into the biblical predictions of the end of human history.

Chapter 13. Rapture: The Rescue of the Church

Many of us have heard of the "rapture," though mostly through popular culture, rather than the Bible. The HBO show *The Leftovers* (2014) depicts a rapture-like event, where 140 million people instantly disappear, including Gary Busey (of all people!). Others have only been exposed to the rapture by Seth Rogen and Jonah Hill in their hit comedy *This is the End* (2013), depicting a squad of comedic celebrities who are "left behind" in James Franco's LA home. And of course, last but not least, Tim LaHaye and Jerry Jenkin's bestselling series *Left Behind* brought the concept of the rapture to millions, recently becoming a movie with actor Nicolas Cage (2014).

But what does the Bible really say about the rapture?

To begin, let's jettison the term "rapture" from our collective vocabularies. This word doesn't even come from the Bible. Instead, it appears in the Latin translation of the NT as *raeptius* in 1 Thessalonians 4:17 for the Greek term *harpazo* ("caught up"). Since modern people don't use the term "rapture" anymore (with the possible exception of the term "rapturous"), we should change the name of this event to a more common word: *rescue*. Moreover, by changing terms, we can avoid much of the sensationalism that enters our minds when we hear the word "rapture."

What exactly is the rescue of the Church?

The Bible teaches that Jesus will return to rescue the Church at some point in the future. When this happens, Christ will call believers to himself (1 Thess. 4:16-17), and he will give them their resurrection bodies (1 Cor. 15:52-53). All theologians agree *that* Jesus will rescue the Church, but they debate *when* he will do so. Will Christ return to rescue believers *before* the Tribulation, or will he return *after*? Is the rescue of the Church the same event as his Second Coming, or are these separate events? Consider these views side by side:

TIMING OF THE RESCUE

Theologians debate the timing of Jesus' rescue of the Church, but several lines of evidence point toward this event occurring *before* the Tribulation.

First, the book of Revelation never mentions the Church in the Tribulation. Revelation mentions the Church (*ekklesia*) 19 times in chapters 1-3, but never mentions it in chapters 4-21. This is an odd omission considering the fact that Revelation 6-16 contains the most detailed description of the Tribulation that we find in the entire Bible; yet it never mentions the Church *once*. Revelation 2-3 repeatedly states, "He who has an ear, let him hear what the Spirit says *to the churches*" (Rev. 2:7, 11, 17, 29; 3:6, 13, 22). And yet, during the Tribulation in Revelation 13:9, we read, "If *anyone* has an ear, let him hear..." There is a conspicuous difference between these two statements. One is directed to the *Church*; the other is directed to *anyone* left on earth.[1]

Second, the NT and OT predict that Israel will face the Tribulation—not the Church. Jeremiah predicted that the Tribulation would be a time of *"Jacob's* distress" (Jer. 30:7), and Daniel stated that the Tribulation would be for "your people" and "your holy city" (Dan. 9:24; cf. 12:1). Jesus predicted that the

---

[1] Post-tribulationalist Craig Blomberg responds by arguing that this would eliminate the Church from heaven as well. He writes, "If its absence from the earthly scenes of these chapters means the church's absence from earth, then, by the same logic, it should be absent from heaven as well." Craig Blomberg. "Chapter Four: The Posttribulationism of the NT: Leaving 'Left Behind' Behind." Craig Blomberg and Sung Wook Chung, *A Case for Historic Premillennialism: An Alternative to "Left Behind" Eschatology* (Grand Rapids, MI: Baker Academic, 2009), 82. However, Revelation 22:16 does mention the churches in heaven—just not in the Tribulation.

Evidence for a pre-tribulational rescue of the Church

Tribulation would exist "in Judea" with a Jewish "temple" (Mt. 24:15-16), and he also claimed that Jerusalem would be trampled underfoot "until the times of the Gentiles are fulfilled" (Lk. 21:24), implying a Jewish regathering. Repeatedly, we find that the Tribulation will be for the Jewish people—not the Church.

Third, no one will be able to die in the Millennium, unless there is a pre-tribulational rescue of the Church. Isaiah predicts, "The youth will *die at the age of one hundred* and the one who does not reach the age of one hundred will be thought accursed" (Isa. 65:20). With this in mind, how is it possible for people to die in the Millennium? When Christ returns, God will give all believers their resurrection bodies making them "immortal" and "imperishable" (1 Cor. 15:51-53), and God will judge *all* non-believers at this time as well (1 Thess. 5:3; 2 Thess. 2:12; Mt. 13:40-42, 49; 24:31, 39-41; Lk. 17:33-35; Rev. 19:21; Isa. 13:9). But if the only people left have immortal and imperishable bodies, then how could anyone die (Isa. 65:20), have children (Isa. 65:23), or rebel against Christ (Rev. 20:7-9) in the Millennium?[2]

---

[2] Post-tribulationalists argue that some non-believers will make it into the Millennium and have children, and these are the people who will die. Grudem writes, "Many will simply surrender without trusting Christ, and will thus enter the millennium as unbelievers. And during the entire period of the millennium no doubt many will be converted to Christ and become believers as well." Wayne Grudem, *Systematic Theology* (Grand Rapids, MI: Zondervan Publishing House, 1994). 1133. Yet this doesn't answer the language of all facing judgment at the return of Christ (1 Thess. 5:3; 2 Thess. 2:12; Mt. 13:40-42, 49; 24:31, 39-41; Lk. 17:33-35; Rev. 19:21; Isa. 13:9).

PROBLEM WITH THE POST-TRIBULATION VIEW

Under this view, the rescue of the church is the Second Coming.

ADVANTAGE OF THE PRE-TRIBULATION VIEW

Fourth, the NT states that the rescue of the Church will be imminent. That is, it could happen at any time. The Corinthians were "awaiting *eagerly* the revelation of our Lord Jesus Christ" (1 Cor. 1:7; cf. Phil. 3:20; Heb. 9:28). James wrote, "The coming of the Lord is *near*" (Jas. 5:8; cf. Phil. 4:5). Paul told Titus that they should be "looking for the blessed hope and the appearing" of Christ (Titus 2:13). But Jesus taught that specific signs would precede his Second

Coming (Mt. 24:4-34). If Jesus comes to rescue the Church *before* the Second Coming, then no signs would be necessary, making his rescue imminent.[3]

Many interpreters assume that the rescue of the Church will occur immediately before the seven year Tribulation, but this isn't necessarily the case. Hitchcock writes, "The Bible never tells us how much time passes between the Rapture and the beginning of the Tribulation."[4] It's possible that Jesus could return to rescue the Church fifty years before the Tribulation, or maybe even a hundred. It could literally happen at any moment.

Fifth, the rescue of the Church contains many differences from the Second Coming. Critics of the pre-tribulational view note that the NT uses the same Greek word for the rescue of the Church and the Second Coming, implying that these are the same events.[5] Yet, as we've already seen in other cases, mere word association doesn't prove that these are the same events. Consider these significant differences below:

The Rescue of the Church	The Second Coming
The *removal* of believers from the Earth (1 Thess. 4:17)	The *coming* of believers to the Earth (Rev. 19:14)
Believers meet Jesus *in the air* (1 Thess. 4:17)	Believers meet Jesus *on the ground* (Zech. 14:4)
Believers are resurrected *during* Jesus' descent (1 Cor. 15:52)	Believers are resurrected *after* Jesus slays enemies, judges the beast and false prophet, and binds Satan (Rev. 20:1-4)
When the message of Jesus' coming is given to the Church, it is given as a *message of comfort* (1 Thess. 4:18; 1 Cor. 1:8; 1 Cor. 5:5; 2 Cor. 1:14; Phil. 1:6)	However, when it is given to Israel, it is a *message of warning and judgment* (Isa. 13:6, 9; 34:8; Ezek. 30:3; Amos 5:18; Zeph. 1:7-13; 1 Thess. 5:2; 1 Thess. 3:2; 2 Thess. 2:2)

---

[3] Post-tribulational interpreters argue that the rescue of the church can't be imminent based on John 21:18, where Jesus predicts that Peter will "grow old." But at most, this is an argument against imminency for the first few decades of the church, but not for today. Of course, the NT letters were written between roughly AD 50 and 90, and Peter would've been old by this time. Thus when the NT authors wrote their letters, imminency would've been a real possibility. Moreover, Herod almost killed Peter in Acts 12—only a few years after Jesus made this prediction. Yet when Rhoda saw Peter alive, the church believed that she was wrong (Acts 12:15-16). Thus they didn't *expect* Peter to live through this situation. Since John didn't write his gospel until AD 90, it's likely that most people hadn't heard of this prediction from Christ.

[4] Hitchcock believes that not much time will occur between the Rapture and the Tribulation. I would agree. But like Hitchcock, I'm open to time passing between the two events. Mark Hitchcock, *The End: A Complete Overview of Bible Prophecy and the End of Days*, 233.

[5] Anthony Hoekema, *The Bible and the Future*, 166.

Some theologians argue that these conflicting accounts can be
harmonized—just as we can reconcile apparent contradictions in the rest of
the Bible. For instance, Douglas Moo writes, "I could name several
apparent inconsistencies in the Resurrection narratives of the Gospels—yet
we know these all depict the same event."[6] Likewise, Riddlebarger writes
that these are merely "different aspects of the same event."[7]

However, it isn't fair to compare the future rescue of the Church with the
past event of the resurrection. If we are committed to inerrancy, the events
of the resurrection *must* be harmonized, because it's impossible for there to
have been *two* resurrections of Christ. However, these future events haven't
occurred yet, so we are not obligated to harmonize them as being the same
events.

Key passages on the rescue of the Church

1 Thessalonians 4:16-17

> For the Lord Himself will descend from heaven with a shout, with
> the voice of the archangel and with the trumpet of God, and the
> dead in Christ will rise first. [17] Then we who are alive and remain
> will be caught up together with them in the clouds to meet the
> Lord in the air. (1 Thess. 4:16-17)

HOW will Christ rescue the Church? Paul uses the Greek word *harpazo*
to describe the rescue of the Church ("caught up"). John uses this word to
refer to Jesus being "*caught up* to God and to His throne" (Rev. 12:5). Of
course, this occurred when Jesus physically rose into heaven (Acts 1:9). Paul
uses the word elsewhere to refer to himself being "caught up" into heaven
(2 Cor. 12:2, 4). Likewise, Luke uses the term to explain how "the Spirit of
the Lord *snatched* Philip away; and the eunuch no longer saw him" (Acts
8:39).

While many people believe that the rescue of the Church will be a silent or
secret coming of Christ, we have no reason to believe this. This is probably
a hangover from the *Left Behind* book series, where believers silently
disappear. The rescue of the Church will not be silent—like a dog whistle
that only Christians can hear. Instead, Paul writes that Jesus will return

---

[6] Douglas Moo, *Three Views on the Rapture*, 101.
[7] Kim Riddlebarger, *A Case for Amillennialism*, 170.

"with a *shout*" (1 Thess. 4:16) and then "the *trumpet* will sound" (1 Cor. 15:52).

WHERE will Christ take the Church? Jesus will take us "in the clouds" and "in the air." We will be physically taken away from the surface of the Earth to meet with Christ.

WHEN will Christ take the Church? If we read Paul's letter to the Thessalonians chronologically, then the rescue of the Church will occur *before* the "day of the Lord" (1 Thess. 5:2). Paul doesn't picture believers as living through this great and terrible period of history.[8] Notice the pronouns in 1 Thessalonians 5. Hitchcock writes, "There's a conspicuous shift from *you* and *we* (the believers) to *they* and *them* (the unbelievers). The shift is significant. The pronouns indicate that when the Day of the Lord arrives, there will be two distinct groups of people. One group will be raptured and escape the wrath, and the other will remain on earth and face its full force."[9]

1 Thessalonians 1:9-10

> You turned to God from idols to serve a living and true God, and to wait for His Son from heaven, whom He raised from the dead, that is Jesus, *who rescues us from the wrath to come.* (1 Thess. 1:9-10)

Some interpreters hold that this refers to our rescue from *Hell.* This is certainly possible, but look at the context. Paul says that we will be rescued—not through the Cross—but through the Second Coming ("to wait for His Son from heaven"). If a believer dies tonight, they will be rescued from the wrath of Hell. But this rescue is different. It will only occur in the *future*, when Christ returns at his Second Coming.

---

[8] When Paul writes, "*We* who are alive and remain," he isn't committing himself to the fact that he will personally be alive when Jesus returns. Instead, he is making use of the editorial "we" or royal "we." For example, a history teacher might say, "*We* took the beach of Normandy in World War II." Or an environmentalist might say, "When *we* destroy the ozone layer, *we* will perish." By this, the environmentalist is not claiming for certain that *he* will be alive at this time, but *humanity* will be alive. If Paul believed that he would certainly be alive at Jesus' Second Coming, then he wouldn't have said *we*; he would have said, "*I* will be alive and remain until the coming of the Lord." Paul didn't know when Jesus *would* return (Mt. 24:36), but he lived in the expectation that he *could* return at any moment.

[9] Mark Hitchcock, *The End: A Complete Overview of Bible Prophecy and the End of Days,* 157.

1 Thessalonians 5:9

> God has not destined us for *wrath*, but for obtaining *salvation*
> through our Lord Jesus Christ. (1 Thess. 5:9)

The NT uses the term "salvation" (Greek *sōtēria*) in multiple senses. Many
times, it refers to being saved from Hell. However, it also refers to being
rescued from the perils of wealth (Lk. 19:9), the evil age (Acts 2:40), Egypt
(Acts 7:25), or even physical danger (Acts 27:34). In 1 Thessalonians 5:9,
salvation does not refer to being saved from *Hell*, but from the *Tribulation* at
the end of human history. Moreover, Paul's use of the word "wrath" fits
precisely with God's wrath during the Tribulation (Rev. 3:10; 6:16; 15:1).

Paul's language here in 5:10 ("whether we are awake or asleep, we will live
together with Him") and 5:11 ("encourage [*parakaleite*] one another")
corresponds with his language in 4:17 ("we who are alive and remain") and
4:18 ("comfort [*parakaleite*] one another with these words"). If these
parallels are sound, they would point to a rescue of the Church *before* the
Tribulation occurs.

2 Thessalonians 2:1-5

> Now we request you, brethren, with regard to the coming of our
> Lord Jesus Christ and our gathering together to Him, that you not
> be quickly shaken from your composure or be disturbed either by
> a spirit or a message or a letter as if from us, to the effect that the
> day of the Lord has come. Let no one in any way deceive you, for
> it will not come unless the apostasy comes first, and the man of
> lawlessness is revealed, the son of destruction, who opposes and
> exalts himself above every so-called god or object of worship, so
> that he takes his seat in the temple of God, displaying himself as
> being God. Do you not remember that while I was still with you, I
> was telling you these things? (2 Thess. 2:1-5)

The Thessalonians believed that they were living in the Tribulation, and
Jesus hadn't rescued them. If these believers were taught a post-tribulation
view, then why would they be "shaken" or "disturbed" at entering the
Tribulation (v.3)? Why wouldn't they be rejoicing, knowing that Jesus would
soon return?

When Paul writes that "*it* will not come," (v.3) what is he referring to? Some
believe that he is referring back to the "coming of our Lord Jesus." But not
so fast! The nearest antecedent for this pronoun ("it") is the "day of the
Lord," not the coming of Christ. For instance, imagine if I said, "I hung out
with my wife today. We picked up her sister. She lives in the city." Who

does the "she" refer to? In context, the nearest antecedent is my wife's sister—not my wife. Similarly, when Paul states "*it* will not come," he is referring to the "day of the Lord," not the "coming of our Lord Jesus."

The "day of the Lord" refers to the Tribulation—not the rescue of Christ (Isa. 13:6, 9; 34:8; Ezek. 30:3; Amos 5:18; Zeph. 1:7-13; 1 Thess. 5:3). Paul argues that the Tribulation cannot come until the Apostasy (v.3) and the Antichrist (v.4) appear. Of course, this aligns with Jesus' teaching regarding the signs of the times (Mt. 16:2-3; Mt. 24:4-34). These events need to occur before the Tribulation begins.

Paul's first letter to the Thessalonians contains his clearest teaching on the rescue of the Church (1 Thess. 4:16-5:10). This makes sense of Paul's mysterious statement: "Do you not remember that while I was still with you, I was telling you these things?" (2 Thess. 2:5) The Thessalonians shouldn't have been "shaken" or "disturbed," because Paul had already taught them the pre-tribulational rescue (1 Thess. 4:16-17).

1 Corinthians 15:51-53

> I tell you a mystery; we will not all sleep, but we will all be changed, in a moment, in the twinkling of an eye, at the last trumpet; for the trumpet will sound, and the dead will be raised imperishable, and we will be changed. For this perishable must put on the imperishable, and this mortal must put on immortality. (1 Cor. 15:51-53)

In this passage, Paul teaches that some believers will not need to physically die ("not all sleep"). "Sleep" is a biblical euphemism for death (cf. Jn. 11:12-14). When Jesus returns, he will not kill the remaining believers, only to immediately raise them from the dead! Instead, God will instantly give this final generation of Christians immortal and imperishable bodies.

The rescue of the Church will be instantaneous ("in a moment, in the twinkling of an eye"). Paul uses the Greek word *atomos* here, which is the root from which we get the term "atom." It literally means "indivisible."[10] Hitchcock writes, "Today, we would translate this 'in an instant,' 'in a split second,' or 'in a flash.'"[11] While this might be difficult to conceive of, we need to remember that God has supernaturally rescued (or at least *transported*) many people exactly like this in the past, including Enoch (Gen.

---

[10] Arndt, W. (et al.), *A Greek-English Lexicon of the New Testament*, 149.
[11] Mark Hitchcock, *The End: A Complete Overview of Bible Prophecy and the End of Days*, 129.

5:24), Elijah (2 Kings 2:1, 11), Jesus (Rev. 12:5; Acts 1:9), Philip (Acts 8:39-40), and Paul (2 Cor. 12:2-4).

Additionally, Paul calls the rescue of the Church a "mystery" (1 Cor. 15:51). But why? The OT repeatedly taught both the Second Coming (Dan. 7:13-14; Zech. 14:1-5) and the resurrection of the dead (Isa. 26:19; Dan. 12:2; Job 19:25-26; Ps. 22:29). He must be saying that the rescue of the Church is a new teaching—not foreseen in the OT Scriptures.[12]

Revelation 3:10

> Because you have kept the word of My perseverance, I also will keep you from the hour of testing, that hour which is about to come upon the whole world, to test those who dwell on the earth. (Rev. 3:10)

When will this hour of testing take place? The hour of testing refers to the Tribulation. The very next verse refers to the Second Coming ("I am coming quickly"), placing it at the end of history.[13] Osborne writes, "The consensus view is that it refers to the final end-time trials that precede the [end of history]."[14]

Is the "hour of testing" global or just for the Philadelphians? Jesus states that this hour of testing will come upon the "whole world," which refers to all people on Earth (Rev. 12:9; 16:14). Revelation always uses this expression ("those who dwell on the earth") to refer to the entire globe.

---

[12] Some interpreters take note of Paul's use of the phrase "at the *last* trumpet." Since the book of Revelation contains a series of trumpets culminating at the *end* of the Tribulation, they reason that Paul must believe in a post-tribulational rescue of the Church. And yet, it's difficult to think that Paul has the book of Revelation in mind, when he wrote to the Corinthians for a very important reason: Revelation wasn't written yet. In fact, John didn't write Revelation until AD 95, and Paul wrote 1 Corinthians in roughly AD 52. Instead, Paul's use of the "last trumpet" comes from the Old Testament. Specifically, in the book of Numbers, the trumpet referred to "summoning the congregation" of Israel to "gather themselves" together and to "set out" (Num. 10:2-5). In Ezekiel, this was also used as a "warning" to the people (Ezek. 33:1-7). Both symbols could be in view here. The rescue of the Church will be both a time of *gathering* for God's people, and it will be a *warning* to the nation of Israel, who remains on Earth. Thus theologian Paul Benware writes, "The trumpet of 1 Corinthians 15 is probably called 'the last' because it is signifying the completion of a program, namely, God's dealings with the church on earth." Paul N. Benware, *Understanding End Times Prophecy*, 271.

[13] Johnson writes, "We can dismiss the view that the 'hour of trial' refers to some general or personal distress that will come upon the Philadelphian community and from which the church will be delivered." Alan Johnson, *Revelation*, 454.

[14] Grant Osborne. *Revelation:* Baker Exegetical Commentary on the New Testament (Grand Rapids, MI: Baker Academic, 2002), 193.

Moreover, John uses this expression twice to refer to judgment for those who have rejected Christ (Rev. 13:8; 17:8). While believers are called to *suffer* for Christ, we are never called to experience his *wrath*.

What does it mean to be kept from the hour of testing? If a teacher told her class, "I will keep you from gym tomorrow during first period," this would mean that the students wouldn't be going to gym class. Likewise, when Jesus promises to keep the Philadelphians from the hour of testing, this means that they won't be in this era of history.

At the same time, this passage might not be that clear. The Greek word *tēreō* can either mean *protection through* or *removal from*.[15] So is Jesus saying that he will remove us from this period of history entirely, or just protect us while we're suffering?

The Greek preposition *ek* literally means "out of" or "from." Jesus prayed, "What shall I say, 'Father, save Me *from* this hour'? But for this purpose I came to this hour" (Jn. 12:27). This usage shows that the term "from" (*ek*) refers to removal from this period of time altogether. Of course, Jesus didn't pray to be removed "from" the Cross. He prayed for the courage to endure *through* the Cross (Lk. 22:42).

In John 17:15, Jesus prays, "I do not ask You to take them out of the world, but to *keep them from* the evil one." This is the only use of *tēreō ek* found anywhere in biblical or extra-biblical Greek. Though elsewhere John uses the term *tēreō*, when he writes, "He who was born of God keeps (*tēreō*) him, and the evil one does not touch him. [19] We know that we are of God, and that the whole world lies in the power of the evil one" (1 Jn. 5:18-19). Both passages make a similar point: While believers are still in Satan's world, we are not "in" the evil one. We have been placed into Christ instead.

Therefore, the expression "keep from" (*tēreō ek*) doesn't refer to *protection* from the hour of testing. Instead it refers to *removal* from it. If Jesus asked to be taken "from" his hour on the Cross, then God would've removed him from it entirely (Jn. 12:27). Just as believers do not belong in Satan (Jn. 17:15; 1 Jn. 5:18), the Philadelphians do not belong in the hour of testing. Jesus won't merely remove the Philadelphians from a *person*, but from this *period of time*.

---

[15] Osborne writes, "It must be admitted that both readings are possible from the language, so context must show which is more likely." Grant Osborne. *Revelation*, 193.

Did John Darby invent the pre-tribulational view?

Barbara Rossing argues that the concept of a pre-tribulational rescue of the Church really originates from one man: John Nelson Darby. Like many critics of the pre-tribulation view, she writes, "The dispensationalist system is a fabrication of Darby... A system invented less than 200 years ago in the British Isles, shipped to America, exported to the world, and that must be challenged today because of its false theology."[16] Surely, John Darby *popularized* the view that Christ would return to rescue the Church before the Tribulation, but he wasn't the first to *originate* this view.

Pseudo-Ephraem (7th century AD). This is a Syrian sermon, which taught a pre-tribulational rescue of the Church. It states, "All the saints and elect of God are gathered together *before the tribulation*, which is to come, and are *taken to the Lord*, in order that they might not see at any time the confusion which overwhelms the world because of our sins."[17]

Brother Dolcino (14th century AD). He was a leader of the Apostolic Brethren. In 1316, an anonymous author of the local diocese wrote of Dolcino and their group: "And that the Antichrist was coming into this world within the bounds of the said three and a half years; and after he had come, that he [Dolcino] and his followers would be transferred into Paradise, in which are Enoch and Elijah. And in this way they will be preserved unharmed from the persecution of the Antichrist."[18] Of course, this fits better with a mid-tribulation view, but it at least shows that Dolcino saw the rescue of the Church before the wrath of the Tribulation.

Morgan Edwards (1722-1795). Edwards was an 18th century Baptist minister. He held that there was at least a 3.5 year period between the rescue of the Church and the start of the Millennium.[19]

---

[16] Barbara R. Rossing, *The Rapture Exposed: The Message of Hope in the Book of Revelation* (New York: Basic, 2004), 30.

[17] Pseudo-Ephraem, "On the Last Times, The Antichrist, or Sermon on the End of the World." Cited in Mark Hitchcock, *The End: A Complete Overview of Bible Prophecy and the End of Days*, 178.

[18] Cited in Mark Hitchcock, *The End: A Complete Overview of Bible Prophecy and the End of Days*, 178.

[19] Morgan Edwards, *Two Academical Exercises on Subjects Bearing the Following Titles: Millennium, Last-Novelties* (Philadelphia: Dobson and Lang, 1788), 5-6.

Furthermore, even if Darby was the first to originate this doctrine, so what? *Time* doesn't determine *truth*. Some heresies are old, and some truths have only been discovered in recent times. The age in which a truth is discovered is irrelevant. Really, if the age of a belief determines its truth, then Amillennialism should be rejected, because (as we've already seen) the early Christian teachers and theologians didn't embrace it. As historian Philip Schaff writes, "The most striking point in the eschatology of the ante-Nicene age [before AD 325] is... the belief of a visible reign of Christ in glory on earth with the risen saints for a thousand years, before the general resurrection and judgment."[20]

Surely, if someone today claimed to discover a *core* Christian doctrine in the Bible which no one had ever seen before, this would be suspicious. But the subject of eschatology is confusing, since it is about the unrealized future. Thus it shouldn't surprise us to have new insights into such a complex subject. Moreover, since the Church largely lost the grammatical-historical hermeneutic from the time of the early Christians until the Reformation (4th to the 17th century), it is no wonder that a pre-tribulational view was also lost. By allegorizing the promises to Israel, it made this doctrine impossible to discover. Thus Benware writes, "Once a literal approach to interpreting the Scriptures began to be rediscovered, these truths started to emerge."[21] Once the proper hermeneutical *tools* were restored, these *truths* quickly emerged.

Is the pre-tribulational rescue of the Church just the result of wanting to avoid suffering?

Many believers can't seem to embrace the pre-tribulational rescue of the Church because it seems to encourage a weak dedication to Christ. I've discussed this subject many times with fellow believers who reject the pre-

---

[20] Philip Schaff, *History of the Christian Church, vol. 2, Ante-Nicene Christianity from the Death of John the Apostle to Constantine the Great*, A.D. 100-325, 5th ed. (New York: Scribner's Sons, 1889; repr., Peabody, MA: Hendrickson, 1996), 614. To argue against this, Amillennialists offer arguments from silence in regards to the views of the church fathers. Amillennialist Sam Storms writes, "The literature that documented early Christian martyrdoms also betrays *the absence of any form of premillennialism.*" C. Samuel Storms, *Kingdom Come*, 175. Yet as historians note, arguments from silence are not persuasive unless it is a *conspicuous* silence. Since the doctrine of a millennial reign was offensive to Roman authorities, many theologians may have omitted this intentionally, in order to avoid persecution. More importantly, many of the early Church Fathers—particularly those in Asia Minor—believed in the millennial reign of Christ in the future. They probably learned this directly from the ministry of the apostle John, who was resident there.
[21] Paul N. Benware, *Understanding End Times Prophecy*, 248.

tribulational view, and they almost always argue that this view is merely the result of wanting to avoid suffering. Apart from the biblical evidence, they can't seem to overcome their suspicion that pre-tribulationists are tickling people's ears, telling them what they want to hear.

Obviously, the pre-tribulational view *is* to our personal advantage. If Christ returns to rescue us before the horrors of the Tribulation, this will certainly spare us from tremendous suffering. But just because this teaching is to our personal advantage, this doesn't invalidate the teaching itself. Think about it: *Most of the Bible's teaching is to our personal advantage!* For instance, salvation by grace through faith is infinitely better than salvation by works. But imagine if someone said, "You only believe in salvation by grace because it is easier for you." This charge would do nothing to invalidate the truth of our belief. While salvation by grace *is* much easier for us, it is still true.

If God doesn't want us to endure the Tribulation, this is his prerogative. We shouldn't seek to suffer beyond what he has called us to. In the meantime, however, God does call on believers to suffer for him (Phil. 1:29; Jas. 1:2; 2 Tim. 3:12; Jn. 16:33).

Doesn't this teach a Second and Third Coming of Christ?

Critics of a pre-tribulation rescue of the Church argue that Dispensationalists really teach a *Second* and a *Third* coming of Christ. Riddlebarger writes, "If dispensationalists are correct about a secret rapture, then Jesus does not have two advents but three."[22]

Of course, Hebrews states that Jesus will appear a "second time" (Heb. 9:28), so for this reason, it's best to think of the rescue of the Church and the Second Coming as one entire event. Since 1 Thessalonians 4:17 implies that Jesus never touches his feet to the ground when he rescues the Church ("[We] will be caught up together with them *in the clouds* to meet the Lord *in the air*"), we can't really consider this event his final return. It is under the large umbrella of the Second Coming, which will be completed when Jesus finally returns to rule the Earth (Acts 1:9-11). Others characterize the rescue of the Church as a *calling* of Christ, rather than a *coming* of Christ. However we capture it, we shouldn't think in terms of two Second Comings.

While Jesus' Second Coming will be complicated, so was his First Coming. Again, consider if you could go back in time and speak with a Jewish rabbi who lived 200 years before the time of Christ. If you had told him that there

---

[22] Kim Riddlebarger, *A Case for Amillennialism*, 171.

would be *two* comings of the Messiah, it's very likely that he would've laughed in your face. It's easy to imagine the rabbi saying, "*Two* comings of the Messiah... That's ridiculous! The Messiah will only come *once*." However, now that Christ has come, it's crystal clear that the OT predicted both a Suffering Servant (Isa. 53; Zech. 12) and a Conquering King (Dan. 7:13-14; Isa. 9:6-7). Similarly, his Second Coming will not be as straightforward as we might think.

Conclusion

It's important to note that the timing of Jesus' rescue is not an essential Christian doctrine. Actually, this doctrine is more of an inference based on the biblical data. While I believe that a pre-tribulational rescue of the Church makes the most sense, the Premillennial position doesn't hinge on the timing of this event. In fact, Premillennialists hold to a wide range of views on this subject, including a pre-tribulation, mid-tribulation, and post-tribulation rescue of the Church.[23]

Discussion questions

1. What might be the dangers of focusing too much on non-essential Christian doctrine like the timing of the rescue of the Church?

2. Jesus could return at any time. As one theologian once quipped, "How many of us wake up in the morning and say, 'Jesus could return today'"? Or who thinks, "Jesus might return this Tuesday"? For discussion, how might this doctrine affect a group of believers if they truly believed in Jesus' imminent return?

3. If Christ could return at any time, does this mean that we should not invest in long term goals? How might you respond to the claim, "We shouldn't invest in our retirement or a college education, because Jesus could return at any moment"?

---

[23] More could have been said in this chapter about the mid-tribulation perspective. Yet the pretribulation and midtribulation views are very similar in that they claim believers will not endure the full wrath of the Tribulation. For proponents of this view, see the work of J. Oliver Buswell, Merrill C. Tenney, or Gleason Archer, who offer the best case in *Three Views on the Rapture*. Others have offered a "prewrath" rescue of the Church. For this perspective, see Robert Van Kampen, *The Rapture Question Answered: Plain and Simple,* (Grand Rapids, MI: Revell, 1997).

Chapter 14. Tribulation (Part I): Overview

War, starvation, and disease have plagued the human race for millennia in its struggle for survival. Nevertheless, the Bible predicts a future period of human history that will contain suffering and judgment on a scale we've never encountered. Theologian Dwight Pentecost frankly states, "No passage can be found to alleviate to any degree whatsoever the severity of this time that shall come upon the earth."[1]

What is the Tribulation?

The Tribulation will be a time of divine judgment, but much of that judgment will be *passive*. God will simply turn humanity over to their own leadership. Through war, destruction of the environment, and persecution, humans will hurtle toward self-destruction. Jesus said, "There will be a great tribulation, such as has not occurred since the beginning of the world until now, nor ever will" (Mt. 24:21), and he even said that if God didn't intervene to rescue humanity during this time that "no life would have been saved" (Mt. 24:22). The prophet Daniel concurs, "There will be a time of distress such as never occurred since there was a nation until that time" (Dan. 12:1). The book of Revelation describes the "great tribulation" (Rev. 7:14) in chapters 6 through 16, culminating in the return of Christ (Rev. 19).

Revelation 6 and Matthew 24 describe the events leading up to the Tribulation. Jesus said that many of these events are simply "birth pangs" (Mt. 24:8). Just as a woman's pain increases in *duration* and *intensity* during labor, many calamities will increase as the end of history approaches. Thus these judgments intensify and build, like a crescendo played by a chaotic symphony. These will consist of war (Rev. 6:4; Mt. 24:6-7), famine (Rev. 6:6; Mt. 24:7), death (Rev. 6:8; Mt. 24:7-9), martyrdom (Rev. 6:9-11; Mt. 24:9, 16-22), the sun and moon darkening (Rev. 6:12; Mt. 24:29), the stars falling (Rev. 6:12-14; Mt. 24:29), and divine judgment on Planet Earth (Rev. 6:15-17; Mt. 24:32-33).

---

[1] J. Dwight Pentecost, *Things to Come*, 235.

When is the Tribulation? (Dan. 9:27)

The Tribulation will occur for seven years just before the return of Christ. Daniel predicted the First and Second Coming of Christ in Daniel 9:

> Seventy weeks have been decreed for your people and your holy city, to finish the transgression, to make an end of sin, to make atonement for iniquity, to bring in everlasting righteousness, to seal up vision and prophecy and to anoint the most holy place. So you are to know and discern that from the issuing of a decree to restore and rebuild Jerusalem until Messiah the Prince there will be seven weeks and sixty-two weeks; it will be built again, with plaza and moat, even in times of distress. Then after the sixty-two weeks the Messiah will be cut off and have nothing, and the people of the prince who is to come will destroy the city and the sanctuary. And its end will come with a flood; even to the end there will be war; desolations are determined. (Dan. 9:24-26)

We saw in an earlier chapter that Jesus fulfilled the first 69 weeks (9:25-26), which predicted his death in AD 33. But remember that Daniel predicted "seventy weeks" total (9:24). What happened to Daniel's 70th week?

> He will make a firm covenant with the many for *one week*, but in the middle of the week he will put a stop to sacrifice and grain offering; and on the wing of abominations will come one who makes desolate, even until a complete destruction, one that is decreed, is poured out on the one who makes desolate. (Dan. 9:27)

Since Daniel made his prediction for "your people and your holy city" (Dan. 9:24), this final "week" (seven years) must refer to a period of time for the nation of Israel.

Dispensationalists believe that the Tribulation will last for seven years based on Daniel 9:27, but additionally, Daniel 7:25 states that the second half of the Tribulation will last for "a time, times, and half a time." Daniel used the expression of "times" to refer to years earlier in his book (Dan. 4:16). This is why Miller writes, "Most scholars interpret 'for a time, times and half a time' to mean three and one half-years."[2] Whether or not they regard these 3.5 years as *symbolic* or *literal*, most agree that Daniel's expression refers to 3.5 years.

The book of Revelation synchronizes with Daniel's prediction. John uses multiple different expressions to explain a period of 3.5 years including

---

[2] Stephen R. Miller, *Daniel*. New American Commentary. Vol. 18. (Nashville, TN: Broadman, 1994), 214.

"forty-two months" (Rev. 11:2; 13:5), "time and times and half a time" (Rev. 12:14), and "one thousand two hundred and sixty days" (Rev. 12:6). Clearly, the time span of 3.5 years must be important. Otherwise, why would these authors articulate this era so many times and in so many different ways if mere symbolism was in view?

Amillennialists claim that this 3.5 year period is symbolic for an intense time of persecution, harkening back to Antiochus Epiphanes' persecution of the Jewish people (167-164 BC).[3] On their view, the 3.5 years served as a staple for a time of persecution in Jewish circles—almost like the numbers "9/11" carry this meaning for Americans today. Storms writes, "It is *not* the *length* but the *kind* of time that is meant."[4]

This interpretation, however, prefers the *extrabiblical* sources (the history of the Maccabees) over the *biblical* sources (the prophet Daniel). We should have no problem appealing to extrabiblical history for insight, but these insights should not trump the biblical allusions themselves, especially when the Apostle John used Daniel so consistently as a primary source in the book of Revelation. Why not interpret this time frame in light of the clear allusion to the book of Daniel, rather than such an obscure reference to extrabiblical literature?

At the end of his book, Daniel states that a 75 day gap will exist between the end of the Tribulation and the beginning of the Millennium (Dan. 12:11-12). Hitchcock writes, "This interval could be likened to the time between the election of a US president in November and the official inauguration in January. During this time, the president-elect appoints cabinet members, prepares his agenda, and doles out the spoils of victory to his faithful supporters."[5] Daniel records that people are "blessed" if they make it through the end of this period (Dan. 12:12). The blessing most likely refers to the fact that they make it into the Millennium—probably limping from the suffering they endured.

Who leads the Tribulation?

Who is the figure who makes a covenant with the Jewish people in Daniel 9:27 ("He will make a firm covenant with the many... he will put a stop to sacrifice and grain offering")? Some interpreters claim that *Christ* fulfills the

---

[3] See C. Samuel Storms, *Kingdom Come*, 485.
[4] C. Samuel Storms, *Kingdom Come*, 486.
[5] Mark Hitchcock, *The End: A Complete Overview of Bible Prophecy and the End of Days*, 393.

70th week, while others believe the *Antichrist* fulfills it. Needless to say, one group is drastically wrong!

Dispensationalists see a gap of time between verses 26 and 27 of Daniel 9. The first reason is that Daniel separates the first 69 weeks from the 70th week in the text. If no gap existed, then why separate these two sets of time?

Second, the rest of the prophecy occurs "even to the end" (v.26), which seems to focus on the end of history.

Third, in verse 26, the Roman army destroyed the Temple ("the people of the prince who is to come will *destroy the city and the sanctuary*"). Yet in verse 27, this future figure ends Temple sacrifices ("he will put a stop to sacrifice and grain offering"), which implies that the Temple has been rebuilt.

Finally, and most importantly of all, Jesus identified the "abomination of desolation" with the Antichrist. In Mark's version of the Olivet Discourse, Jesus uses the masculine singular participle (Mk. 13:14), saying that the Antichrist will be "*standing* where it should not be."[6]

Amillennialists criticize the notion of seeing a gap here. Riddlebarger writes, "Where is the gap found in the text? Dispensationalists must insert it."[7] Instead of a gap, Amillennialists see the 70th week as a continuation of Jesus' ministry—not the Antichrist's desolation of the Temple. Storms writes, "He who, literally, 'causes a covenant to prevail' is Jesus."[8] Amillennialists argue that Christ (not the Antichrist) was the one to "put a stop to sacrifice and grain offering" (Dan. 9:27), when he died "once for all" (Heb. 9:12; 10:10), fulfilling the sacrificial system. Moreover, Christ (not the Antichrist) inaugurated the New Covenant ("he will make a firm covenant with the many") halfway through the final week after his three and a half years of ministry was completed at the Cross ("in the middle of the week he will put a stop to sacrifice and grain offering"). Jesus said, "This is My blood of the covenant, which is poured out for many for forgiveness of sins" (Mt. 26:28). Thus the "desolation" of Daniel 9:27 refers to the destruction of the Jewish Temple in AD 70. Jesus, they argue, put an end to the Temple sacrifices at the destruction of the Temple (Heb. 9:26). Since Revelation 12:14 relates the second half of the week to the Tribulation ("time and times and half a time"), this must refer to the Church Age.

---

[6] Osborne writes, "Perhaps the first NT reference to a coming Antichrist is found in the Olivet discourse, where Jesus speaks of the abomination of desolation as a person (Mark 13:14), using the masculine participle (*hestēkota*, standing) in contrast to the neuter (*bdelygma*, abomination) that it modifies." Grant Osborne. *Revelation*, 493.

[7] Kim Riddlebarger, *A Case for Amillennialism*, 181.

[8] C. Samuel Storms, *Kingdom Come*, 85.

But just for a moment, imagine walking through the desert and seeing a watery oasis on the horizon. From afar, this looks attractive to the naked eye, but as you walk closer, you discover that this was merely a mirage. Similarly, at first glance, the Amillennial view seems attractive, but when you examine it closer, you discover that it contains many problems.

For instance, Amillennialists have a problem with seeing a gap in Daniel's prediction, yet they see no problem equating 3.5 years with the 2,000 year Church Age! Thus Riddlebarger writes, "The final three and a half years of the seventieth week, as interpreted by John, *are symbolic of the church on earth during the entire time of its existence.* It also is a reference to the tribulation depicted in Daniel."[9] Furthermore, Storms writes, "The destruction of Jerusalem and its temple in AD 70 is the middle of the week, and the present church age is the latter half."[10] Thus Amillennialists take the first 69 weeks as *literal* measurements of time,[11] but take the final 70th week as symbolic of two millennia!

Moreover, to fit their view, Amillennialists take these predictions out of order. For instance, when Daniel writes, "He will make a firm covenant with the many for one week" (Dan. 9:27), how can this covenant refer to the New Covenant of Jesus' blood, when it takes place *after* the desolation of the Temple (mentioned in verse 26)? Thus in order for these interpreters to avoid a gap in the text, it seems that they need to take these predictions as *non-sequential* and also *non-chronological*—even though the text specifies both sequence and chronology.

Preterists also see a problem with a gap between verses 26 and 27. DeMar objects, "Is there *any* gap in this seventy-year period? No! It is the near termination point of this seventy-year period."[12] And yet, even under the Preterist view, a gap still must exist between Jesus' death in AD 33 and the destruction of the Temple in AD 70. DeMar sees the inconsistency of this view, when he states that a short gap is at least better than a long gap: "Could we not assume that a forty-year gap is much more logical than a gap of indeterminate length?"[13] Nonetheless, a gap is still a gap. While

---

[9] Kim Riddlebarger, *A Case for Amillennialism*, 183.
[10] C. Samuel Storms, *Kingdom Come*, 90.
[11] Many Amillennialists do not even take the first 69 weeks as literal. For instance, Storms writes, "The seventy weeks are not designed to establish precise chronological parameters for redemptive history. Rather, they serve to evoke a *theological image*, namely, that in 'Messiah Jesus' God will work to bring about the final jubilee of redemptive history." C. Samuel Storms, *Kingdom Come*, 90.
[12] Emphasis his. Gary DeMar, *Last Days Madness*, 330.
[13] Gary DeMar, *Last Days Madness*, 333.

Dispensationalists hold to a longer gap, both interpreters must see a gap in this prophecy somewhere.[14]

Therefore, after considering all of these views, we should conclude that the Antichrist will arise in this future period of time (seven years, according to Daniel 9:27). He will make a peaceful agreement with the nation of Israel ("your people" and "your holy city") to allow for temple sacrifices. But halfway through this period of seven years, "he will put a stop to sacrifice and grain offering" (Dan. 9:27), betraying his contract with Israel.

Remember, type-gap prophecies help us to understand how these predictions will be fulfilled: If the first abomination occurred from a pagan and wicked ruler (i.e. Antiochus Epiphanes IV), then the second abomination will follow the same pattern—only to a further extreme (i.e. the Antichrist).

Worship in the Tribulation (Rev. 11:1-2)

> Then there was given me a measuring rod like a staff; and someone said, 'Get up and measure the temple of God and the altar, and those who worship in it. Leave out the court which is outside the temple and do not measure it, for it has been given to the nations; and they will tread under foot the holy city for forty-two months.' (Rev. 11:1-2)

Revelation depicts a Jewish Temple during the Tribulation (Rev. 11:1-2), but theologians debate if this is a *literal Temple* or a *symbolic picture of the Church*.

Amillennialists argue that John's Temple symbolically refers to the Church. Earlier in Revelation, Jesus said, "He who overcomes, I will make him a pillar *in the temple of My God*" (Rev. 3:12). John also uses the term "holy city" to refer to believers (Rev. 21:2, 10; 22:19; c.f. 3:12; 20:9), and Paul equates the Church as the fulfillment of the Temple (1 Cor. 3:16; 6:19; 2 Cor. 6:16).

Dispensationalists note that John sees a difference between a literal Temple on Earth and a spiritual Temple in heaven. John sees "the temple of God," as well as "those who worship in it." Thomas rightly notes, "If the sanctuary

---

[14] DeMar claims that no gap exists on his view. He argues that *Daniel* did not predict the end, but he predicted that *Jesus* would predict it in the 70th week ("desolations are determined"). That is, Jesus predicted the destruction of the Temple in Matthew 23:38. But the reader can clearly see that DeMar is really reaching here. On Daniel's prediction, halfway through the 70th week, the Romans would destroy the Temple; yet this was *not* fulfilled seven years after Jesus' death. Daniel doesn't write that desolations *will be* determined; he says that they *are* determined. Gary DeMar, *Last Days Madness*, 333.

represents the church..., who are the worshipers?"[15] Even in Revelation 11, John sees both an *earthly* Temple (vv.1-2) and a *heavenly* Temple (v.19). Clearly, two temples are in view.

In addition, John depicts worshippers *in* the Temple (Rev. 11:1). This doesn't seem to fit with believers *being* the Temple, because John sees them as separate from it. In his Olivet Discourse, Jesus predicted, "They [the Jews] will fall by the edge of the sword, and will be led captive into all the nations; and Jerusalem will be trampled under foot by the Gentiles *until the times of the Gentiles are fulfilled*" (Lk. 21:24). This statement surely implies that the Jewish people will regain Jerusalem once the Gentiles are taken out of the way. This would make sense of John's comment that the nations "will tread under foot the holy city for forty-two months" (Rev. 11:2). Paul (2 Thess. 2:4), Jesus (Mt. 24:15), Daniel (Dan. 9:27), Isaiah (Isa. 56:7; 66:20), Jeremiah (Jer. 33:18), Zechariah (Zech. 6:12; 14:21), and Malachi (Mal. 3:3-4) all predicted a Jewish Temple during this time.

Finally, why does John measure the city if it is only symbolic for the Church? When prophets measured their cities in the OT, this was symbolic for God's protection or his destruction (Zech. 2:1-5; 2 Kings 21:13; Isa. 34:11; 2 Sam. 8:2; Lam. 2:8). But while measuring the Temple surely had symbolic implications, they were still literally measuring the city of Jerusalem. Furthermore, in Revelation 11, John is recreating one of Ezekiel's visions. As in Revelation 10:8-10 (where John eats the bitter scroll; c.f. Ezek. 3:1-3), John's act of measuring the Temple harkens back to Ezekiel's vision of measuring the third Temple in Jerusalem (Ezek. 40:3, 5).

Based on the biblical evidence then, a restored Temple will exist in Jerusalem during the time of the Tribulation.

Who is in the Tribulation? *Israel or the Church?* (Rev. 12:1-2)

> A great sign appeared in heaven: a woman clothed with the sun, and the moon under her feet, and on her head a crown of twelve stars; and she was with child; and she cried out, being in labor and in pain to give birth. (Rev. 12:1-2)

Who is the woman described here?

Dispensationalists identify the woman as the nation of Israel, which brought about Christ (Rom. 9:5; Mic. 5:2-3). The imagery of the sun, moon, and

---

[15] Robert L. Thomas, *Revelation 8-22: An Exegetical Commentary* (Chicago: Moody, 1995), 81.

stars refers to the nation of Israel in the OT. Joseph said, "I have had still another dream; and behold, *the sun and the moon and eleven stars were bowing down to me*" (Gen. 37:9). Osborne writes, "In Jewish literature 'twelve stars' often refers to the twelve patriarchs or the twelve tribes."[16] Moreover, the image of being protected by eagle's wings refers to Israel. In Exodus 19:4, we read, "You yourselves have seen what I did to the Egyptians, and *how I bore you on eagles' wings*, and brought you to Myself." This seems to fit with the language in Revelation 12:14, where we read, "The two wings of the great eagle were given to the woman, so that she could fly into the wilderness to her place, where she was nourished." Daniel pictured the end of history to be centralized around "*your* people and *your* holy city" (Dan. 9:24), which fits with Israel as well.

Daniel 12 predicts that Michael would rise up at this time to protect Israel—not the Church (Dan. 12:1). We see a fulfillment of this, when John writes, "There was war in heaven, Michael and his angels waging war with the dragon" (Rev. 12:7). Finally, the man-child of Revelation 12:5 must refer to Jesus—not the Church—when he rules the nations with a rod of iron (Rev. 19:15).

Amillennialists argue that the woman is the Church. The NT authors call the Church a woman (2 Cor. 11:2; Eph. 5:25-27, 32; 2 Jn. 1, 5; 3 Jn. 9), and the early Christian commentaries call her a woman as well.[17] Moreover, Revelation 2:26-27 promises the church of Thyatira that they would reign with Christ with a rod of iron, which seems to match John's promises that the son of the woman "is to rule all the nations with a rod of iron" (Rev. 12:5). However, since Jesus will "strike down the nations" and "will rule them with a rod of iron" (Rev. 19:15), this interpretation puts the Amillennialist in the awkward position of believing that the Church gave birth to Jesus. Can we really hold to such a view? Surely this puts the cart before the horse! Additionally, if the woman is the Church, then who are "the rest of her children" (v.17) mentioned later?

[16] Grant Osborne. *Revelation*, 456.
[17] *Hermas* V.1.i-ii. See Alan Johnson, *Revelation*, 514.

Witnesses of the Tribulation (Rev. 11:3-12)

Theologians have offered various explanations for the identity of the two witnesses,[18] but two broad interpretations typically dominate the discussion. Should we view these two witnesses as future, historical people? Or should we interpret them in a symbolic fashion to refer to the witnessing of the Church?

Dispensationalists argue that these two witnesses are literal—perhaps Moses and Elijah. After all, both figures appear to be human. They have bodies (v.8), they have feet (v.11), and they are placed in a tomb at death (v.9). Moreover, they wear sackcloth, which was the garb of prophets (v.3; cf. 2 Kings 1:8; Isa. 20:2; Zech. 13:4).

Furthermore, God took both Elijah and Moses bodily into heaven: Elijah went directly into heaven before death (2 Kings 2:11), and Michael (the archangel) confiscated the body of Moses into heaven as well (Jude 9). Why would God care about Moses' dead body, unless he had a future purpose for it? Furthermore, at the Mount of Transfiguration, both Moses and Elijah bodily appeared to Christ and the disciples (Mt. 17:3). Could it be that they will both appear again at the end of history?

Malachi predicted that Elijah would appear before "the great and terrible day of the Lord" (Mal. 4:5-6; c.f. 3:1-3). Jesus also said that "Elijah is coming and will restore all things" (Mt. 17:11; cf. Mk. 9:11-13). While John the Baptist was a partial fulfillment of this prophecy, this was contingent on whether or not the nation of Israel would receive Christ (Mt. 11:14). Of course, John the Baptist denied that he was the fulfillment of these passages about Elijah (Jn. 1:21)—even though he did come "in the spirit and power of Elijah" (Lk. 1:17).

Dispensationalist interpreters do not believe that Elijah's return is absolutely necessary, but are inclined to believe so. Dwight Pentecost writes, "The fact that John could have fulfilled it, even though he was not personally Elijah, seems to indicate that Elijah need not come personally to fulfill the prophecies. During the period preceding the second advent, and prior to the outpouring of judgments upon the earth, there will be a ministry by one

---

[18] Enoch and Elijah, Jeremiah and Elijah, James the bishop of Jerusalem and the apostle John, two Christian prophets martyred by Titus, Peter and Paul martyred by Nero, two individual prophets modeled after Joshua and Zerubbabel, the two olive trees of Zech. 4:1-2, linked with the priestly Messiah (Aaron) and the lay Messiah (Israel) of Qumran. See Grant Osborne. *Revelation*, 417.

in the spirit and power of Elijah, which will fulfill this prophecy."[19]
Therefore, this could be an "Elijah-like" figure, if not Elijah himself.

Finally, the language of causing a draught and turning the rivers into blood
seems to fit with Elijah and Moses (v.6). Elijah prayed to cause a draught in
Israel (1 Kings 17:1), and Moses turned the Nile into blood (Ex. 7:17). The
language of "every plague" seems to fit with the plagues of the Exodus as
well. God originally protected Elijah's ministry with fires from heaven (1
Kings 18:38; 2 Kings 1:11-12), which would fit with John writing, "If
anyone wants to harm them, fire flows out of their mouth and devours their
enemies; so if anyone wants to harm them, he must be killed in this way"
(Rev. 11:5).

However, it is also possible that this isn't literal. John could be explaining
that their words are the words of judgment. In Jeremiah 5:14, God tells the
prophet, "Because you have spoken this word, behold, *I am making My words
in your mouth fire and this people wood*, and it will consume them." Later in
Revelation, we see that the fire of judgment is for those who rejected their
message (Rev. 20:11-14). Thus the *message* of a literal future judgment could
be what is in view here.

Amillennialists advocate a more symbolic interpretation: These two witnesses
represent the evangelism of the Church. Others argue that perhaps these
two witnesses are symbolic for the Law and the Prophets of the OT (Jn.
5:45). They find it strange that the Beast would need to wage war on just
two witnesses (v.7). On the other hand, Dispensationalists point out that
God was supernaturally protecting these two individuals (v.5), who had
supernatural control over the weather patterns (v.6). Therefore, it may take
an actual war to destroy these two.

Additionally, the Amillennial view faces serious difficulties when the
authorities kill the two witnesses (Rev. 11:8-9). If the witnesses are the
Church, then this would mean that the Church will be wiped out during this
period of history, which Jesus claimed is impossible (Mt. 16:18). To avoid
this problem, Beale holds that the "death" of the prophets is really
hyperbole for being "driven underground" and that "a universal silence will
fall on the church at the very end of history."[20] Such an interpretation,
however, falls short of the language in Revelation 11, where the prophets lie
dead—not *dormant*.

---

[19] J. Dwight Pentecost, *Things to Come*, 313.
[20] G.K. Beale, *The Book of Revelation* (Grand Rapids, MI. William B. Eerdmans Publishing
Company, 1999), 590.

Amillennialists also argue that the two witnesses are called "lamps" and "olive trees" (v.4). They note that Revelation 1:20 identifies the seven "lampstands" as the Church. However, the lamps are also identified with the Holy Spirit (Rev. 4:5), Christ, (Rev. 21:23), and God (Rev. 22:5). Therefore, this symbolism is inconsistent. Moreover, this imagery of "lamps," "olive trees," and "witnesses" is more likely drawn from Zechariah 4. There, Zechariah sees seven lamps and two olive trees (vv.2-3). The angel interprets this vision for Zechariah, saying that these are "two anointed ones" (v.14)—that is, two literal people.

Conclusion

The purpose of this chapter was to offer a quick flyby of the "great tribulation" (Rev. 7:14). As we saw, the Tribulation will be a time where God judges the Earth to an unparalleled degree. If this understanding is correct, the Tribulation will be led by a future tyrant whom the Bible calls the "Antichrist" or the "Beast," and he will reign on Earth for seven years. He will make an agreement with Israel to allow her to practice Temple sacrifices once again, but will double-cross the Jewish people halfway through his reign, calling himself God and demanding worship. During this time, two prophets will return to call Israel back to faith in God (Moses and Elijah?), and the Jewish people will realize their drastic error.

In the following chapters, we will look closer at this dreadful period of human history.

Discussion questions

1. Without cheating by looking back into the book, answer the following questions with Scripture. Feel free to offer alternate interpretations of each and assess their merits:

> What is the Tribulation?
>
> When is the Tribulation? How long will it last?
>
> Who leads the Tribulation?
>
> Worship in the Tribulation?
>
> Will Israel or the Church be in the Tribulation?
>
> Who are the two witnesses?

2. The Tribulation will be a time of intense suffering: Why do you think God would permit this sort of suffering on Earth? What reasons do you think he might have for permitting this?

3. What is the significance of God sending two prophets during this awful era of history?

Chapter 15. Tribulation (Part II): World Empires & World Warfare

In an earlier chapter, we saw that Daniel accurately predicted the four world empires that conquered Israel, culminating with the Roman Empire. Yet portions of this final empire have not yet been fulfilled. In his final description of the Roman Empire, we read:

> In that you saw the feet and toes, partly of potter's clay and partly of iron, *it will be a divided kingdom*; but it will have in it the toughness of iron, inasmuch as you saw the *iron mixed with common clay*. As the toes of the feet were partly of iron and partly of pottery, so *some of the kingdom will be strong and part of it will be brittle*. And in that you saw the iron mixed with common clay, they will combine with one another in the seed of men; but they will not adhere to one another, even as iron does not combine with pottery. (Dan. 2:41-43)

> Behold, a fourth beast, *dreadful and terrifying and extremely strong*; and it had large iron teeth. It devoured and crushed and trampled down the remainder with its feet; and it was different from all the beasts that were before it, and *it had ten horns*. While I was contemplating the horns, behold, another horn, a little one, came up among them, and three of the first horns were pulled out by the roots before it; and behold, this horn possessed eyes like the eyes of a man and a mouth uttering great boasts. (Dan. 7:7-8)

> As for the ten horns, *out of this kingdom ten kings will arise*; and another will arise after them, and he will be different from the previous ones and will subdue three kings. (Dan. 7:24)

Many commentators believe that Daniel is only predicting the ancient Roman Empire here. But if this is so, then many of these predictions are simply false. The original Roman Empire had *one* king—not *many* as Daniel 7:24 predicts ("ten kings"). Ten kingdoms never came out of the ancient Roman Empire. Moreover, Daniel describes anatomical distinctions between the two parts of the statue. Daniel 2:40 explains the iron legs of the statue, while Daniel 2:41-43 describe the iron and clay feet and toes. Thus the final portion of Daniel's prediction must still be arriving in the future.

Amillennialists sometimes suggest that "the ten horns are any and conceivably all of the pagan empires that emerged subsequent to the fall of

Rome."[1] Since this is a round number ("ten"), it refers to the
"completeness" of human empires from Rome until today. Yet since
Daniel's other predictions have been fulfilled literally, we should expect the
unfulfilled portions to transpire in the same way.

What will God's kingdom be like?

In his vision of the world empires, Daniel predicts a final kingdom that will
crush all of the others. He writes,

> In the days of those kings *the God of heaven will set up a kingdom*
> which will never be destroyed, and that kingdom will not be left
> for another people; *it will crush and put an end to all these kingdoms*, but
> it will itself endure forever. (Dan. 2:44)

Amillennialists hold that the Church "destroyed" the ancient Roman Empire
through the spread of the gospel. While ancient Rome has disappeared, the
Church still remains and "it will itself endure forever" (Dan. 2:44). Thus
Storms writes, "The point is that the establishment of the messianic
kingdom and the destruction of the pagan empires is not an instantaneous
event."[2]

Dispensationalists, on the other hand, point to the language of Daniel 2:44,
which states how God's kingdom will "crush" this final world empire. This
doesn't describe the *peaceful* spread of the gospel; instead it describes a
violent and drastic overthrow ("it will *crush* and put an end to all these
kingdoms").

Historically, the Roman Empire *slowly* deteriorated for over a millennium.
The western part of the Roman Empire fell in AD 476, but the eastern
portion didn't meet its demise until AD 1453. Hitchcock observes, "A more
gradual process could hardly be imagined. This is neither the sudden
destruction of the image's feet (Daniel 2:34) nor the ten-horn stage of the
beast (Daniel 7:7) that Daniel predicted. This prophecy remains
unfulfilled."[3] Moreover, if all of the other empires were literal (e.g. Babylon,
Media-Persia, Greece, Rome), it seems to follow that the final kingdom of
God will be literal as well (i.e. the Millennial Kingdom).

One of the best ways to discover if we're interpreting prophecy accurately is
to appeal to correlation. If other biblical authors interpret prophecy the

---

[1] C. Samuel Storms, *Kingdom Come*, 104.
[2] C. Samuel Storms, *Kingdom Come*, 109.
[3] Mark Hitchcock, *The End: A Complete Overview of Bible Prophecy and the End of Days*,
247.

same way, it fortifies our interpretation. We find this in Revelation 13 and 17:

> I saw a beast coming up out of the sea, having *ten horns*. (Rev. 13:1)
>
> The *ten horns* which you saw are *ten kings* who have not yet received a kingdom. (Rev. 17:12)

John must be thinking of Daniel's prophecy, because he uses the exact same imagery of "ten horns" being "ten kings." But John believes that this hasn't happened yet ("not yet received a kingdom"). He writes,

> The seven heads are seven mountains on which the woman sits, and they are seven kings; five have fallen, one is, the other has not yet come; and when he comes, he must remain a little while. The beast which was and is not, is himself also an eighth and is one of the seven, and he goes to destruction. (Rev. 17:9-11)

At the time that John wrote this (AD 95), the "five fallen" kings were Egypt, Assyria, Babylonia, Persia, and Greece. The king that "now is" would be Rome, which ruled the world in the first-century. Finally, John explains that the other "has not yet come," which must refer to the future Roman Empire. Thus the eighth king (v.11) must be the Antichrist coming out of that final kingdom.

Amillennialists and *Preterists* hold that John's reference to the "seven mountains" (NASB) or "seven hills" (NIV) must refer to the ancient Roman Empire. Ancient authors often referred to Rome as the city built on seven hills.[4]

While this view seems plausible at first, the Greek word *oros* should be rendered "mountains" (NASB, ESV), not "hills" (NIV, NLT). Johnson writes, "In the seven other instances of the word *orē* in Revelation, it is always rendered 'mountain,' except here in 17:9, where it is translated 'hills.' Is this a case where previous exegesis has influenced even the best translations?"[5] Moreover, if John's reference to the "seven mountains" referred to Rome, why would it require a "mind which has wisdom" (Rev. 17:9)? Johnson rightly observes, "Any Roman soldier who knew Greek could figure out that the seven hills referred to Rome. But whenever divine wisdom is called for, the description requires theological and symbolical discernment, not mere geographical or numerical insight."[6]

---

[4] Osborne cites Cicero, *Letters to Atticus.* 6.5; Pliny, *Natural History.* 3.66—67. Grant Osborne. *Revelation*, 617.
[5] Alan Johnson, *Revelation*, 559.
[6] Alan Johnson, *Revelation*, 558.

John must be thinking of Daniel's statement of "a great mountain" that "fills the whole earth" (Dan. 2:35). The "great mountain" is a world empire. John interprets the seven mountains in exactly this way, calling them "seven kings" (Rev. 17:10). Who are these seven kings? Some commentators hold that the seven kings are ancient Roman Emperors, but aligning these with ancient Roman emperors "is incredibly difficult."[7] If you ask *five* commentators where we should begin the reign of emperors, you will likely receive *six* different answers!

THE SEVEN KINGS
REVELATIONS 17:9-11

Revelations 17:9-11	Dispensational View	Amillennial View
"Seven mountains"	Seven kingdoms (Egypt, Assyria, Babylonia, Persia, and Greece, Rome, and future Rome)	Seven Roman kings (Roman emperors)
"Five have fallen"	Egypt, Assyria, Babylonia, Persia, Greece	Five Roman emperors prior to the one in power
"One is"	Rome I (First century)	Current Roman emperor (Nero? Domitian?)
"The other has not yet come"	Rome II (End of human history)	The final world empire? First-century Rome?

John tells us that the Antichrist (or Beast) comes out of the seventh king (or kingdom). He writes, "The beast which was and is not, is himself also an eighth and is one of the seven" (Rev. 17:11). This must mean that the Antichrist arises from the regathered Roman Empire. Thus as history reaches its end, we should expect some sort of revived Roman Empire with ten kingdoms, as both Daniel and Revelation predict.

Armageddon

The "battle of Armageddon" is really a misnomer. Multiple battles will occur during this time. Benware writes, "It is not a single battle but rather a whole series of conflicts that culminate with the Second Coming of Christ. The Greek word *polemos*, translated 'battle' in Revelation 16:14, signifies a war or campaign… [This] indicates that Armageddon is really a campaign made up of numerous conflicts among a number of nations over a period

---

[7] Grant Osborne. *Revelation*, 617.

of time at the end of the tribulation."[8] Thus the "battle of Armageddon" really refers to a series of battles that occur against the nation of Israel at the end of history. A superhuman (the Antichrist) and a superpower (the unified nations of the world) will gather to destroy Israel.

While several passages describe this world war, (Ps. 2; Isa. 34:1-16; 63:1-6; Joel 3:1-17; Zech. 12:1-9; 14:1-15; Dan. 11:36-45; Ezek. 38-39; Mal. 4:1-5; Rev. 14:14-20; 16:12-16; 19:19-21), we will focus on just a few.

Who will participate in Armageddon?

The beginning of Daniel 11 (vv.1-35) describes Antiochus Epiphanes IV, but we see a gap in between verses 35 and 36: Daniel places this event "at the end time" (v.40). He states, "There will be a time of distress such as never occurred since there was a nation until that time" (Dan. 12:1), and he places this event during the time of the resurrection (Dan. 12:2). Furthermore, while Antiochus Epiphanes IV remained loyal to the Greek gods, this individual "will show no regard for the gods of his fathers or for the desire of women, nor will he show regard for any other god; for he will magnify himself above them all" (Dan. 11:37). Surely this entire passage cannot refer only to Antiochus.

Daniel predicted that a king from the south of Israel will dominate the land (Dan. 11:40-41). This king will destroy Egypt (Dan. 11:43), but eastern and northern nations will eventually destroy him (Dan. 11:44-45). The arrival of kings "from the East" correlates with the release of the four angels "who are bound at the great river Euphrates" (Rev. 9:14) who bring a "two hundred million" man army (Rev. 9:16). This would further correlate with John's statement of the river Euphrates drying up "so that the way would be prepared for *the kings from the east*" (Rev. 16:12). John later states that this prepares the world for the battle at "Har-Magedon" (Rev. 16:16).

The prophet Ezekiel offers the most detail regarding the nations that will be involved in this ferocious battle (Ezek. 38-39).

> Son of man, set your face toward *Gog* of the land of *Magog*, the prince of *Rosh*, *Meshech* and *Tubal*, and prophesy against him [3] and say, 'Thus says the Lord God, "Behold, I am against you, O *Gog*, prince of *Rosh*, *Meshech* and *Tubal*... [5] *Persia*, *Ethiopia* and *Put* with them, all of them with shield and helmet; [6] *Gomer* with all its troops; *Beth-togarmah* from the remote parts of the north with all its troops—many peoples with you. (Ezek. 38:2-3, 5-6)

---

[8] Paul Benware, *Understanding End Times Prophecy* (Moody: Chicago, 2006), 31.

Who are these nations? Some of these locations are difficult to identify. When this is the case, we should exercise restraint in our assessment.

Gog

Besides Ezekiel 38-39, the OT only mentions "Gog" in 1 Chronicles 5:4, which doesn't help us in identifying this nation. Ezekiel calls Gog the "prince of Rosh" (Ezek. 38:2; 38:2), so a person might be in view, who rules these other nations. Though Gog's identity is not certain,[9] Allen writes that Gog "seems to relate to one known to the Greeks as Gyges and to the Assyrians as Gugu, who was a powerful king of Lydia in west Asia Minor in the first half of the seventh century. As with the national names, so here a great figure of the past is evidently used to define a future threat, as we might speak fearfully of a new Hitler."[10] Daniel Block concurs that "the most likely explanation derives Gog from Gyges (668-631 BC)."[11] While Yamauchi associates Gog with the kingdom of Gyges, he writes, "Various attempts to explain the background of Gog and Magog have not won universal consent."[12]

Since the Assyrian "Gugu" rebelled against the empire and was quickly killed, Duguid doesn't see him as a major historical figure, describing him as "mere roadkill on the highway of the empire."[13] Instead, Duguid contends that Ezekiel is not focusing on the *historical importance* of Gog, but rather the *character* or *nature* of this man. Herodotus tells us that Gugu (Gog) took the throne from his master by killing him.[14] Thus Duguid writes, "The Gog of Ezekiel transcends historical categories and takes on mythical proportions, rather like the figure of Arnold Schwarzenegger in the movie *The Terminator*."[15] In other words, the reference to "Gog" might be symbolic for a future tyrant, who sadistically takes control of these other kings and rulers.

---

[9] Alexander lists six possible solutions, but concludes, "None of the proposed solutions have sufficient support to warrant their acceptance as the identity of the term 'Gog.'" Ralph Alexander. *Ezekiel.* In F. E. Gaebelein (Ed.), *The Expositor's Bible Commentary: Isaiah, Jeremiah, Lamentations, Ezekiel.* Vol. 6. (Grand Rapids, MI: Zondervan Publishing House, 1986), 929.

[10] Leslie Allen, *Ezekiel 20–48.* Vol. 29. (Dallas: Word, Incorporated, 1998), 204-205.

[11] Daniel Block, *The Book of Ezekiel: 25-48*, 433.

[12] Edwin Yamauchi, *Foes from the Northern Frontier: Invading Hordes from the Russian Steppes* (Grand Rapids, MI: Baker Book House, 1982), 24.

[13] Iain Duguid, *The NIV Application Commentary: Ezekiel* (Grand Rapids, MI: Zondervan, 1999), 447.

[14] The king of Lydia (Candaules) had Gyges (his general) stare at his wife naked to show off her beauty. As revenge, the Queen had Gyges kill her husband by hiding in the same place he viewed her nakedness. See Herodotus, *Histories.* 1.8-13.

[15] Iain Duguid, *The NIV Application Commentary: Ezekiel*, 447.

Assessment: The location of Gog is not certain. This nation must be to the north of Israel (Ezek. 38:15). If we associate it with the Greek (Gyges) and Assyrian (Gugu), this would place Gog in modern-day Turkey. It's also possible that Ezekiel is only thinking of a *man*—not a *nation*—when he refers to Gog.

Magog

Josephus states that the ancient Scythians lived in Magog.[16] This would place Magog in "a mountainous region around the Black and Caspian seas."[17] Yamauchi states, "In the broad sense the word Scythian can designate some of the many other tribes in the vast steppes of Russia, stretching from the Ukraine in the west to the region of Siberia in the east."[18]

Assessment: Magog can be identified with the region around the Black Sea in the broad area of Russia. Garland notes that "this position is generally accepted."[19]

Rosh

Considerable debate has surrounded identifying Rosh. Some Dispensational authors assumed that Rosh should be identified with "Russia." The arguments given were often based on the word association between "Rosh" and "Russia." However, more recently, other evangelical authors have dismissed this assertion. Because so much debate surrounds the identity of Rosh, we will consider this question carefully.

Should "Rosh" be understood as a proper noun or as an adjective?

Modern English translations disagree on whether to take "Rosh" as a proper *noun* (i.e. the title of a nation) or as an *adjective* (i.e. the description of Gog). When we compare translations, we discover that the NASB, NKJV, and ASV render this Hebrew word as a proper noun ("Rosh"), while the KJV, ESV, NIV, NRSV, NLT, and NET translate it as an adjective

---

[16] Josephus, *Antiquities of the Jews*, 1.6.1.
[17] Ralph Alexander. *Ezekiel*. In F. E. Gaebelein (Ed.), *The Expositor's Bible Commentary: Isaiah, Jeremiah, Lamentations, Ezekiel*. Vol. 6. (Grand Rapids, MI: Zondervan Publishing House, 1986), 929.
[18] Edwin Yamauchi, *Foes from the Northern Frontier*, 64.
[19] David E. Garland (et al.), *Jeremiah-Ezekiel* (Grand Rapids, MI: Zondervan, 2010), 853.

("prince" or "ruler" of the nations).[20] The case for translating Rosh as a proper noun can be soundly supported for a number of reasons.

First, Hebrew grammarians understand Rosh as a proper noun.[21] For instance, Wilhelm Gesenius is "generally considered by modern Hebrew scholars to have been one of the greatest scholars of the Hebrew language."[22] Gesenius writes that Rosh is a "proper noun of a northern nation, mentioned with Meshech and Tubal; undoubtedly the Russians, who are mentioned by the Byzantine writers of the tenth century, under the name the Ros, dwelling to the north of Taurus... as dwelling on the river Rha (Wolga)."[23] Billington writes, "The grammatical arguments for the translation of 'Rosh' as a proper noun in Ezekiel 38-39 are conclusive and not really open for serious debate... Few Hebrew scholars today maintain that Rosh in Ezekiel 38-39 should be translated as 'chief.'"[24]

Second, ancient Greek translations render this Hebrew term as a proper noun—not an adjective. The Septuagint, Symmachus, and Theodotian (other ancient Greek translations of the OT) rendered Rosh as a place or nation—not a title.[25]

Third, Jerome's translation of the Latin Vulgate erroneously popularized the adjectival translation. Jerome couldn't identify the Rosh people, so he went against grammatical rules to render Rosh as an adjective.[26] As a result, Jerome's translation greatly influenced the King James Bible of 1611, and other English translations have (erroneously) followed in this tradition.

Is there any historical connection between Rosh and modern-day Russia?

Many scholars claim that no connection exists between Rosh and Russia historically or etymologically. For instance, the eminent historian Edwin

---

[20] For proponents of this adjectival usage, see David E. Garland (et al.), *Jeremiah-Ezekiel* (Grand Rapids, MI: Zondervan, 2010), 854. Block favors seeing Rosh as a "common noun" and an appositional usage. See Daniel Block, *The Book of Ezekiel: 25-48*, 435.

[21] For an exhaustive treatment of the subject, see James Price. "Rosh: An Ancient Land Known to Ezekiel." *Grace Theological Journal*, 6.1 (1985). 67-89. See also C. F. Keil, *Ezekiel, Daniel, Commentary on the Old Testament* (Grand Rapids: Eerdmans Publishing Company, 1982), 159-160.

[22] Clyde E. Billington, Jr. "The Rosh People in History and Prophecy," (Part One), *Michigan Theological Journal* 3:1 (Spring 1992). 61.

[23] Friedrich Heinrich Wilhelm Gesenius, *Thesaurus Linguae Hebraeae et Chaldaeae Veteris Testamenti* (Lipsiae: Sumtibus Typisque, Fr. Chr. Guil. Vogelii, 1835), vol. III, p. 1253. Cited in Clyde E. Billington, Jr. "The Rosh People" 62.

[24] Clyde E. Billington, Jr. "The Rosh People" 56.

[25] Clyde E. Billington, Jr. "The Rosh People" 60.

[26] Clyde E. Billington, Jr. "The Rosh People" 60.

Yamauchi writes, "[Rosh] can have nothing to do with modern 'Russia.' This would be a gross anachronism, for the modern name is based upon the name *Rus*, which was brought into the region of Kiev, north of the Black Sea, by the Vikings only in the Middle Ages."[27]

On the other hand, in his three part journal article series, scholar Clyde Billington offers a different perspective. He notes that identifying the Rosh people is difficult because different cultures spelled and pronounced this term differently. Moreover, the Rosh people were nomadic, travelling from place to place, so it's difficult to locate them precisely.[28] Nevertheless, Billington offers several lines of evidence that place the Rosh people in modern-day Russia:

Many ancient historical sources identify Rosh. Remember, since the Rosh people were nomadic, we shouldn't expect them to stay in the same geographic location. This is why we find them appearing in multiple areas:

1. Ancient Egyptian inscriptions (~2,600 BC) identify a place called "Rash," but these sources do not give us a location.[29]

2. The Hatshepsut's inscription (~1500 BC) refers to "Reshu," located to the north of Egypt. Billington states that this inscription "is almost certainly to be identified with the name 'Rosh' mentioned in Ezekiel 38-39."[30] This would place Rosh in northern Egypt—south of Israel.

3. The Eblaites, Ugarites, Hittites, and Assyrians all mention a city called "'ursbu/ Rish/ Urash' located somewhere in northwest Syria. It is very likely that the name of this city is directly connected to the name Rosh mentioned in Ezekiel 38-39."[31] Billington adds, "There is even one cuneiform document from the reign of the Assyrian King Sargon II (ruled 722-705 B.C.) which actually names all three peoples [Rosh, Meshech, Tubal] mentioned by Ezekiel 38–39."[32] He notes, "Assyrian documents from the 9th-7th centuries B.C. mention a group of Rosh people living in Mesopotamia to the east of the Tigris River."[33]

---

[27] Edwin Yamauchi, *Foes from the Northern Frontier*, 20.
[28] Clyde E. Billington, Jr., "The Rosh People in History and Prophecy (Part Two)," *Michigan Theological Journal* 3:2 (Fall 1992). 143-145.
[29] Clyde E. Billington, Jr., "The Rosh People in History and Prophecy (Part Two)," 145.
[30] Clyde E. Billington, Jr., "The Rosh People in History and Prophecy (Part Two)," 146.
[31] Clyde E. Billington, Jr., "The Rosh People in History and Prophecy (Part Two)," 153.
[32] Clyde E. Billington, Jr., "The Rosh People in History and Prophecy (Part Two)," 170.
[33] Clyde E. Billington, Jr., "The Rosh People in History and Prophecy (Part Two)," 170.

4. The Rosh people lived in the Caucasus Mountains. Billington notes, "There is solid evidence linking one group of Rosh People to the Caucasus Mountains."[34] He adds, "It should be noted that there were also bands of Meshech, Tubal, and Rosh peoples living in or north of the Caucasus Mountains in what is today Russia, Georgia, Azerbaijan, and Armenia."[35]

5. Later, Byzantine Christians placed the Rosh people in Russia. Billington writes, "As early as 438 AD, Byzantine Christians placed Gog, Magog, Meshech, Tubal and Ros peoples to the north of Greece in the area that is today Russia."[36]

Historians dispute how far back the term "Russian" existed. Some hold that it only goes back as far as the ninth century AD with the Varangian Rus people. However, these people *adopted* this name from the preexistent people who lived there.[37] Billington concludes that given the nomadic nature of the Rosh people, they started in the Caucasus Mountains, but spread to India and Eastern Mesopotamia. A group in the sixth century was in the north of the Black Sea in Ukraine.[38]

Biblical evidence supports the existence of an ancient nation that eventually became Rosh. Genesis 10:2 identifies the sons of Japheth with "Gomer and Magog... Tubal and Meshech and Tiras," which later grew into nations. This passage mentions all of the major nations from Ezekiel 38, but what about "Rosh"? Billington links "Tiras" with "Rosh," noting that the ancient Akkadian language dropped "t" sounds when these preceded "r" sounds, leaving us with "Ras."[39] Of course, when Ezekiel wrote his book, he was captive in Babylon (which spoke Akkadian), so it would make sense for him to call this nation "Rosh" rather than "Tiras."

The book of Judges references the Cushan-rishathaim (of Mesopotamia), who conquered the Jewish people temporarily. These people connect us with the Egyptian texts mentioned earlier. Billington writes, "There are strong reasons for identifying the 'country of Reshet' and the 'land of Reshu' mentioned in New Kingdom Egyptian texts with the country of the Rishataim people mentioned in Judges 3:8-11. There are also strong reasons

---

[34] Clyde E. Billington, Jr., "The Rosh People in History and Prophecy (Part Two)," 170.

[35] Clyde E. Billington, Jr., "The Rosh People in History and Prophecy (Part Two)," 172.

[36] Clyde E. Billington, Jr., "The Rosh People in History and Prophecy (Part Three)," *Michigan Theological Journal* 4:1 (Spring 1993). 48.

[37] Clyde E. Billington, Jr., "The Rosh People in History and Prophecy (Part Three)," 54-55.

[38] Clyde E. Billington, Jr., "The Rosh People in History and Prophecy (Part Two)," 173.

[39] Clyde E. Billington, Jr., "The Rosh People in History and Prophecy (Part Two)," 167.

for identifying the Reshu/Rishataim people with the ruling class of Indo-Aryans in the Kingdom of Mitanni."[40]

Assessment: There are overwhelming reasons for taking Rosh as a proper noun—not an adjective. As to the location of these people, we are not certain. However, several lines of evidence would point toward modern-day Russia.

Meshech & Tubal

Ezekiel 27:13 states that Meshech and Tubal were trading partners with Tyre (in modern-day Lebanon). Alexander writes, "The biblical and extrabiblical data, though sparse, would imply that Meshech and Tubal refer to geographical areas or countries in eastern modern Turkey, southwest of Russia and northwest of Iran."[41] Mark Hitchcock,[42] Leslie Allen,[43] and John Gammie[44] all agree with this identification of Meshech and Tubal.

Some Dispensational authors still believe that Meshech and Tubal should be identified with Moscow and Tobolsk—two major cities of Russia. However, Alexander writes, "There is no etymological, grammatical, historical, or literary data in support of such a position."[45]

Assessment: Meshech and Tubal can be identified with modern-day Turkey.

Persia

Scholars overwhelmingly agree that Persia later became the modern state of Iran. Hitchcock writes, "The ancient land of Persia became the modern nation of Iran in March 1935, and then the name was changed to the Islamic Republic of Iran in 1979."[46]

---

[40] Clyde E. Billington, Jr., "The Rosh People in History and Prophecy (Part Two)," 153.

[41] Ralph Alexander. *Ezekiel.* In F. E. Gaebelein (Ed.), *The Expositor's Bible Commentary: Isaiah, Jeremiah, Lamentations, Ezekiel.* Vol. 6. (Grand Rapids, MI: Zondervan Publishing House, 1986), 930.

[42] Mark Hitchcock, *The End: A Complete Overview of Bible Prophecy and the End of Days*, 298.

[43] Leslie Allen, *Ezekiel 20–48.* Vol. 29. (Dallas: Word, Incorporated, 1998), 204.

[44] John G Gammie and Paul Achtemeier, *Harper's Bible dictionary* (San Francisco: Harper & Row, 1985), 629.

[45] Ralph Alexander. *Ezekiel.* In F. E. Gaebelein (Ed.), *The Expositor's Bible Commentary: Isaiah, Jeremiah, Lamentations, Ezekiel.* Vol. 6. (Grand Rapids, MI: Zondervan Publishing House, 1986), 930.

[46] Mark Hitchcock, *The End: A Complete Overview of Bible Prophecy and the End of Days*, 298.

Assessment: Persia can be identified with modern-day Iran.

Cush

Alexander,[47] Block,[48] and Garland[49] identify Cush with Ethiopia and Nubia. Hitchcock writes, "Ancient Cush was called Kusu by the Assyrians and Babylonians, Kos or Kas by the Egyptians, and Nubia by the Greeks. Secular history locates Cush directly south of ancient Egypt, extending south past the modern city of Khartoum, which is the capital of modern Sudan. Thus, modern Sudan inhabits the ancient land of Cush."[50] Sudan is the largest African nation (26 million in population), and currently holds firm alliances with Iran (Persia).

Assessment: Cush can be identified with Sudan or its neighbor Ethiopia.

Put

Garland states that Put is "normally identified as Libya or some African country."[51] Hitchcock writes, "From the Babylonian Chronicles, tablets that recorded ancient Babylonian history, it appears that Put was the 'distant' land to the west of Egypt, which would be modern-day Libya and could possibly include nations farther west such as modern Algeria and Tunisia. The Septuagint renders the word Put as Libues."[52]

Assessment: Put can be identified with modern-day Libya, or possibly Algeria and Tunisia.

Gomer

Allen identifies Gomer with the ancient Cimmerians,[53] as does Alexander,[54] Block,[55] Yamauchi,[56] and Garland.[57] Homer located the Cimmerians with

---

[47] Ralph Alexander. *Ezekiel.* In F. E. Gaebelein (Ed.), *The Expositor's Bible Commentary: Isaiah, Jeremiah, Lamentations, Ezekiel.* Vol. 6. (Grand Rapids, MI: Zondervan Publishing House, 1986), 931.

[48] Daniel Block, *The Book of Ezekiel: 25-48,* 439.

[49] David E. Garland (et al.), *Jeremiah-Ezekiel* (Grand Rapids, MI: Zondervan, 2010), 855.

[50] Mark Hitchcock, *The End: A Complete Overview of Bible Prophecy and the End of Days,* 298.

[51] David E. Garland (et al.), *Jeremiah-Ezekiel* (Grand Rapids, MI: Zondervan, 2010), 855. See also Daniel Block, *The Book of Ezekiel: 25-48,* 439.

[52] Mark Hitchcock, *The End: A Complete Overview of Bible Prophecy and the End of Days,* 298.

[53] Leslie Allen, *Ezekiel 20–48,* 205.

the "Crimean peninsula on the north shore of the Black Sea."[58] Hitchcock writes, "Ancient history identifies biblical Gomer with the Akkadian Gimir-ra-a and the Armenian Gamir. Beginning in the eighth century BC, the Cimmerians occupied territory in what is now modern Turkey. Josephus noted that the Gomerites were identified with the Galatians who inhabited what today is central Turkey."[59]

Assessment: Gomer can be identified with modern-day Turkey.

Beth-togarmath

Beth means "house" in Hebrew. Alexander identifies Beth-togarmath as "possibly the ancient Til-garimmu southeast of the Black Sea."[60] Hitchcock writes, "Ancient Togarmah was also known as Til-garamu (Assyrian) or Tegarma (Hittite), and its territory is in modern Turkey, north of Israel. Again, Turkey is identified as part of this group of nations that attack Israel to challenge the group of ten."[61] Allen identifies Beth-togarmath as the people of Armenia—the neighbors of Turkey.[62]

Assessment: Beth-togarmath can be identified with the people of Armenia or Turkey.

Piecing together Ezekiel's prophecy

While not all of the nations mentioned in Ezekiel 38 can be identified precisely, some of these are fairly certain. If this reconstruction above is

---

[54] Ralph Alexander. *Ezekiel*. In F. E. Gaebelein (Ed.), *The Expositor's Bible Commentary: Isaiah, Jeremiah, Lamentations, Ezekiel*. Vol. 6. (Grand Rapids, MI: Zondervan Publishing House, 1986), 931.

[55] Daniel Block, *The Book of Ezekiel: 25-48*, 439.

[56] Yamauchi writes, "Biblical *Gomer* (Gen. 10:2-3; Ezek. 38:6) may be associated with the invading tribe from Russia known in nonbiblical sources as the Cimmerians." Edwin Yamauchi, *Foes from the Northern Frontier*, 49.

[57] David E. Garland (et al.), *Jeremiah-Ezekiel* (Grand Rapids, MI: Zondervan, 2010), 855.

[58] See Homer, *Odyssey*, 11.13-19. Cited in Edwin Yamauchi, *Foes from the Northern Frontier*, 49.

[59] Mark Hitchcock, *The End: A Complete Overview of Bible Prophecy and the End of Days*, 299.

[60] Ralph Alexander. *Ezekiel*. In F. E. Gaebelein (Ed.), *The Expositor's Bible Commentary: Isaiah, Jeremiah, Lamentations, Ezekiel*. Vol. 6. (Grand Rapids, MI: Zondervan Publishing House, 1986), 931.

[61] Mark Hitchcock, *The End: A Complete Overview of Bible Prophecy and the End of Days*, 299.

[62] Leslie Allen, *Ezekiel 20–48*, 205.

correct, then the nations of this gruesome battle could be illustrated in this way below:

Ezekiel does not give an exhaustive list of nations. He writes that there will be *"many* peoples with you" (Ezek. 38:6). Thus other unnamed nations are surely in view as well.

When will this battle take place?

Israel will be in a state of peace and security when this battle occurs (Ezek. 38:8, 11). Ezekiel predicts that multiple nations will all invade Israel including Russia, Iran, Sudan, and many others (Ezek. 38:16). God will supernaturally rescue the nation of Israel with an earthquake and fire from heaven, and the number of casualties will be so massive that it will take seven months to bury the bodies (Ezek. 39:11-12). Surely we would've noticed if this battle had already occurred! Furthermore, since Ezekiel wrote this, Israel has never felt the security to go defenseless in her own land as Ezekiel 38:11 suggests. Thus instead of looking into the past for a fulfillment, Ezekiel places this event "after many days" (Ezek. 38:8) and "in the last days" (Ezek. 38:16), expressions which refer to the end of history. Yet it isn't exactly certain *when* Armageddon will occur—even if we are sure it will happen sometime in the future. Several options have been given:[63]

---

[63] Rhodes shows *seven* different views on when event will occur. See Chapter Seven, "Can We Know When the Ezekiel Invasion Will Occur?" Ron Rhodes, *The 8 Great Debates of Bible Prophecy* (Eugene, OR: Harvest House, 2014), 69-83.

Before the rescue of the Church. If God destroys this invasion of Israel before the rescue of the Church, then this would explain how the Jewish people could rebuild their Temple over the Dome of Rock. It would also explain why it takes seven years to burn the weapons after the battle (Ezek. 39:9).

After the rescue of the Church but before the Tribulation. This view explains how Israel could rebuild the Temple on the Dome of the Rock, as well as the destruction of the weapons for seven years (Ezek. 39:9). This view would also militarily castrate Russia and the Arabs, lifting Europe to the forefront of global politics.

Halfway through the Tribulation. This would align the events of the Tribulation with the northern aggressor of Daniel 11:40. It would also make sense of Israel living securely in the false peace of the Antichrist (Ezek. 38:8; cf. Dan. 9:27). This view has difficulty explaining why the weapons would be burned for seven years (Ezek. 39:9).

At the end of the Millennium. This would make sense of John's statement that Gog and Magog will invade Israel at the end of the Millennium (Rev. 20:7-9). Yet it doesn't fit with the chronology of Ezekiel's prophecy: Ezekiel pictures this battle *after* the regathering of Israel (Ezek. 37) but *before* the Temple sacrifices in the Millennium (Ezek. 40-48). Of course, John states that there will be "no temple" in the New Heaven and Earth (Rev. 21:22). Moreover, it seems strange to have the Jewish people spending seven months burying all of the dead bodies (Ezek. 39:12) and seven years burning all of the weapons (Ezek. 39:9), if Christ will immediately return to raise them for judgment.

Ezekiel states that Gog will only come from "the remote parts *of the north*" (Ezek. 38:15; 39:2), while John writes that Gog and Magog will come from "the four corners of the earth" (Rev. 20:8). Thus John and Ezekiel may be seeing two separate events—not one. Rhodes writes, "The apostle John may have been using the terms Gog and Magog as a shorthand metaphor, just as we do today. For example, the name Wall Street is now a metaphor for the stock market. Likewise, in New Testament times, terms like Corinthian and Nazarene became metaphors for people with less-than-desirable qualities. When John used the terms Gog and Magog in Revelation 20:7-10, his readers no doubt immediately drew the right connection and understood that this invasion at the end of the millennium would be similar to what Ezekiel described—a confederation of nations will attack Israel but will not succeed."[64]

Why do they use *ancient* weapons, if this is a *future* battle?

Ezekiel foresees that the battle of Armageddon will be fought with "horses" (Ezek. 38:4, 15), "swords" (Ezek. 38:4, 21; 39:23), "bows and arrows" (Ezek. 39:9, 3), and "war clubs and spears" (Ezek. 39:9). If this battle occurs in the future, why would Ezekiel see such ancient weapons and warfare?

Preterists argue that the battle of Ezekiel 38-39 must have already occurred (perhaps in Esther 9),[65] and the presence of ancient weapons only confirms that this is a past event—not a future one. Thus DeMar argues, "The weapons of choice are swords, bows and arrows, and spears, indicators of an ancient battle in a pre-industrial age. It is amazing to read what some people will do to make this obvious ancient battle fit into a modern context."[66]

Some futurists argue it's possible that humanity could revert to ancient weapons at this time. After the world sees such tragic destruction and despair, we may not have access to the type of weapons we have today. After all, as Albert Einstein once said, "I know not with what weapons World War III will be fought, but World War IV will be fought with sticks

---

[64] Ron Rhodes, *The 8 Great Debates of Bible Prophecy* (Eugene, OR: Harvest House, 2014), 81.

[65] In addition to ignoring all textual cues that this event occurs at the end of history, several other problems confront the Preterist interpretation: First, Ezekiel predicts an invasion of Israel (38:16), while Esther records invasion throughout cities in the Persian Empire outside of Israel (9:2). Second, Ezekiel predicts supernatural earthquakes and fire from heaven (38:19-22), while Esther records normal warfare (9:3-5). Third, Ezekiel predicts multiple nations as far as Libya (38:5), while Esther records the Persian Empire in more remote locations (8:9). Fourth, Esther never cites Ezekiel's fulfillment, and no Jewish commentaries associate this with a fulfillment of Ezekiel 38-39. Hitchcock argues, "One important question we might ask at this point is, if Ezekiel 38-39 was fulfilled in the events of Esther 9, why did this escape the notice of everyone in Esther's day? Why is there no mention in Esther of this great fulfillment of Ezekiel's prophecy? And why are there no Jewish scholars in that day or subsequently who recognized this fulfillment? The answer seems quite clear." See footnote. Mark Hitchcock, *The End: A Complete Overview of Bible Prophecy and the End of Days*, 302.

[66] Gary DeMar, *Last Days Madness*, 367.

and stones."[67] Because this battle will be fought over mountainous terrain, perhaps these armies would prefer horses to tanks.

Another option is that Ezekiel could be using ancient imagery for a future event. Even today, a modern general might use the expression, "Send in the *cavalry*" or "They're going to die by the *sword*." Similarly, Hebrew words were used more for their *function*, rather than their *definition*. Chuck Missler states that these words could be a case of synecdoche, whereby the specific term can be used in the general sense or vice-versa. A snake is literally a "hisser" and a horse is literally a "leaper."[68] Thus these words may have more of a semantic range that might include modernized weapons. Other Dispensationalists have criticized this view.[69]

A third option rests in the possibility that Ezekiel is only mentioning some of the weapons, but not all of them. Ezekiel never states that they will *only* use primitive weapons; modernized weapons might be in view which he simply fails to mention. In Ezekiel 38:9, the prophet uses the language of simile to describe this army: "You will come *like a storm*; you will be *like a cloud covering the land*, you and all your troops, and many peoples with you." Naturally, "storms" and "clouds" come from up above, so perhaps aerial warfare could be in view.

In the end, this remains a difficulty. Walvoord rightly concludes, "The final answer to explain the weapons is unknown."[70]

Conclusion

Many points of controversy surround the battle (or battles) of Armageddon. However, while the details are difficult to discern, the central message remains clear: A massive world war awaits the Earth.

Discussion questions

1. Which portions of the battle of Armageddon are the clearest to you? Which are the most difficult to discern?

---

[67] Albert Einstein in an interview with Alfred Werner. *Liberal Judaism* 16 (April-May, 1949), 12. Cited in Albert Einstein and Alice Calaprice, *The New Quotable Einstein* (Princeton, NJ: Princeton UP, 2005), 173.
[68] Chuck Missler, *The Magog Invasion* (Palos Verdas, CA: Western Front, 1995), 174.
[69] See Ice, Thomas. "Ezekiel 38-39: Part VIII."
[70] John Walvoord, *Every Prophecy in the Bible: Clear Expectations for Uncertain Times* (Colorado Springs, CO: David C. Cook Publications, 2011), 188.

2. How much weight should we place on identifying the nations of Ezekiel 38? Are we over-interpreting the text when trying to identify these nations? How important is it to identify these nations?

3. How realistic do you find the Bible's prediction of this future world war? Is this plausible or unrealistic?

Chapter 16. Tribulation (Part III): The Antichrist

If you enjoy campy horror flicks, you've probably heard of the Antichrist, and if you've ever argued about presidential candidates, I'm sure you've heard (or used!) the title before. But few people are aware of how the Bible depicts this epic figure. Hitchcock writes, "More than one hundred passages of Scripture describe the origin, nationality, character, career, conquest, and doom of the final world ruler known as the Antichrist. Clearly God wants His people to know something about the coming prince of darkness."[1] What can we know about this future figure?

He will be a single individual

Some interpreters argue that the Antichrist is merely a symbol for the evil of human empires in rebellion against God. They note that John describes him as the combination of Daniel's images for the world empires (Dan. 7:5-6). Yet John uses imagery of the nations to describe the Antichrist from Daniel 7 (e.g. the leopard, lion, bear) due to the fact that the Antichrist represents and rules the nations. Daniel, Jesus, and the apostles depict the Antichrist as a singular person—not as a symbol for world empires.

Daniel uses the term "little horn" (a single person) in Daniel 7:8 and 7:25 ("this horn possessed... a mouth uttering great boasts... He will speak out against the Most High and wear down the saints of the Highest One... they will be given into his hand for a time, times, and half a time"). *Jesus* uses the masculine singular participle in Mark 13:14, saying that the Antichrist will be "*standing* where it should not be."[2] And finally, *Paul* expected a singular person in 2 Thessalonians 2:4 ("the *man* of lawlessness"), as did John, when he distinguished *the* Antichrist from "*many* antichrists" (1 Jn. 2:18).

---

[1] Mark Hitchcock, *The End: A Complete Overview of Bible Prophecy and the End of Days*, 253.

[2] Osborne writes, "Perhaps the first NT reference to a coming Antichrist is found in the Olivet discourse, where Jesus speaks of the abomination of desolation as a person (Mark 13:14), using the masculine participle (*hestēkota*, standing) in contrast to the neuter (*bdelygma*, abomination) that it modifies." Grant Osborne. *Revelation*, 493.

He will arise from the revived Roman Empire

Daniel predicts that a person, whom he calls the Little Horn, will arise from the Roman Empire (the "fourth beast"), and he will reign over it (Dan. 7:7-8, 11). At the same time, Daniel distinguishes the Little Horn from the ten kings. According to Daniel, the Little Horn arises after the ten kings come into power, and he deposes three of them. This person comes from the fourth beast (Rome). He also "boasts" (Dan. 7:8) against God himself (Dan. 7:25), attacking and persecuting God's people (Dan. 7:21).

John uses this imagery of the "beast" (Rev. 13:1-2; 17:3), who persecutes God's people (Rev. 13:7) and whom Christ destroys at his Second Coming (Rev. 19:19-20; cf. 2 Thess. 2:8). He also mentions that the "ten horns" are "ten kings" (Rev. 17:12), and he records that this figure will reign for 3.5 years (Rev. 13:5). When we compare these two figures side by side, we see that Daniel's Little Horn is one and the same as John's prediction of the Beast.

Comparison of the Little Horn and the Beast	
Daniel 7	**Revelation 13 & 17**
The Little Horn is called a "beast" (Dan. 7:7, 11, 19, 23).	The figure in Revelation is called the "beast" (Rev. 13:1-2; Rev. 17:3).
The Little Horn persecutes the saints (Dan. 7:25).	The beast persecutes the saints (Rev. 13:7).
The Little Horn is destroyed by the return of Christ (Dan. 7:26-27).	The beast is destroyed by the return of Christ (2 Thess. 2:8; Rev. 19:19-20).
(Dan. 7:8) "Another horn, a little one, came up among them [the 10 horns]" (c.f. v.20, 24).	(Rev. 17:12) "The ten horns you saw are ten kings who have not yet received a kingdom, but who for one hour will receive authority as kings along with the beast." (c.f. Rev. 13:1; 17:3, 16).
(Dan. 7:25) "[Authority] will be given into his hand for a time, times, and half a time."	(Rev. 12:6, 14) "There she would be nourished for one thousand two hundred and sixty days… where she was nourished for a time and times and half a time." (Rev. 13:5) "The beast was given… to exercise his authority for forty-two months."

(Dan. 7:21) "I kept looking, and that horn was waging war with the saints and overpowering them."	(Rev. 13:7) "He was given power to make war against the saints and to conquer them."
(Dan. 7:8) "This horn possessed eyes like the eyes of a man and a mouth uttering great boasts."	(Rev. 13:5) "There was given to him a mouth speaking arrogant words and blasphemies."

Interestingly, the book of Revelation never calls this figure the Antichrist. We get the term "Antichrist" from John's first letter, where he writes that the "antichrist is coming" (1 Jn. 2:18). Revelation uses the term "the beast" to describe this man (Rev. 19:19-20), and Paul refers to this figure as the "man of lawlessness" and the "son of destruction" (2 Thess. 2:3). All of these names describe the same horrific person who will be the first and last ruler of the world before Jesus returns.

He will be a Gentile

John states that the Antichrist will come "out of the *sea*" (Rev. 13:1), a symbol used for the nations of the world. Daniel states that he will show "no regard for the gods of his fathers or for the desire of women, nor will he show regard for any other god; for he will magnify himself above them all" (Dan. 11:37). This means that he will not hold to biblical theism or even paganism. Instead, he will deify himself. Remember, Daniel states that Antiochus Epiphanes IV was a type (or foreshadowing) of the Antichrist, and he was a Gentile—not a Jew.

He will be a powerful speaker

Daniel tells us that this figure will have "a mouth uttering great boasts" (Dan. 7:8; cf. 7:11). Later Daniel explains that he "will speak monstrous things against the God of gods" (Dan. 11:36). John mirrors this imagery when he writes, "There was given to him a mouth speaking arrogant words and blasphemies" (Rev. 13:5). Just as charismatic figures have led the world astray with their words in the past (e.g. Adolf Hitler), this future figure will do the same.

He will bring world peace

All of us yearn for peace on Earth, and the Tribulation will begin with what we've always wanted. But just as humanity finally believes that they have made peace apart from God, the world will collapse into utter anarchy. Paul writes, "You yourselves know full well that the day of the Lord will come just like a thief in the night. [3] While they are saying, 'Peace and safety!' *then destruction will come upon them suddenly like labor pains upon a woman with child, and they will not escape*" (1 Thess. 5:2-3).

The conflict in the Middle East is currently a tinder box, waiting to ignite. Modern people wonder if peace will ever occur in the Israeli-Palestinian conflict. This charismatic figure will be so persuasive and powerful that he will return the Temple to the Jewish people in Israel, causing the people to enter into a contract with him. Daniel predicts, "He will make a firm covenant with the many for one week [seven years]" (Dan. 9:27 NIV). Halfway through this period of "peace," this figure will betray the Jewish people. Daniel writes, "In the middle of the 'seven' he will put an end to sacrifice and offering. And on a wing of the temple he will set up an abomination that causes desolation, until the end that is decreed is poured out on him" (Dan. 9:27 NIV).

He will claim to be God incarnate

Daniel predicted that this figure will "magnify himself above" pagan gods, deifying himself (Dan. 11:37). Paul writes that this man "will oppose and will exalt himself over everything that is called God or is worshiped, so that he sets himself up in God's temple, proclaiming himself to be God" (2 Thess. 2:4). Revelation states that this man will accept worldwide worship (Rev. 13:8).

Amillennialists often (though not always) believe in a future Antichrist, but they deny that he will be in a literal temple. Instead, they argue that the "temple" really refers to the Church.[3] Riddlebarger writes, "When Paul referred to the man of sin 'sitting' in the temple, he was referring to the church on earth when the apostasy occurs and when the man of sin is revealed... The five other times Paul used the word *temple* (*naos*), it clearly referred to believers (the church), who constitute the temple of God."[4] Hoekema states, "The expression is probably best understood as an apocalyptic description of the usurpation of the honor and worship which is properly rendered only to God."[5]

No matter the interpretation, we see the inconsistency of their view: They take the return of Christ, the apostasy, and the Antichrist to be *literal*, but

---

[3] See C. Samuel Storms, *Kingdom Come*, 532-534.
[4] Kim Riddlebarger, *A Case for Amillennialism*, 151.
[5] Anthony Hoekema, *The Bible and the Future*, 160.

interpret the future Temple to be *symbolic*. Moreover, in the five other instances where Paul uses the term "temple" (*naos*) to describe the Church (1 Cor. 3:16, 17; 6:19; 2 Cor. 6:16; Eph. 2:21), every time he makes it clear from the context that believers are the Temple. In this passage, however, Paul makes no such clarification.

He will be aided by the False Prophet

Satan regularly uses false teachers to distort the person, work, and message of Christ. If we include Jesus' letters to the Seven Churches in Revelation 2 and 3, the NT mentions false teaching in 17 out of 22 letters (Rom. 16:17-18; 1 Cor. 15:12; 2 Cor. 2:17; 11:13-15; Gal. 1:6-9; 5:10-12; Phil. 3:2; Col. 2:16-23; 2 Thess. 2:1-2; 1 Tim. 1:3ff.; 4:1-5; 6:3-5; 2 Tim. 3:1-8; Titus 1:10-16; 3:9-11; Heb. 13:9; 2 Pet. 2:1-22; 1 Jn. 2:18-26; 4:1-6; 2 Jn. 1:7-9; 3 Jn. 1:9-10; Jude 1:4ff.; Rev. 2:2, 15, 20). Jesus himself taught, "Beware of the false prophets, who come to you in sheep's clothing, but inwardly are ravenous wolves" (Mt. 7:15).

While Jesus claimed that many false teachers would arise at the end of human history (Mt. 24:24), one will be unique. Revelation refers to *the* False Prophet three times (Rev. 16:13; 19:20; 20:10), calling him the second beast (Rev. 13:11-18). Just like Joseph Goebbels served as the Minister of Propaganda for Hitler's Nazi regime, the False Prophet will support the Antichrist's claims to authority and power through the vehicle of some sort of false religion. This figure will recreate the miracles of the Exodus (Rev. 13:13-14), just as the false prophets mimicked Moses' miracles in Egypt (Ex. 7:11-13, 22; 8:7). The False Prophet will create an idol of the Antichrist in the Temple (Rev. 13:14-15; Mt. 24:15).

What does the 666 mean? (Rev. 13:18)

> Here is wisdom. Let him who has understanding calculate the number of the beast, for the number is that of a man; and his number is six hundred and sixty-six. (Rev. 13:18)

Here we come to the ten-million-dollar question that has boggled biblical readers for centuries: *What does the number 666 mean?* Prophecy fanatics have offered various interpretations of this passage,[6] much to the embarrassment of both themselves and Christ. Ironically, John writes that we need

---

[6] Hitchcock writes, "The day after Barack Obama was elected president, the Pick 3 number in the Illinois lottery was 666, leading some to irresponsibly view this as a harbinger that he's the Antichrist." Mark Hitchcock, *The End: A Complete Overview of Bible Prophecy and the End of Days*, 338.

"wisdom" and "understanding" to interpret this passage—two virtues these interpreters have ironically lacked! Many interpretations have been offered:

The Unholy Trinity. Riddlebarger argues that the "666" represents "the beast, who along with the dragon (Satan) and the second beast (or false prophet) mimics the Holy Trinity but is condemned to fall short of completeness. The beast can never rise above humanity to attain the deity it so desires."[7]

Symbolic for fallen humanity. Those who hold this view claim that this "number is that of *man*," that is, humanity in general. Since the Greek word for "man" (*anthropon*) lacks the article, it may only refer to humanity in general. Since "seven" is symbolic of God's perfected creation (Gen. 1-2), these commentators hold that "666" falls one step short of humans being 777 or "perfect." Leon Morris,[8] David Aune,[9] G.K. Beale,[10] and George Ladd[11] all hold to this view.

Symbolic for falling short of Jesus Christ. The *Sibylline Oracles* (1.324-329) calculate Jesus' name as "888." Under this view, the number "666" falls one short of the perfect number for humans, which is "777."

Emperor Nero. Preterists interpret the "666" to refer to Emperor Nero in the first century. Hanegraaff goes so far as to say that we "can be *absolutely certain* that 666 is the number of Nero's name and that Nero is the beast who ravaged the bride of Christ."[12] Since Hebrew, Latin, and Greek letters have numeric equivalents (called *gematria*), Hanegraaff argues that "Kaisar Neron" (Caesar Nero in Hebrew) adds up to the number 666:

---

[7] Kim Riddlebarger, *A Case for Amillennialism*, 153.

[8] Leon Morris, *Revelation: An Introduction and Commentary* (Downers Grove, IL: InterVarsity Press, 1987), 168.

[9] David E. Aune, *Revelation 6–16* (Dallas: Word, Incorporated, 1998), 769.

[10] G.K. Beale, *The Book of Revelation* (Grand Rapids, MI. William B. Eerdmans Publishing Company, 1999), 722-724.

[11] Ladd holds very loosely to this view, but isn't certain of it. See George Ladd, *A Commentary on the Revelation of John* (Grand Rapids, MI: William B. Eerdman's Publishing Company, 1972), 187.

[12] Hank Hanegraaff, *The Bible Answer Book: Volume 2* (Nashville, TN: Thomas Nelson, 2006), #78 "What is the Meaning of 666?"

| Does 666 represent Nero? ||
Letter	Numeric Equivalent
K	100
S	60
R	200
N	50
R	200
O	6
N	50
Total?	**666**

Yet it's strange that Hanegraaff transliterates Nero's name into Hebrew before adding up the numbers. Morris writes, "No one has shown why a Hebrew name with an unusual spelling should be employed in a Greek writing."[13] Why couldn't we just add up the numerical value in *Greek?* If John wanted us to change Nero's name into Hebrew, he would've specified this, as he did for other names in Revelation (Rev. 9:11; 16:16). Moreover, it isn't clear that we should transliterate Nero's name in this way. Osborne writes, "The major problem is that the primary spelling of 'Caesar' in Hebrew is קיסר, and the added *yodh* would make the tally 676."[14]

Finally, if this interpretation was so obvious, why wasn't it discovered by the early Christian teachers? Osborne writes, "The greatest problem of linking 666 with 'Nero Caesar' is the absence of such an interpretation in the church fathers."[15] This makes us wonder if we're really *discovering* a meaning, or if we're *creating* one. Dr. George Salmon aptly criticizes this approach:

> First, if the proper name by itself will not yield it, add a title; secondly, if the sum cannot be found in Greek, try Hebrew, or even Latin; thirdly, do not be too particular about the spelling... We cannot infer much from the fact that a key fits the lock if it is a lock in which almost any key will turn.[16]

Some Preterists argue that John encoded his message about Nero being the Antichrist, because he wanted to avoid persecution. However, other

---

[13] Leon Morris, *Revelation: An Introduction and Commentary,* 168.
[14] Grant Osborne. *Revelation,* 520.
[15] Grant Osborne. *Revelation,* 521.
[16] George Salmon, *A Historical Introduction to the Study of the Books of the NT,* 230-231. Cited in G.K. Beale, *The Book of Revelation* (Grand Rapids, MI. William B. Eerdmans Publishing Company, 1999), 721.

Preterists like David Chilton believe that this is "obviously false," because John would already be persecuted for claiming Jesus was Lord over the kings of the Earth in chapter 1.[17] If John was already writing a subversive letter, why not just go the whole way and implicate Nero as the Beast?

So, what does the 666 mean? *We don't know!* Since the "man of lawlessness" will not be revealed until after the Rescue of the Church (2 Thess. 2:2-3), we should not try to discover who this person is. Instead of wasting time (and credibility) in discovering the meaning of the 666, we should trust that later generations will understand its meaning, as history comes to a close.

Will the Antichrist be fatally wounded? (Rev. 13:3)

> I saw one of his heads as if it had been slain, and his fatal wound was healed. And the whole earth was amazed and followed after the beast. (Rev. 13:3)

Historically, prophecy fanatics have identified this fatal wound with Mussolini, Hitler, Stalin, and even JFK![18] These wild speculations should be avoided. Instead, let's consider some of the more common interpretations:

Preterists interpret this fatal wound with the "Nero redivivus" view (Latin for "Nero who came to life again"). Because of his failure to properly run the Roman Empire (due to his insanity), the Roman senate censured Nero on June 8, AD 68. Immediately after this, Nero committed suicide by thrusting a dagger into his own throat. Later, rumors circulated that Nero had returned to life after his suicide, and this became a popular legend in the 80s AD.[19] Preterists argue that this is reminiscent of the beast having a "fatal wound [that] was healed" (Rev. 13:3) having "the wound of the sword" but "[coming] to life" (Rev. 13:14).

However, this myth doesn't fit with the language of Revelation 13:3, which states that the wound was to the *head*—not the *throat*. Moreover, if we hold to this view, then we would need to believe that John actually believed these myths and legends which are highly questionable. Like the rest of Preterism, this interpretation wasn't held by those Christians nearest to Nero's death.

---

[17] David Chilton, *The Days of Vengeance: An Exposition of the Book of Revelation* (Ft. Worth, TX: Dominion, 1987), 35.
[18] Walvoord writes, "Among the more common suggestions are Nero, Judas Iscariot, and in modern times such personages as Mussolini, Hitler, and Stalin. The multiplicity of suggestions seems to be evidence in itself that these explanations are not the meaning of the passage." John Walvoord, *The Revelation of Jesus Christ*, 199.
[19] Grant Osborne. *Revelation*, 496.

Indeed, none of the early Christians entertained this view until it was "first suggested by Victorinus and made explicit by Augustine."[20] Christian commentators—like Minear—argue that this view is simply non-historical and doesn't fit with the wound of Revelation 13:3.[21]

This perspective also doesn't fit with Paul's description of Christ slaying the Antichrist. Paul writes, "That lawless one will be revealed whom the Lord will slay with the breath of His mouth and bring to an end by the appearance of His coming" (2 Thess. 2:8). If Nero is the Antichrist, then in what sense did Jesus slay him at his coming—especially since Nero killed himself? Remember, Preterist interpreters believe that Jesus' coming occurred in AD 70, when the Roman Empire destroyed the Jewish Temple. However, this would have been two years *after* Nero committed suicide.

Some Dispensationalists argue that the "fatal wound" refers to the death and resurrection of the Antichrist.[22] They note that the language of being "slain" (*esphagmenon*) in Revelation 13:3 is identical with Christ being "slain" at the Cross (Rev. 5:6). Moreover, the language of being raised to "life" (*ezesen*) in Revelation 13:14, also describes Jesus' resurrection earlier in the book (Rev. 2:8).

Still other interpreters (like myself) note that we have already interpreted the "heads" to refer to nations—not individuals. John equates the "seven heads" with the "seven mountains" and "seven kings" (Rev. 17:9-10). Thus this would refer to the "resurrection" of the Roman Empire at the end of history. Walvoord argues,

> The wounding of one of the heads seems instead to be a reference to the fact that the Roman Empire as such seemingly died and is now going to be revived. It is significant that one of the heads is wounded to death but that the beast itself is not said to be dead. It is questionable whether Satan has the power to restore to life one who has died, even though his power is great. Far more probable is the explanation that this is the revived Roman Empire in view.[23]

---

[20] Robert L. Thomas, *Revelation 8-22: An Exegetical Commentary* (Chicago: Moody, 1995), 158.

[21] See Paul S. Minear, *I Saw a New Earth: An Introduction to the Visions of the Apocalypse* (Washington: Corpus, 1968), 228-60.

[22] Robert L. Thomas, *Revelation 8-22: An Exegetical Commentary* (Chicago: Moody, 1995), 158-159.

[23] John Walvoord, *The Revelation of Jesus Christ* (Chicago, IL: JFW Publishing Trust, 1966), 199.

The beast is both personal and the empire itself; so also is the head. The revival of the future empire is considered a miracle and a demonstration of the power of Satan.[24]

Therefore, this "wound" (*plege*) is not a *gunshot* or a *stab wound*—though the word can certainly carry this meaning. Instead, the word "everywhere in Revelation means 'plague,' in fact, a divinely inflicted judgment (9:18, 20; 11:6; 15:1ff; 16:9, 21; 18:4, 8; 21:9; 22:18)."[25] So this would describe the judgment and resurrection of the Roman Empire.

He could exist in any generation

No one knows when Jesus will return—not even Satan (Mt. 24:36). Therefore, Satan might have a candidate for the Antichrist in every age. Consequently, this shouldn't lead Christians to search for this figure. As Hitchcock writes, "Since the identity of the Antichrist cannot be known until after the Rapture, no one today should spend time trying to figure out who he is or come up with possible candidates. All such attempts are speculative and futile. I like to tell people, 'If you ever do figure out who the Antichrist is, I've got bad news: you've been left behind.'"[26]

Discussion questions

1. Many people have heard of the "Antichrist" from popular culture. How did your pre-understanding about the Antichrist differ from the Bible's teaching on this person? In other words, in what ways do popular teachings on the Antichrist differ from the Bible's descriptions?

2. Why do you think the Bible offers more than 100 passages to describe the Antichrist? How important do you think it is to understand this component of biblical prophecy?

[24] John Walvoord, *The Revelation of Jesus Christ*, 200.

[25] Alan Johnson, *Revelation*, 526.

[26] Mark Hitchcock, *The End: A Complete Overview of Bible Prophecy and the End of Days*, 258.

Chapter 17. Tribulation (Part IV): Is it Plausible?

Sensationalists take a "newspaper approach" to biblical prophecy, whereby every event in the news corresponds to biblical prophecy. Surely this is unwarranted. As Hitchcock observes, "The problem is that when everything becomes a sign, then nothing is a sign."[1] Instead of claiming *certainty* in regards to the fulfillment of biblical prophecy, it's better to merely show *plausibility*.

Are the events of the Tribulation plausible in our modern world?

Ecological catastrophes (Mt. 24:7-8; 1 Thess. 5:3; Rom. 8:22)

The Bible foresees that ecological disasters will increase as history reaches an end. Jesus refers to these events as "birth pangs" (Mt. 24:8). Likewise Paul writes, "The whole creation groans and suffers the pains of childbirth together until now" (Rom. 8:22; cf. 1 Thess. 5:3). Just as a woman's pain increases in duration and intensity during labor, many calamities will increase as the end of history approaches.

According to a recent Yale study, "Since 1970 there have been more than 9,800 natural disasters worldwide, killing more than 3.7 million people, affecting more than 5.8 billion people, and causing more than $1.7 trillion in estimated damages, *and the numbers are steadily increasing*."[2] This study argues that there has been a fivefold increase in natural disasters since 1970. According to the International Disaster Database, natural disasters have been causing more and more costs in damages over the last 30 to 40 years.[3]

Experts in the field of climate studies do not offer optimistic predictions about the next four decades either. Jorgen Randers (a policy analyst and President Emeritus of the Norwegian School of Management) explains, "The negative impacts will be significant—but not disastrous, at least not before 2052. There will be more droughts, floods, extreme weather, and

---

[1] Mark Hitchcock, *The End: A Complete Overview of Bible Prophecy and the End of Days*, 107.
[2] Emphasis mine. Derek Kellenberg and A. Mushfiq Mobarak. "The Economics of Natural Disasters Annual Review of Resource Economics." Vol. 3: 298. (October 2011)
[3] http://www.emdat.be/disaster-trends.

insect infestations."[4] Then, as a result of increased global temperature, he writes, "Humanity will experience an increasing number of bothersome climate effects over the decades to come. These will be extreme weather events like untypical floods, recurring droughts, landslides in new places, and uncommon trajectories for tornadoes, hurricanes, and cyclones... Each event will lead to public outrage and create fear for the future."[5]

Is this ecological evidence incontrovertible?

Other experts retort that there are merely more people today—not more disasters.[6] Thus when an earthquake or tsunami strikes, it affects more people and has a worse effect than in previous years. Others argue that our *documentation* of global catastrophes has increased—not the events themselves. These observations carry weight. However, the data still correlates with biblical prophecy in an interesting way, and it is worth noting. Moreover, this evidence shows us that ecological disasters are not getting any better.

Overpopulation (Rev. 9:16)

The Bible predicts a unique state of overpopulation at the end of human history. John writes, "The number of the armies of the horsemen was *two hundred million*; I heard the number of them" (Rev. 9:16). When John wrote this, there were roughly this many total people on Earth.[7] To put this in perspective, the Roman army of the first century had only 125,000 soldiers.[8]

---

[4] Jorgen Randers, *2052: A Global Forecast for the Next Forty Years* (White River Junction, VT: Chelsea Green, 2012), 47.
[5] Jorgen Randers, *2052: A Global Forecast*, 120.
[6] Richard Heinberg, *The End of Growth: Adapting to Our New Economic Reality* (Gabriola Island, B.C.: New Society, 2011), 145.
[7] The *Encyclopedia Britannica* explains, "By the beginning of the Christian era, 8,000 years later, the human population approximated 300,000,000, and there was apparently little increase in the ensuing millennium up to the year ad 1000."
http://www.britannica.com/EBchecked/topic/470303/population/60687/Trends-in-world-population
[8] Mark Hitchcock, *The Amazing Claims of Bible Prophecy* (Eugene, OR: Harvest House, 2010), 143-144.

To further compare, during World War II, roughly 85 million soldiers served in all the armies on Earth combined.[9]

All of this is to say that the world has never seen an army of 200 million people—a figure too staggering to be realistic in any other time before our own. Yet today, an army of this size is feasible. According to the *Central Intelligence Agency Factbook*, China contains 385 million fit for military service (males between the ages of 16-49), adding 10 million people per year.[10]

The perils of exponential population growth

Due to the nature of exponential growth, the human population stayed relatively static for millennia, but in the last century, it has grown rapidly.

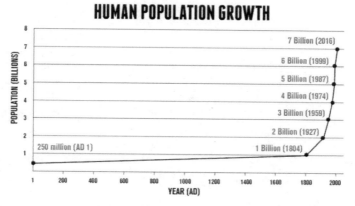

HUMAN POPULATION GROWTH

Humanity took thousands of years to reach one billion people. But it only took a little over a century to reach two billion—and then only 30 years to

---

[9] Several factors complicate the question of how many troops fought in World War II: (1) Are the numbers reliable? Some governments kept better records than others. The USSR often inflated their numbers. (2) Is the number a total number of soldiers from start to finish? Some give a number of standing soldiers at one time. Others give a complete number. (3) Who counts as a soldier? Some military police, medics, and administrative workers are often counted or not counted, affecting the number. (4) Should we count only major countries like USA, Russia, Germany, France, Britain, etc., or should minor countries count also? At most, a nation can mobilize 10% of their people for war. For instance, Russia mobilized this many because they were fighting for absolute survival, but historians believe that this is unsustainable. To put this in perspective, the United States mobilized 4% of their population for World War II. I'm indebted to my friend Joe McCallum for these insights.

[10] https://www.cia.gov/library/publications/the-world-factbook/geos/ch.html.

reach three billion and so forth. As you can see, while exponential growth starts slowly, it can quickly accelerate out of control. To illustrate, a Persian legend tells of a man who gave an expensive chessboard to the king. In return, he asked that the king would give him a grain of rice on the first square, two on the second, four on the third, and so on. By the tenth square, there were 512 grains, and by the fifteenth square there were 16,384. By the forty-first square? The board would've contained one trillion grains of rice.[11]

Exponential population growth points toward a dismal conclusion: *Humanity cannot continue growing like this without serious consequences.* Richard Heinberg writes, "No one seriously expects human population to continue growing for centuries into the future. But imagine if it did—at just 1.3 percent per year (its growth rate in the year 2000). By the year 2780 there would be 148 trillion humans on Earth—one person for each square meter of land on the planet's surface."[12] Clearly, Heinberg doesn't believe that this will happen. But that's the point: something will arise to counteract exponential growth of this kind. He writes, "Population 'blooms' (or periods of rapid growth) are nearly always followed by crashes and die-offs."[13] Something catastrophic will need to occur in order to curb overpopulation. As Randers writes, "[Current factors project the] global population to reach a maximum of some 8.1 billion people in the early 2040s. Thereafter the global population will decline at accelerating speed."[14]

According to experts in this field, overpopulation is only going to become more demanding in years to come. For instance, Colin Sullivan of *Scientific American* states, "Earth's human population is expected to coast upward to 9.6 billion by 2050 and 10.9 billion by 2100, up from 7.2 billion people alive today."[15]

Famine (Rev. 6:6-8)

As history reaches its conclusion, the Bible predicts that food shortages will be at an all-time high. John predicts that people will say, "Two pounds of wheat for a day's wages, and six pounds of barley for a day's wages, and do not damage the oil and the wine!'" (Rev. 6:6 NIV) In ancient times, this

---

[11] Jorgen Randers (et al.), *Limits to Growth*, 21.
[12] Richard Heinberg, *The End of Growth: Adapting to Our New Economic Reality* (Gabriola Island, B.C.: New Society, 2011), 14.
[13] Richard Heinberg, *The End of Growth*, 15.
[14] Jorgen Randers, *2052: A Global Forecast*, 62.
[15] Colin Sullivan, "Human Population Growth Creeps Back Up." *Scientific American* (June 14, 2013).

much wheat could only feed one man for one day.[16] Imagine paying a full day's wage for only two pounds of wheat! Beale notes that these prices were "eight to sixteen times the average prices in the Roman Empire at the time (cf. Cicero, *In Verrem*, 3.81)."[17] No doubt, food will be scarce if inflation occurs to this extent.[18]

Our modern age finds this vision all too familiar. Food shortages are part and parcel with the problem of overpopulation. Heinberg writes,

> Demand for food is slowly outstripping supply. Food producers' ability to meet growing needs is increasingly being strained by rising human populations, falling freshwater supplies, the rise of biofuels industries, expanding markets within industrializing nations for more resource-intensive meat and fish-based diets; dwindling fisheries; and climate instability. The result will almost inevitably be a worldwide food crisis sometime in the next two or three decades.[19]

Sir John Beddington (the chief science adviser to the U.K. government) told a symposium of scientists in 2011, "By 2030 we are going to need 50% more food, 40% more available fresh water, and something on the order of 50% more low-carbon energy... We need a radical redesign of global food systems."[20] Lester R. Brown of *Scientific American* notes that we use 70% of our freshwater for the purpose of irrigation.[21] If freshwater supplies evaporate (no pun intended), then so will food production.

---

[16] Herodotus, 7.187.

[17] G.K. Beale, *The Book of Revelation* (Grand Rapids, MI. William B. Eerdmans Publishing Company, 1999), 381.

[18] Most commentators would agree with this interpretation of John's vision. Osborne writes, "A 'denarius' was the average days' wage for a laborer. A quart of wheat was enough food for one person for a day, and three quarts of barley were barely enough for a small family (there were few small families except among the wealthy in the ancient world). Therefore a man's entire earnings were barely enough to feed himself, let alone his family, and all the other costs like home or incidentals could not be met. These were famine prices, about ten to twelve times the going rate according to ancient records (Mounce 1998: 144 cites Cicero, *Verr.* 3.81)." Grant Osborne. *Revelation*, 280.

[19] Richard Heinberg, *The End of Growth*, 136-137.

[20] Roehr, Bob. "Researchers at AAAS Annual Meeting Explore the Challenge of Feeding 9 Billion People." *American Association for the Advancement of Science* (AAAS). February 25, 2011. *http://news.aaas.org/2011_annual_meeting/0225post-17.shtml*

[21] Lester R. Brown, *Scientific American*. 300 (5). May, 2009. 50-57.

Disease (Rev. 6:8)

John sees a vision for the end of history, where many will die by "famine and plague, and by the wild beasts of the earth" (Rev. 6:8 NIV). Ancient people feared the invisible and unknown terror of disease, but is such a fear really realistic today? After all, we have modern medicine and vaccinations. While an ancient writer like John might've feared disease, is it really plausible today?

Catastrophic diseases abound in our modern age: Ebola, HIV, West Nile Virus, Lyme Disease, SARS, Bird Flu, Swine Flu—the list could continue. Joshua Lederberg (the Nobel Prize winner for medicine) writes, "The single biggest threat to man's continued dominance on the planet is a virus."[22] Matson and Pavlus of *Scientific American* write, "Humankind is more vulnerable than ever to a devastating, Black Death—style pandemic," placing the possibility at 50/50 in the next thirty years.[23]

Antibiotics like penicillin, methicillin, and vancomycin historically protected us from deadly and infectious strains of bacteria. However, antibiotic-resistant strains have developed almost as fast as the antibiotics themselves. Maryn McKenna of *Scientific American* writes,

> Many lethal infections that antibiotics have held at bay for decades might soon return with a vengeance... For almost every antibiotic developed to date, bacteria have evolved a resistance factor that protects them from the drug's attack. For almost every resistance factor, pharmaceutical companies have produced a tougher drug— until now. Over the decades the battle has gradually tilted to the side of the organisms, like a seesaw slowly shifting out of balance. Bacteria, after all, have evolution on their side. It takes them 20 minutes to produce a new generation. It takes a decade or more to research and develop a new drug.[24]

Fred Guterl (the executive editor of *Scientific American*) explains that influenza rapidly changes to spread in the human body:

> The virus, by recombining with other viruses, swapping genes, and taking on random mutations in its genetic code, keeps trying to find this jackpot combination—a bug that spreads easily and quickly, but strikes with deadly virulence. It's possible that the

---

[22] D. Crawford, *The Invisible Enemy: A Natural History of Viruses* (New York, NY: Oxford University Press, 2003), 2.
[23] John Matson and John Pavlus, *Scientific American*. 303 (3). September, 2010. 82.
[24] Mayrn McKenna, *Scientific American*. 304 (4). April, 2011. 46-53.

genetic slot machine hasn't yet produced its worst—and that the deadliest human influenza virus awaits us.[25]

Regarding the H1N1 virus of 1918, Guterl notes that this virus killed between 50 and 100 million people in two years.[26] Likewise, in the 14th century, the Black Death absolutely devastated Europe. He writes, "It killed about a third of the population—as much as 60 percent in some places. The population of China dropped 50 percent."[27] Imagine if such plagues appeared today in an age of world travel. Gibbs and Soares of *Scientific American* write, "[An influenza pandemic] will cause severe and sometimes fatal illness, resulting in a pestilence that could easily claim more lives in a single year than AIDS did in 25. Epidemiologists have warned that the next pandemic could sicken one in every three people on the planet, hospitalize many of those and kill tens to hundreds of millions."[28]

Drying up of the Euphrates River (Rev. 16:12)

The Euphrates River stretches 1,700 miles long. For years, it functioned as one of the largest rivers on Earth. Nevertheless, John predicted that this great river would dry up before the end of human history (Rev. 16:12). Incidentally, in 2009, *Time* magazine reported,

> Throughout the marshes, the reed gatherers, standing on land they once floated over, cry out to visitors in a passing boat. 'Maaku mai!' they shout, holding up their rusty sickles. 'There is no water!' The Euphrates is drying up. Strangled by the water policies of Iraq's neighbors, Turkey and Syria; a two-year drought; and years of misuse by Iraq and its farmers, the river is significantly smaller than it was just a few years ago. Some officials worry that it could soon be half of what it is now. *The shrinking of the Euphrates, a river so crucial to the birth of civilization that the Book of Revelation prophesied its drying up as a sign of the end times,* has decimated farms along its banks, has left fishermen impoverished and has depleted riverside towns as farmers flee to the cities looking for work... Along the river, rice and wheat fields have turned to baked dirt. Canals have dwindled to shallow streams, and fishing boats sit on dry land.

---

[25] Fred Guterl, *The Fate of the Species: Why the Human Race May Cause Its Own Extinction and How We Can Stop It* (New York: Bloomsbury, 2012), 16.
[26] Fred Guterl, *The Fate of the Species*, 19.
[27] Fred Guterl, *The Fate of the Species*, 25-26.
[28] W. Wayt Gibbs and Christine Soares. *Scientific American*. 293 (5). November, 2005. 44-54.

> Pumps meant to feed water treatment plants dangle pointlessly over brown puddles.[29]

It is interesting to note that the Euphrates is drying up, and that *Time* magazine would notice this in regards to biblical prophecy.

Global Government (Rev. 13:7-8)

> It was also given to him [the Beast] to make war with the saints and to overcome them, and *authority over every tribe and people and tongue and nation was given to him.* [8]All who dwell on the earth will worship him. (Rev. 13:7-8)

For years, this passage seemed absolutely impossible: *How could one man be in charge of the entire world?* Historically, world governments have been so set on independence that this seemed utterly incomprehensible.

Today, however, political scientists propose a different perspective. In his article "Why a World State is Inevitable," Alexander Wendt (professor of Political Science at The Ohio State University) writes,

> My guess is that a world state will emerge within 100 years. As long as a structure exists that can command and enforce a collective response to threats, a world state could be compatible with the existence of national armies... it would not even require a world 'government,' if by this we mean a unitary actor with one person at the top whose individual decisions are final... In short, as long as it has a common power, legitimacy, sovereignty, and subjectivity we should not prejudge the form a world state might take. The EU is already not far from meeting these requirements on a regional level. Were a 'completed' EU-like structure to be globalized it would be a world state.[30]

Global problems face the modern world: ecological catastrophes, over-population, food shortage, and disease. In order to solve these problems, we need *international* and *global* solutions. Experts are all too aware of these conclusions. Randers writes,

> All in all this will mean *bigger government in the decades ahead*: a larger role for the state, higher taxes, and a larger share of investments in the GDP.[31]

---

[29] Emphasis mine. Campbell Robertson, "Iraq Suffers as the Euphrates River Dwindles." *Time.* July 13, 2009.
[30] Emphasis mine. Alexander Wendt, "Why a World State is Inevitable." *European Journal of International Relations* (December, 2003), 491-542.
[31] Emphasis mine. Jorgen Randers, *2052: A Global Forecast,* 167.

The prime example is the climate challenge. It is a truly global problem; the temperature will rise everywhere, irrespective of who was the source of the emissions. And it is a truly long-term problem: the temperature will not react (that is, deviate from its current path) until thirty years after the initiation of the effort (as long as that effort is of realistic proportions). *Such truly global, truly long-term problems are hard to solve if one restricts oneself to using the powers of the 'free' market only.*[32]

Elsewhere, Meadows and Randers write, "There must be greater respect, caring, and sharing *across political boundaries.*"[33] In 2006, Joseph Stiglitz (Nobel Prize winning economist, former chief economist of the World Bank, and professor at Columbia) writes,

We need …international frameworks and international courts… As the countries of the world become more closely integrated, they become more interdependent. *Greater interdependence gives rise to a greater need for collective action to solve common problems…* As the world becomes more globalized, more integrated, there will be more and more areas in which there are opportunities for cooperative action, and in which *such collective action is not only desirable but necessary…* In effect, economic globalization has outpaced political globalization. We have a chaotic, uncoordinated system of global governance without global government… *There is a clear need for strong international institutions to deal with the challenges posed by economic globalization;* yet today confidence in existing institutions is weak.[34]

Warfare and genocide devastated Europe, leading to a hunger for world peace. Yet the League of Nations couldn't stop another world war, being too weak to enforce peace. After the Second World War, the United Nations (UN) replaced the League of Nations, exerting more authority. However, many still complain that the UN cannot adequately exert enough authority to solve world crises. Eventually, the need for protection will only lead to higher control in these world unions.

In the last several decades, we've witnessed the creation of the European Union (EU). In their book *The European Union* (2014), McCormick and Olsen explain some of the remarkable features of this unified confederacy:

---

[32] Emphasis mine. Jorgen Randers, *2052: A Global Forecast,* 248.
[33] Emphasis mine. Jorgen Randers (et al.), *Limits to Growth: The 30-Year Update* (White River Junction, VT: Chelsea Green, 2004), xv.
[34] Emphasis mine. Joseph E. Stiglitz, *Making Globalization Work* (New York: W.W. Norton &, 2006), 207; 280; 281; 21.

Frustrated and appalled by war and conflict, many Europeans argued over the centuries in favor of setting aside national differences in the collective interest.[35]

The European Union today is the largest economic bloc in the world, accounting for one-fourth of global gross domestic product (GDP) and about 20 percent of global trade... There is now virtually unlimited free movement of people, money, goods, and services among most of its member states.[36]

The EU today is a very different actor on the international stage than it was in its early years. It is a global powerhouse: the world's largest economy, its second largest exporter and importer, and—with a population of more than 500 million—significantly larger than the United States... When one speaks of 'Europe' today what is meant is the EU.[37]

When the EU inaugurated the "euro" in 2002 "for the first time since the Roman era, much of Europe had a single currency."[38] This seems to fit with the notion of a revived Roman Empire at the end of human history.

Other massive political entities have fallen into place as well. China used to be largely agrarian, closed, and "backward" by Western standards. Today, they command the role of being one of the strongest powers on Earth. Moreover, the presence of a strong Arab presence around Israel seems to fulfill the nations which will surround her at the end of human history (Ezek. 38-39). Isn't it interesting that when we turn on the nightly news, reporters focus on the political hornet's nest in Israel? For centuries, Israel didn't play into global concerns, but this has all changed in the last half-century.

Obviously, we do not know if these global powers fulfill the Bible's predictions. Yet at the very least, their presence shows the plausibility of these predictions.

---

[35] John McCormick and Jonathan Olsen, *The European Union: Politics and Policies*. 5th ed. (Boulder, CO: Westview, 2014), 3.

[36] John McCormick and Jonathan Olsen, *The European Union: Politics and Policies*. 5th ed., 6.

[37] John McCormick and Jonathan Olsen, *The European Union: Politics and Policies*. 5th ed., 77-78.

[38] John McCormick and Jonathan Olsen, *The European Union: Politics and Policies*. 5th ed., 82.

Why isn't the United States mentioned in biblical prophecy?

Many students of Scripture ask why the Bible makes no mention of the United States. Of course, the question itself might reveal an ethnocentric bias—that is, *most* nations aren't mentioned in biblical prophecy. Instead, prophecy usually refers to the many "nations" of the world in more of a general sense (Zech. 12:2-3; Hag. 2:6-7; Isa. 66:18-20). Nonetheless, since the United States commands such a strong political presence in the world, we might expect it to be mentioned. Students of prophecy often propose a number of speculative answers to this question:

The United States could be included with Europe. Many nationalities and ethnicities have influenced the United States in its short history. At the same time, we have been mostly influenced by European and Roman culture. In fact, historians see many parallels between the Roman Empire and the United States. Thus the United States might be under the prophetic umbrella of "Rome."

The United States might SLOWLY lose its stake as a political superpower. As we speak, we might argue that this is already happening. Other nations and superpowers have arisen as formidable forces in the 21st century, and this might continue on into the future. Other superpowers have faded into the dust of history—why not the United States? This isn't meant to predict doom and gloom, but rather to consider this as an entirely plausible reality.

The United States might CATASTROPHICALLY lose its stake as a political superpower. As terrorism rises or as nuclear war occurs, catastrophic events could cripple the United States. Moreover, if a pre-tribulational Rescue of the Church occurs, the United States could become a ghost of its former self. It's difficult to assess the number of true Christians in America, and surely many nominal Christians exist. Nonetheless, it's possible that a pre-tribulational Rescue of the Church could cripple the United States worse than in other nations.

Conclusion

For years, the Bible's predictions of the future might've seemed ridiculous. But today? As human history reaches its shocking conclusion, we discover that these predictions are clearer than ever before.

Discussion questions

1. Do you find the biblical prophecies about the future to be plausible, as this chapter argued? How do you think you might assess these biblical predictions if you were living one hundred or two hundred years ago?

2. Which of the areas of predictive prophecy in this chapter did you find to be the most plausible? Which do you find the least plausible?

3. What would happen if some of this evidence for the plausibility of predictive prophecy started to turn in the opposite direction? How would this affect your interpretation of biblical prophecy?

Chapter 18. Tribulation (Part V): Technological Advancement

The biblical authors wrote their books long before the technological revolution of the last century. In their day, armies fought with swords, spears, and stones. Communication occurred by horseback or messengers on foot. Yet they repeatedly foresaw technological advancements that wouldn't exist for millennia.

Universal control of money (Rev. 13:16-17)

[The beast] causes all, the small and the great, and the rich and the poor, and the free men and the slaves, to be given a mark on their right hand or on their forehead, [17]and he provides that no one will be able to buy or to sell, except the one who has the mark, either the name of the beast or the number of his name. (Rev. 13:16-17)

The Romans used the term "mark" (*charagma*) as "a term for the images or names of emperors on Roman coins, so it fittingly could apply to the beast's emblem put on people."[1] The Egyptian ruler Ptolemy Philopator I "branded Jews, who submitted to registration, with an ivy leaf in recognition of their Dionysian worship (cf. 3 Macc. 2:29)."[2] Nevertheless, the "mark of the beast" has not occurred yet in history. Ladd rightly points out, "We know of no ancient practice which provides adequate background to explain the mark of the beast in historical terms."[3]

Preterists claim that this mark refers to the religious authorities excluding Christians from buying or selling in the Temple without betraying Christ.[4] Yet this passage teaches that *the beast* will control the money of believers— not the *religious authorities*. The Romans never kept the Christians out of the

---

[1] Robert L. Thomas, *Revelation 8-22: An Exegetical Commentary* (Chicago: Moody, 1995), 181.
[2] Robert L. Thomas, *Revelation 8-22*, 181.
[3] George Ladd, *A Commentary on the Revelation of John*, 185.
[4] DeMar writes, "Revelation 13:16-17 is not describing the control of financial transactions but rather access to the temple controlled by the Jewish anti-Christian religious establishment. The key to interpreting the passage is the prohibition 'to buy or to sell' (13:17) if a worshipper does not have the mark of the beast." Gary DeMar, *Last Days Madness*, 249. DeMar also speculates that the "666" should be interpreted in light of Solomon's 666 talents of gold (1 Kin. 10:14), whereby Solomon violated the law and sold himself to foreign interests. DeMar, *Last Days Madness*, 261.

Temple. The Jewish authorities did. Moreover, the Romans never had a state-wide control of money like this.[5] Ladd writes, "The practice of branding was not a common one and is not known in connection with emperor worship."[6] Since this mark has not been fulfilled, we should expect a fulfillment in the future.

We currently don't know what the mark of the beast is, but whatever it is, it monitors and controls trade and commerce. How could anyone control buying and selling in the first century to this degree? Trade occurred on such a personal level that this would be impossible. But today? Technology of this kind not only *could* exist soon, but rather, it *does* exist now.

Radio-frequency identification (RFID) utilizes electromagnetic fields to transfer data—such as identification. The tag or "chip" is about the size of a grain of rice, and these RFID tags are currently used for animal tracking. This concept of "somatic surveillance" is already an escalating concern. Monahan and Wall write, "RFID implants function through the subcutaneous embedding of small RFID chips into the arms of individuals. These chips contain unique numerical identifiers, which can be scanned by automated readers, medical staff, or others."[7] The UFDA approved RFID chips for humans in 2004. Presently, two hospitals in the US actively use RFIDs with patients who consent and pay to be a part of the system, and as of June 2006 about 100 people had been 'chipped' for medical purposes.[8] Monahan and Wall write,

> RFID implants have already distinguished themselves as being multi-purpose and highly controversial. Aside from their uses in medical settings, in 2004 the Mexico Attorney General's Office implanted workers to regulate access to secure areas (Associated Press, 2006). Over 1,000 Mexican citizens have been chipped in efforts to facilitate finding children and others who might, at some point, be kidnapped... A US security company, CityWatcher.com, has also required the chipping of employees wishing special clearance to work on high-level, secure projects (Associated Press, 2006; Libbenga, 2006). A subsequent media firestorm over this

---

[5] Osborne writes, "As several point out, the Roman government persecuted but did not use economic sanctions against Christians, so this is probably built on local persecutions." Osborne, G. R. *Revelation*, Baker Exegetical Commentary on the New Testament, (Grand Rapids, MI: Baker Academic, 2000), 518.
[6] George Ladd, *A Commentary on the Revelation of John*, 185.
[7] Torin Monahan and Tyler Wall. "Somatic Surveillance: Corporeal Control Through Information Networks." *Surveillance & Society*. Special Issue on 'Surveillance and Criminal Justice' Part 1, 4(3): 164.
[8] Torin Monahan and Tyler Wall. "Somatic Surveillance," 165.

case sparked state legislation currently in Wisconsin, but being considered elsewhere, prohibiting the involuntary chipping of anyone (Songini, 2006). This of course does not directly address the coercion associated with companies demanding RFID implants as a necessary condition for work. CityWatcher.com, subsequently clarified its position, stipulating that no employees will be fired for not being implanted, but employees may not be able to work on the best—and presumably higher-paying—projects if they do not agree to be chipped. Finally, RFID implants have also gained notoriety for their use by the Baja Beach Club in Barcelona, where implanted patrons can carry their credit card information around in their arms, obviating the need for purses, wallets, or much clothing (McHugh, 2004). If customers desire a drink, all they need to do is have their arms scanned for payment. In some senses, the human embodiment of capitalism that theorists have traditionally spoken about metaphorically has now become quite literal.[9]

It's difficult to believe that people would allow such invasive and controlling technologies upon themselves. In particular, Americans seem much too autonomous to allow such a practice.

On the other hand, if desperation increased, we might take a different perspective on the matter. Consider the controversial "Patriot Act" as a microcosm. After the terrorist attack of September 11, 2001, the American people cried for justice and protection. The "Patriot Act" took away many liberties of the American people, so that it could protect the nation in a time of crisis. About a month later, President George W. Bush signed the "Patriot Act" into law on October 26, 2001. The Senate voted 98 to 1 in favor of this law.[10]

Debate surrounded this controversial act. Some felt that it was an affront to our liberty, while others felt it was a necessary measure to counter terrorism and protect our nation. I don't know what your thoughts are on the Patriot Act (and frankly, it's irrelevant). My point is not to affirm or critique this law, but only to show that in times of crisis, people have historically surrendered liberties for the sake of protection.[11]

---

[9] Torin Monahan and Tyler Wall. "Somatic Surveillance," 165-166.
[10] www.senate.gov/legislative
[11] Another historical argument for this principle can be found in the Weimar Republic in Germany. Hitler's thugs (the Brown Shirts) were just as tough as the Communist gangs, and the German people were willing to give over their rights to be protected.

Now imagine if the world really *was* coming to an end—not in a figurative but a literal way. And consider if a charismatic and strong leader stepped to the forefront of world politics, claiming he could save the world from famine, disease, and war. Wouldn't you be willing to surrender some of your liberties in such a scenario? You'd be crazy not to, right? Most people (myself included) are willing to give away our information to the grocery store in order to save a few bucks on food and gas. What if you needed to give your identity to the government to protect yourself from impending disaster?

Identity theft costs businesses $221 billion per year.[12] When someone steals our identity, the credit card company or bank almost always covers the cost. But imagine if businesses could no longer afford to cover the cost of cybercrime. What if banks stopped reimbursing identity fraud unless the member allowed such an invasive procedure? We can very easily imagine the logic becoming unavoidable.

Of course, the way that this scenario unfolds is pure speculation. Christians shouldn't react to this by going "off the grid," living off of canned goods in the mountains somewhere. Instead the point is this: such a scenario is not at all bizarre considering our modern political and technological climate.

Worldwide viewing ability (Rev. 11:8-9)

After the two prophets die, John writes that everyone on Earth will stare at their dead bodies:

> Their dead bodies will lie in the street of the great city which mystically is called Sodom and Egypt, where also their Lord was crucified. [9] Those from *the peoples and tribes and tongues and nations will look at their dead bodies for three and a half days*, and will not permit their dead bodies to be laid in a tomb. (Rev. 11:8-9)

How is it possible for people from all over the world to look at these two dead men for three and a half days? In the first-century, such an event could not be fathomed. For nineteen hundred years afterward, this prediction would've still seemed outrageous. But today, with satellite technology, 24 hour news stations, and the Internet, we can easily picture such an event taking place.

---

[12] http://credit.org/blog/how-much-does-identity-theft-cost-infographic/

Destruction of all life on Earth

The Bible predicts a state of affairs in the future that could lead to global extinction. Jesus taught, "Unless those days had been cut short, *no life would have been saved*; but for the sake of the elect those days will be cut short" (Mt. 24:22). Isaiah writes that people will die with "their faces aflame" making "mortal man scarcer than pure gold" (Isa. 13:8, 12). Later he writes, "The inhabitants of the earth are burned, and few men are left" (Isa. 24:6), and the Earth shook violently as a result of this final world war (Isa. 24:19-20).

While some of these statements could be poetic, these predictions seem to fit better with modern warfare, rather than ancient warfare. In biblical times, armies still fought with swords and spears—not with weapons that could end all life on Earth. Today, even small scale nuclear warfare could have catastrophic effects on human life. Robock and Toon observe, "New analyses reveal that a conflict between India and Pakistan, for example, in which 100 nuclear bombs were dropped on cities and industrial areas—only 0.4 percent of the world's more than 25,000 warheads—would produce enough smoke to cripple global agriculture. A regional war could cause widespread loss of life even in countries far away from the conflict."[13]

Zechariah writes that a plague will strike all the nations that surround Israel at the end of history. He writes, "Their flesh will rot while they stand on their feet, and their eyes will rot in their sockets, and their tongue will rot in their mouth" (Zech. 14:12). Ancient people were familiar with diseases that would rot the flesh, eye sockets, and tongue. But notice the language: this occurs "while they stand on their feet." Before they have a chance to hit the ground, their flesh will rot off their bones. While this is speculative, modern people are certainly familiar with this in the pictures of Hiroshima and Nagasaki.

Additionally, John writes, "A great star fell from heaven, burning *like a torch*, and it fell on a third of the rivers and on the springs of waters… *many men died from the waters, because they were made bitter* (Rev. 8:10-11). Why would an ordinary torch turn the freshwater supplies "bitter," poisoning the water for human beings? But remember, John doesn't say that this *was* a torch; he says it was *like* a torch. Is it possible that he was seeing a vision of modern warfare? Again, this is speculation, but if you were an ancient man seeing visions of modern warfare, how else would you describe a missile?

---

[13] Alan Robock and Owen Brian Toon, "Local Nuclear War, Global Suffering," *Scientific American*. 302 (1), January, 2010. 74.

Meteorites (Rev. 8:8)

Something like a great mountain burning with fire was thrown into the sea and a third of the sea became blood,[9] and a third of the creatures which were in the sea and had life, died; and a third of the ships were destroyed. (Rev. 8:8)

Again, John uses the language of analogy (e.g. "like" or "as"). What must he have been seeing to write this? How else would you describe a meteorite if you'd never seen one before? Though planet-killing asteroids are not likely,[14] depending on its size, it's possible that a meteorite could cause this much damage. Cosmologist Sir Martin Rees writes,

Almost sixty-five million years ago Earth was hit by an object about ten kilometres across. The resultant impact released as much energy as a million H-bombs; it triggered mountain-shattering earthquakes around the world, and colossal tidal waves; it threw enough debris into the upper atmosphere to block out the Sun for more than a year. This is believed to have been the event that wiped out the dinosaurs... *If we knew several years in advance that an NEO [Near Earth Object] was on course to hit Earth, nothing could be done about it today.*[15]

Fred Guterl (executive editor of *Scientific American*) writes,

NASA scientists might alert us to the event a few weeks ahead of time, calculate the trajectory of the object, and demand an audience with the president and go on talk shows and news programs in a campaign to get funding for an anti-asteroid program. Perhaps, if we were really lucky, the NASA folks would have gotten a bead on the meteor a few months ahead of time, giving us at least a prayer of launching a nuclear-tipped missile that might have been able to break up the meteor into smaller parts that would fall relatively harmlessly in the atmosphere, or knock it off course enough to miss Earth. U.S. Congress mandated in 2005 that NASA find nine of every ten asteroids that could strike Earth, and do some damage, so that we could perhaps have years of warning before a potential impact and prepare a plan for dealing

---

[14] Matson and Pavlus place the likelihood at one in a million in the next century. John Matson and John Pavlus, *Scientific American*. 303 (3). September, 2010. 82.

[15] Emphasis mine. Martin J. Rees, *Our Final Hour: A Scientist's Warning: How Terror, Error, and Environmental Disaster Threaten Humankind's Future in This Century on Earth and Beyond* (New York: Basic, 2003), 90, 94.

with one. But with a measly $4 million budget, NASA's asteroid watch is likely to fall short. Still, that's more than *T. rex* had.[16]

Dispensationalists have gone too far in interpreting these images about the end of history. Many see the locusts in Revelation 9 as helicopters, and they see an airlift in the eagle's wings of Revelation 12. Surely we need to show some interpretive restraint in trying to understand the Bible's symbols and images about the future.

But it's also true that other interpreters haven't gone far enough to wrestle with these predictions. Or else they try to squeeze the fulfillments into narrow events from history that do not really reflect the language of these prophecies. Remember Jesus fulfilled many OT prophecies about himself, and these were exact. Why would we expect a hazy fulfillment for the rest of biblical prophecy?

Many interpreters find it odd that the biblical authors would describe technology that hadn't existed in their day. But why? If God knows the future, then knowing visions of battles at the end of history would be no more difficult than knowing our favorite color or our shoe size. Moreover, the biblical authors have predicted future technology before. David, Isaiah, and Zechariah predicted Jesus' death by crucifixion—a form of death that wouldn't exist until centuries after they wrote their books (Ps. 22:16; Zech. 12:10; Isa. 53:5). Of course, they didn't go into the detail we might like, but they still predicted it. Surely their immediate audience scratched their heads about piercing the man's "hands and feet" (Ps. 22:16), but now that we've seen the Cross, this prediction makes perfect sense. Could something similar be happening in these predictions about future technology and warfare?

Conclusion

We should take a final moment to marvel at the Bible's predictions of the end of human history. We generally delight in science fiction authors who accurately speculate about technological inventions that are *decades* or *centuries* in the future, but what about the biblical authors who wrote *millennia* before the events in question?

Consider the film-series *Back to the Future*. Screenwriters speculated about technology in the year 2015. While the film was very enjoyable in the year 1985, now that we've seen the world in 2015, we find that most of the

---

[16] Fred Guterl, *The Fate of the Species*, 33-34.

futuristic inventions haven't come to fruition (For instance, I'm *still* waiting for Marty McFly's "hoverboard" to be invented!).

And yet, time and time again, the biblical authors foresaw what the world would look like as history reached its conclusion. Indeed, they predicted an entire global scenario that is hauntingly clear.

Discussion questions

1. Do you think it's wrong to speculate about the Bible's picture of the events at the end of history? What are ways to guard us from becoming fanatical about our speculations?

2. If you don't agree with some of these speculations, what do you believe these passages predict?

3. What application should these predictions produce in us as believers in Christ? What application should not be derived as a result?

Chapter 19. The Second Coming: The Return of the King

If Jesus never comes back, Christianity would be built upon a lie—a broken promise from a deadbeat Dad who will forever neglect his children. The NT mentions the Second Coming roughly 300 times—in 23 out of the 27 books.[1] For every time the Bible predicts the First Coming of Christ, it predicts the Second Coming eight times.[2] Jesus promised, "I will come back and take you to be with me that you also may be where I am" (Jn. 14:3 NIV). If we can believe anything in the Bible, we can believe this: Jesus is coming back for us.

For centuries, Christians have prayed that God's will would be done on Earth, just as it is in heaven (Mt. 6:10). In this great day, that prayer will finally be answered.

Jesus will return the same way that he left

Christ *left* in a physical and visible way, and he will *return* the same exact way. The angels told the disciples, "This Jesus, who has been taken up from you into heaven, will come in just the same way as you have watched Him go into heaven" (Acts 1:11). The author of Hebrews explains that Jesus "will appear a second time for salvation without reference to sin, to those who eagerly await Him" (Heb. 9:28). Just as Jesus "appeared" (*epephane*) to bring salvation (Titus 2:11), he will "appear" (*epiphaneian*) again at his Second Coming (Titus 2:13). Hoekema writes, "If the first appearing of Christ... was visible—as no one would care to deny... the Second Coming will be as visible as the first."[3]

Jesus will return to end Armageddon

Just before the battle of Armageddon reaches its chaotic climax, Jesus will appear to subdue the anarchy on Earth. Without divine intervention, humanity would have wiped itself out of existence. In predicting his return,

---

[1] Robert Saucy, "The Eschatology of the Bible." In F. E. Gaebelein (Ed.), *The Expositor's Bible Commentary, Volume 1: Introductory Articles* (Grand Rapids, MI: Zondervan Publishing House, 1979), 110.
[2] Emphasis mine. Mark Hitchcock, *The End: A Complete Overview of Bible Prophecy and the End of Days*, 4.
[3] Anthony Hoekema, *The Bible and the Future*, 171-172.

Jesus said, "Unless those days had been cut short, no life would have been saved" (Mt. 24:22). Christ will enter human history to fight against the nations who are trying to slaughter believers in Israel (Zech. 14:3), and "His feet will stand on the Mount of Olives" (Zech. 14:4).

It's a beautiful picture: Perhaps millions or billions of Gentile believers returning with Christ to rescue the nation of Israel (Rev. 19:14; Zech. 14:5). After millennia of anti-Semitism and persecution from Gentiles, in the end, these Gentile believers will rescue the nation from her enemies.

We can't quite fathom what this day will be like. Only lesser events in history can even begin to compare. We might think of "VE Day" or "VJ Day" at the end of World War II. After years of bloody and brutal war, the papers celebrated the victory in Europe and later in Japan. Newspapers across the world printed the headline: **"THE WAR IS OVER!"** Men returned from battle to marry their girlfriends; families reunited after being separated for years on end; people threw confetti from windows on the masses below who flooded the streets to celebrate. Hoekema writes, "The first coming of Christ was like D-day, in that it was the decisive battle of the war, guaranteeing the enemy's final defeat. The Second Coming of Christ will be like V-day, in which the enemy finally lays down its arms and surrenders."[4]

In William Golding's classic book *The Lord of the Flies*, a group of young boys wash up on an island in the Pacific Ocean. Because no adults survive the crash, the boys learn to govern themselves. But as the story unfolds, self-government ultimately fails, and anarchy rapidly takes over the group. The boys turn into savages as they chase their former leader, Ralph, through the jungle, burning the wildlife behind him. Just one page before the end of the book, the island transforms into a living hell. Disorder, violence, and fear consume the story, as Ralph runs for his life.

But on the last page of the book, the British navy lands on the island.

In an instant, the story changes dramatically. As Ralph and the boys look at the officer, the savage spell is broken. The boys drop their sticks and spears at the sight of the military man, bursting into tears and reverting back to being mere children—not violent savages. Before the officer appeared, the boys felt like kings and chiefs of the island, and in their limited context, they certainly were. Yet after the officer arrives, they look like scared and pathetic children, playing war with pointy sticks.

I wonder if humanity might look similar on the day Jesus returns. Like the boys on the island, some people will immediately burst into tears (Rev. 1:7;

---

[4] Anthony Hoekema, *The Bible and the Future*, 29.

18:19). Others will cheer (Rev. 19:1ff). Whatever their emotional reaction, Paul states that "every knee will bow" and "every tongue will confess that Jesus Christ is Lord" (Phil. 2:10-11). Some will meet Christ as their Savior, and others will meet him as their Judge.

Jesus will return as the revealed King

I recently watched a YouTube video of a professional athlete who dressed as an elderly man in disguise. Makeup artists used cosmetics and haggard clothing to make him look 80 years old. Yet beneath the veneer he was a pro athlete in his prime. As he took to the court, the men's eyes lit up as the athlete ran circles around them. Finally, at the end of the game, the athlete pulled off the disguise, revealing his true identity.

Similarly, though to a much greater degree, Jesus disguised his complete divine identity in his First Coming. Paul writes, "He took the humble position of a slave and was born as a human being" (Phil. 2:7 NLT). The Creator didn't enter his universe as a glorified King, instead "there was nothing beautiful or majestic about his appearance, nothing to attract us to him" (Isa. 53:2 NLT). When Jesus appeared before, he swung a hammer as a poor carpenter, but at his Second Coming, he will pull back the veil, swinging a sword. As John writes, "We will see him as he really is" (1 Jn. 3:2 NLT).

As he entered Jerusalem the week before he died, Jesus rode a donkey (Mt. 21:7), but when he returns, he will ride a white stallion (Rev. 19:11), charging into battle. When the authorities captured Jesus, soldiers forced a crown of thorns into his scalp (Mt. 27:29), and blood soaked through the gaudy robe they threw over his bleeding shoulders (Mt. 27:28). Yet when Christ returns, he will wear a King's crown (Rev. 19:12) and a robe covered with the blood of his attackers (Rev. 19:13). Instead of being *abandoned* by his closest friends in that day (Mt. 26), Christ will be *surrounded* by a massive army of believers (Rev. 19:14). The soldiers ridiculed Jesus for being a weakling at the crucifixion (Mt. 27:29), but on this day, he will reveal his authority as the true King (Rev. 19:16). Instead of taking judgment for their sins onto himself (2 Cor. 5:21), Christ will bring judgment upon them.

When Jesus entered the world the first time, he experienced the suffering of humanity in "all things" (Heb. 2:17). He knew what it was like to get picked on as a kid (Jn. 8:41), live in poverty (Lk. 2:7; Mt. 8:20), grow up without a dad (Mt. 13:55), never get married, suffer civil injustice (Mt. 27:11ff), grow up in a dysfunctional family (Mt. 1:19; Jn. 7:5; Mk. 3:21), be nervous and anxious (Mt. 26:38; Lk. 22:44), suffer public humiliation (Lk. 23:35; Jn. 19:25ff), go without food, water, and sleep (Mt. 4:2; 8:24; Jn. 19:28), see loved ones suffer and die (Jn. 11:33, 35; Mt. 14:13; Acts 9:4), and even face death himself (Lk. 23:46). As the author of Hebrews writes, "[Jesus] understands our weaknesses, for he faced all of the same testings we do, yet he did not sin" (Heb. 4:15 NLT).

In his First Coming, humanity judged Jesus in a kangaroo court, nailing him to a wooden cross. But when he returns, Jesus will judge humanity. The One who offered forgiveness through the Cross will be the same One who judges humanity in the end (Mt. 25:31-46; John 5:21-29; Acts 10:42; 17:31; 2 Cor. 5:10; 2 Tim. 4:1).

Jesus will return as the perfect King

Throughout the OT, we see a repeated problem: the leaders of God's people are fallen and corruptible. Who can possibly have the *power* to lead the people, but also have the *character* to keep from becoming abusive and corrupt? Israel's first king, Saul, was a powerful and charismatic leader: Tall, dark, and handsome—standing a full foot over the other men around him (1 Sam. 9:2). Consequently, Saul's power corrupted him, nearly destroying the entire nation. David was an even greater king, but his success led him to adultery and murder (2 Sam. 11:1ff). In fact, as we read through the Bible or even through today's news, we wonder: Who could have the power to secure justice, but still have the integrity to lead? The desire for this sort of a King finds its fulfillment in Jesus Christ: the humble King (Mt. 11:29). The One who will judge humanity also took the judgment of humanity; the One who rules the kings of the Earth, also humbled himself beneath their rule; the One who suffered injustice on Earth will also bring justice to the Earth.

We all yearn for a king like this, and there's good news: *He's coming!*

Jesus will return to throw a party

Scripture describes the return of Christ as an ecstatic party on Earth. I've been to some great parties in my life: Good weather, loud music, and great friends. Yet all of these experiences will pale in comparison to the party God will throw in this day. After judgment occurs (Isa. 24:17-23), God will throw a banquet for all those who chose to trust in him. God "will prepare a feast of rich food for all peoples, a banquet of aged wine—the best of meats and the finest of wines" (Isa. 25:6 NIV). I'm not sure what kind of steak and wine will be served at this dinner, but if Jesus Christ is throwing this party, it's probably the best food and drink you've ever tasted. The last time Jesus supplied a party like this, a snobby wine steward said, "You have saved the best [wine] until now!" (Jn. 2:10 NLT)

Some Christians (particularly in America) deny that Jesus turned water into *wine*; rather he turned water into *grape juice*. Yet the Greek word for wine (*oinos*) occurs throughout the Bible, and it never refers to "grape juice." Paul writes, "Do not get drunk with wine (*oinos*)" (Eph. 5:18). If Christians could get drunk from *grape juice*, this would be more of a miracle than Jesus turning water into wine in the first place!

God not only promised to throw this party, but Jesus will sit down and drink a glass of wine with us. Jesus promised, "I will not drink wine again *until the day I drink it new with you in my Father's Kingdom*" (Mt. 26:29 NIV). Imagine what it will be like to sit down at a party with Christ, sharing a drink in celebration of his completed work on Earth.

Jesus will return to experience joy

The author of Hebrews wrote that Jesus endured the Cross "for the joy set before Him" (Heb. 12:2). What was this "joy" set before Christ?

Some interpreters believe that it was the Cross itself. But surely this cannot be the case. There was nothing joyful about enduring torture and crucifixion! Moreover, this verse states that Christ endured the Cross *because* of the joy set before him. Therefore, his joy occurred after the Cross—not during it.

Others believe Jesus endured the Cross because of the joy of Heaven. Yet this interpretation doesn't make much sense either. Jesus lived in Heaven with the Father before he came to Earth. If Heaven was his motivating joy, then why would he leave Heaven in the first place?

No, Jesus endured the Cross for another joy entirely. The explanation of his motivating joy is shocking.

It was *you*.

Christ endured the Cross because we was looking forward to being with you. As he suffered, he had you on his mind. That's what motivated him to suffer so intensely.

As I reflect on the return of Christ, my heart fills with longing and anticipation. What will it be like to be in the presence of Jesus? Like a child going to sleep on Christmas Eve, we can hardly stand waiting to meet with Christ on this day. I often picture it as a time of intense emotion and deep joy…

But how do you think Jesus will feel? He's been waiting eons to be with us. He endured the Cross for us. If we will burst into tears of joy when we see Christ, how will he react when he finally sees us?

Conclusion

The early Christians prayed about the return of Christ often. They used the Aramaic term *Maranatha*, which means, "Come, Lord Jesus!" Commentators believe that this "may be the earliest known prayer of the church."[5] We see the same language (in Greek—not Aramaic) at the end of the book of Revelation (22:20).

Those who have met Christ have no reason to fear his return, because he "will also confirm [us] to the end, blameless in the day of our Lord Jesus Christ" (1 Cor. 1:8), and "at that time each will receive his praise from God" (1 Cor. 4:5).

While this book covered many details and intricacies about the return of Christ (and might've raised more questions than answers at times!), I hope it's helped you to keep your eyes fixed on his return. Jesus could return this Tuesday. He could return next month. We're not sure.

In the meantime, I pray that you would "keep yourselves in God's love as you wait for the mercy of our Lord Jesus Christ to bring you to eternal life" (Jude 21 NIV).

Discussion questions

1. In their book *The Underground Church* (2014), Bach and Zhu note that the Chinese government will not let "official churches" teach about the Second Coming of Christ. (As a result, many Chinese Christians have gone "underground" into unofficial house churches.) Why do you think the Second Coming of Christ would be such a controversial doctrine? In your opinion, how important is this doctrine to the Christian faith?

2. Why do you think Christ has waited so long to return at his Second Coming?

3. When Jesus returns, he will bind Satan (Rev. 20:2-3). Why do you think God has permitted Satan to be let loose to such a degree in this present era of history?

4. How often do you find yourself thinking or praying about the Second Coming of Christ? What might be some ways to develop a focus on this biblical teaching?

5. What does it look like to be ready for the Second Coming of Christ? How would we know if we were ready?

---

[5] Alan Johnson, *1 Corinthians* (Downers Grove, IL: InterVarsity Press, 2004), 322.